12/23

Radiant Infrastructures

SIGN, STORAGE, TRANSMISSION
A series edited by Jonathan Sterne
and Lisa Gitelman

Radiant Infrastructures

Media, Environment,
and Cultures of Uncertainty

Rahul Mukherjee

Duke University Press   Durham and London   2020

© 2020 Duke University Press
All rights reserved
Printed and bound by CPI Group (UK) Ltd, Croydon, CR0 4YY
Designed by Drew Sisk
Typeset in Garamond Premier Pro and SangBleu Sunrise by
Westchester Publishing Services

The Cataloging-in-Publication Data is available at the Library of Congress.

ISBN 9781478009016 (ebook)
ISBN 9781478007623 (hardcover)
ISBN 9781478008064 (paperback)

Cover art: Amirtharaj Stephen, *Fishermen proceeding towards the Koodankulam
Nuclear Power Plant to lay a siege on World Fishermen Day*, 2011; courtesy of
the artist. Cell antennas atop Hotel Supreme; photo by Rahul Mukherjee.

Duke University Press gratefully acknowledges the University of Pennsylvania,
which provided funds toward the publication of this book.

CONTENTS

Acknowledgments vii

Introduction Radiant Energies and Environmental Controversies 1

01 Debating Cell Towers 39

02 Contested Nuclear Imaginaries 70

03 Emissions 106

04 Exposures 138

05 Styling Advocacy: Activism and Citizenship 163

Conclusion 192

Notes 219

References 241

Index 259

ACKNOWLEDGMENTS

Radiant Infrastructures has benefited from many mentors, critics, research collectives, and institutions. Parts of the book have been nurtured in various intellectual contexts, and there is much debt to be radiated to the fellow research travelers.

During my graduate days at UC Santa Barbara, I worked closely with a marvelous committee: Lisa Parks, Rita Raley, Chuck Wolfe, Colin Milburn (UC Davis), and Bhaskar Da (Bhaskar Sarkar). Their guidance has helped me emerge with theoretical/methodological patchworks for examining environmental publics. Shiv Visvanathan and Radhika Gajjala prepared me for my dissertation research endeavor while I was at Dhirubhai Ambani Institute for Information and Communication Technology and Bowling Green State University, respectively, before coming to UCSB. Their work continues to inspire me. Thanks to the Department of Film and Media Studies at UCSB for taking a chance with me when I was a computer science student who wanted to write on media and culture. In UCSB's campus, I learned much from participating in classes taught by Peter Bloom, Anna Everett, Swati Chattopadhyay, Miriam Metzger, Bruce Bimber, Jennifer Holt, Greg Siegel, Bishnu Di (Bishnupriya Ghosh), Cristina Venegas, Constance Penley, Janet Walker, and Michael Curtin. Graduate school was a wonderful conversation with my colleagues in the Department of Film and Media Studies and the wider campus: Athena Tan, David Gray, Joshua Neves, Nicole Starosielski, Dan Reynolds, Carlos Jimenez, Hannah Goodwin, Teddy Pozo, Lindsay Palmer, Steve Witkowski, Siladitya, Ramya Yeluri, Sarah Harris, Jade Petermon, Jetti Allen, Maria Corrigan, Lindsay Thomas, Lindsay Palmer, Anne Cong-Huyen, Erik Berg, and Seokwon Choi. They are extraordinary thinkers and writers, and it is wonderful to follow their academic and other professional careers.

Five years ago, the Cinema and Media Studies program at the University of Pennsylvania made me its own by their collegiality and hospitality. Tim Corrigan, Peter Decherney, Karen Redrobe, Meta Mazaj, Kathy DeMarco Van Cleve, and Nicola Gentili are a dream team. As part of the English department,

I benefited from the generosity and guidance of two of its chairs: Amy Kaplan and Jed Esty. My colleagues at the Latitudes group—Suvir Kaul, Ania Loomba, Chi-Ming Yang, Rita Barnard, David Eng, and Jennifer Ponce De Leon—have sparked many a conversation about South-South solidarities. Bethany Wiggin, Paul Saint-Amour, and Etienne Benson have kept the Penn Program in Environmental Humanities alive and responsible at Penn. Projit Mukharji, Nikhil Anand, and Lisa Mitchell designed innovative works-in-progress workshops on matters related to South Asia. Jo Park, J. C. Cloutier, Tsitsi Jaji, Ian Fleishman, Emily Steinlight, Heather Love, and Pearl Brilmyer have provided the intellectual companionship and affective sustenance necessary to keep producing scholarship. Two research collectives (colloquium groups)—Penn Humanities Forum (themed year: Translation) and Humanities+Urbanism+Design—brought together interlocutors who enriched the arguments in the book. Jim English, David Brownlee, and Eugenie Birch moderated sessions wisely. Conversations with students in my graduate courses on publics, environmental media, and global media theory have proved extremely helpful in reexamining the many layers of challenging concepts. In particular, I want to thank Orchid Tierney, Knar Gavin, Iggy Cortez, Kerry McAuliffe, and the two student reading groups—Latitudes, and Anthropocene and Animal Studies—for shaping my ideas about ecological and infrastructural approaches to literature, media, and arts. Spread across Drexel and Penn was my writing group of friends and interlocutors: Linda Kim, Debjani Bhattacharya, Beatrice Jauregui, and Alden Young, you know what the book was before it was a book.

The Atkinson Center for Sustainable Futures Fellowship at Cornell University's Society for the Humanities and the Short Stay Fellowship at Utrecht University provided intellectual camaraderie and precious writing time. I profited immensely from interactions with Rosi Braidotti and Berteke Waaldijk in Utrecht. At Cornell's SHUM, Emily Parsons and Paul Fleming organized fascinating conversations and events over delicious lunches. Amy Sara Carroll, Ricardo Dominguez, Conerly Casey, Chairat Polmuk, Ayelet Ben-Yishai, Erik Born, Robert Travers, and Amie Parry were an amazing group of fellows, emitting sincerity, engagement, laid-backness, and generosity in equal measure. Durba Ghosh, Tim Murray, Renate Ferro, Patti Zimmerman, and Lucinda Ramberg gave my book project their attention and me their inquisitive companionship. I fondly remember afternoon tea meetings with Monika Mehta discussing global media theory in various cafés of Ithaca.

Over the years, colleagues and friends in the fields of environmental media and science and technology studies have gifted many conversations and endless encouragement. Melody Jue, Mel Hogan, Kate Brown, Kath Weston, Monamie Bhadra Haines, Jennifer Beth Spiegel, Itty Abraham, Kavita Philip, Ranjit Singh, Rafico Ruiz, Stacy Alaimo, Brooke Belisle, Ravi Sundaram, Yuriko Furuhata, and Ben Mendelsohn have introduced me to new considerations about data, saturation, intimacy, atmospherics, aesthetics, and matter in my own research on media, infrastructures, and the environment. I still remember that on the sidelines of a conference at the University of Virginia, the inimitable Kath Weston asked me to carefully think about the terms "dosage" and "interference," without which chapter 4 of this book would not be possible.

Courtney Berger is a remarkably insightful editor whose suggestions throughout the writing and revision process have been illuminating and made a huge difference to the final book. Sandra Korn, Jenny Tan, Lalitree, Liz Smith, and the editorial staff at Duke University Press have been fantastic with their guidance and precision. I am deeply indebted to the two reviewers who gave so much of their time to read the book and provide incisive comments and rigorous feedback. I also am grateful to Jonathan Sterne and Lisa Gitelman for including *Radiant Infrastructures* within the Sign, Storage, Transmission series, a series I have long admired. At an earlier stage of the writing process, Brian Larkin and Arvind Rajagopal read a draft of my book as part of a book workshop organized by Tim Corrigan and Jed Esty at Penn. At this workshop, Brian's terrific suggestion that I work to conceptualize "radiant infrastructures" (instead of using the term as a descriptor) inspired a reorganization of the chapters of the book. Arvind's wise reformulation (as summary) of my manuscript draft gave me ideas for the conclusion of this book.

Parts of the book have been presented in conferences at venues such as the Society for Cinema and Media Studies, the Society for Social Studies of Science, the American Anthropology Association, and the International Communication Association. Some sections of chapter 1 and chapter 3 have appeared in modified form as part of journal articles in *Television and New Media* and *Media, Culture and Society*: "'City Inside the Oven': Cell Tower Radiation Controversies and Mediated Technoscience Publics," *Television and New Media* 18 (1) (2017): 19–36; "'You are the first journalist and you are the last journalist who will ever come here': Nuclear Secrets and Media Practices of Access-Trespass," *Media, Culture and Society* 38 (5) (2016): 647–663. Speaking invitations at the University of California, Berkeley (Medium/Environment conference), Concordia University (Global Emergent Lab "Concepts" Seminar), Cornell University ("Sustainable Futures" talk), the University of

Acknowledgments

Virginia (Environmental Humanities symposium), Yale University ("Aggressive Image" conference), the University of Michigan (Digital South Asia conference), and Princeton University (Postcolonial Studies colloquium) were occasions to tinker with the book project and to have interlocutors point out emergent possibilities. I am grateful to Weihong Bao, Joshua Neves, Paul Fleming, Stephanie Bernhard, Ido Lewit, Aswin Punathambekar, and Daniel Hazard for the kind invitations, and to their respective departments and programs for hosting my visits. In particular, visits to the University of Michigan and Concordia University have led to sustained conversations with Josh, Aswin, and Marc Steinberg. It is a rare privilege for a junior scholar like me to have such mentors as friends.

The project has been sustained by fellowships from the UCSB Affiliates and the Interdisciplinary Humanities Center. Travel grants from the Department of Film and Media Studies and the Graduate Division supported fieldwork visits to India. At Penn, the Wolf Chair and the Humanities+Urbanism+Design collective offered research funds to help with further fieldwork. Numerous research contacts—actors, stakeholders, artists, journalists, scientists, photographers, filmmakers, and communities involved in the environmental debates that form a part of my book—helped me to comprehend the complexity of the arguments I studied and the way in which interactions aided media practices. Without their time and assistance, this project would not have been possible. These many research interviewees include Shipra Mathur, Vibha Varshney, S. P. Udaykumar, Amirtharaj Stephen, Tridip Mandal, Anubha Bhonsle, Shriprakash, R. P. Amudhan, Pallava Bagla, Anumita Roychowdhury, Latha Jishnu, Prakash Munshi, Fathima Nizaruddin, Sarah Irion, and Kumar Sundaram. I am especially thankful to friends and relatives who hosted me in various cities. My sister Rohini and her partner Pratyush were understanding and lovely with the strange schedules of my fieldwork assignments. They take Indian hospitality to another level. My school friends Rohan, Ankur, Vishesh, and Abhigyan continue to watch over me and exchange opinions about life and work. To my relatives (blood and alternate families) spread across Ranchi, Philadelphia, Delhi, London, and Bangalore, I remember with great debt your love and care over many years. Iggy Cortez and Alessandra Mirra have been a key part of my Philadelphia support system; they know they are very special.

Without my teachers Lisa Parks and Bhaskar Sarkar, I could not have written this book. Lisa has taught me that there is always a different, evocative angle from which to approach infrastructures. Bhaskar Da has trained me to have radical intellectual openness to a wide range of scholarship and affectionately nudged me to pursue ambitious projects.

Jenn Wilson has kept our life together lively and full of happenings. It is a treat to have one's work be read by such a delectable writer as Jenn. I cannot think of anybody more adorable, more endlessly curious. This book is for Ma and Baba, who have cultivated in me both an enthusiasm for science and a proclivity to quarrel with it. They are the most generous people in my life.

Radiant Energies and Environmental Controversies

In mid-2011, fishermen in Koodankulam, India, a coastal area in the southern state of Tamil Nadu, began complaining about a mysterious decrease in their fish yields. They blamed it on radiation from the nuclear reactor being built there. Urbanites in Mumbai rushed to buy radiation detectors, anxious that the cell towers by their apartment complexes were emitting unsafe levels of radiation. Around this time, I was conducting research about science reporting related to environmental issues in India. I had expected that the journalists and scientists I met would tell me about climate change, genetically modified crops, and e-waste management—the usual topics. Instead, they overwhelmed me with anecdotes about cell towers and nuclear reactors. Since the nuclear disaster in Fukushima, Japan, earlier that year, fishermen and farming communities in rural India had been agitating against the continued construction of nuclear reactors. Meanwhile, in urban centers, Indian citizens were deeply concerned about news reports that residents living in close proximity to mobile phone towers were being diagnosed with cancer. Of course, there were other stories about toxic environments: air pollution in Indian cities was a serious issue with city dwellers—who often developed asthma, chronic bronchitis, and other respiratory ailments—but one could see and smell the unbearable smog in New Delhi, the capital of India and the world's most polluted city (see Daigle 2011).[1] In stark contrast, reactors and towers emitted imperceptible radiation, and this imperceptibility seemed to amplify both the apprehension people felt about its health effects and the imperative journalists felt to mediate it, to make invisible radiation visible.

Owing to radiation's ability to evade the human senses, popular news programs in India characterized cell tower signals as *khamosh khatra*, or silent danger.[2] What was common in the coverage of both controversies was the way the invisible radiation became associated with the very visible atomic power

DATA POWER FOR **1.2 BILLION** INDIANS

FIGURE I.1 Reliance Jio ad with references to "Digital India" and data for
1.2 billion Indians

plants and mobile towers. These structures embodied the dreams of modernity for many Indians, and therefore could not just be brought down. To halt the construction of power plants or evict cell antennas represented an emotionally charged retrenchment from the promise of development.

Urban India is composed of radiant cities: bustling metropoles where radio waves emanate from thousands of cell antennas, keeping millions of mobile phones (and people) connected. Prime Minister Narendra Modi's "Digital India" program aims at connecting all of India's 1.2 billion people to spur innovation, and cell towers embody the promise of that plan. Reliance Jio, the rapidly rising cellular operator launched in 2016, has been building cell towers very quickly and believes an infrastructural investment in antennas using 4G LTE technology is crucial to bringing "data power" to all Indians through smartphones, thus realizing Modi's vision. In this ad, digital data accessed on Jio smartphones provide new freedom to Indians as they run across beaches, unfettered and joyous (figure I.1). Nuclear energy is also heavily symbolic. Many Indians believe it has the potential to illuminate every home in the country. Radiation and radiance, atomic prowess and national glory have long been synonymous.[3] A 2012 ad released by the Nuclear Power Corporation of India Limited (NPCIL) claims that electricity generated by nuclear reactors helped create a bumper crop harvest. Happy children run across a glorious wheat field as NPCIL's campaign slogan reads, "Brightening millions of lives" (figure I.2).

FIGURE I.2
NPCIL ad and
slogan, "Brightening
millions of lives"

Despite these aspirations, over the last seven years, cell towers and nuclear reactors have come to be perceived as emitting uncontrolled, unruly, and unsafe radiation. News programs have expressed concern that cell tower radiation might be a health hazard (figure I.3). In Koodankulam (also spelled Kudankulam), antinuclear activists and affected communities organized a long and enduring protest to stop nuclear reactors from being constructed.[4] The French corporation Areva was planning to build the world's largest nuclear reactor in Jaitapur on India's Arabian Sea coast. Villages like Sakhri-Nate were vehemently opposed. The village water wells and tea stalls were plastered with graffiti that proclaimed, "Areva Go Back" and, in the Marathi language, "Nako annu urja" (no atomic energy) (figures I.4 and I.5).

Although both reactors and towers emit invisible radiation and play an important role in India's development, they are rarely discussed in tandem. During the period of my study (2010–2017), it would have been extremely difficult to find a newspaper article or a television news segment about cell tower radiation that also referred to nuclear reactors and vice versa. Even as the two controversies were unfolding almost simultaneously in India, these "radiant infrastructures" were not being compared. This lack of comparison, or even citation, struck me as strange.

There are, however, some key differences between cell towers and nuclear reactors. For one, they emit different kinds of radiation—ionizing (nuclear) and nonionizing (cell antennas)—and one could argue that technical specificity matters. Another difference of great consequence is that their locations and affected communities vary vastly. Nuclear reactors are being constructed in rural areas, displacing fishermen and farming communities. Cell towers remain an urban problem, with mostly middle-class populations organizing campaigns

FIGURE I.3 NDTV program discussing cell tower radiation

to evict towers from their neighborhoods. The state, policy makers, and media organizations view rural fishermen and the urban middle class very differently.

I want to juxtapose two examples of the mediations of these controversies to reveal just how divided the social fabric of India is. I have met documentary filmmakers shooting in rural India, and also journalists working on lifestyle shows about urban health problems. The committed documentary filmmakers make an argument against nuclear reactors, while the lifestyle shows take up the plight of upper-middle-class urban residents who do not want cell antennas in their backyards. R. P. Amudhan, who made a trilogy of documentaries on nuclear energy programs in India called *Radiation Stories*, told me that his films are poor people's *mela* (fair or festival), and upper-middle-class elites who have political connections have no place in his documentaries. Shows like CNN-IBN's *Living It Up* are about privileged lifestyles, arguing, for example, that talking relentlessly on the phone is an urban addiction just like eating potato chips. Documentary filmmakers interested in bringing social change do not feel inspired to make films regarding cell tower radiation (and the anxieties of the privileged class), and lifestyle shows assume that rural fishermen have only livelihoods, not lifestyles. The mediations of reactors and towers are imbricated with the political economy, public perception, and government policy regarding these radiant infrastructures.

FIGURES I.4 AND I.5 Antinuke protest graffiti in Sakhri-Nate (Screen grab from *Are-Vah!*)

By examining a series of environmental controversies associated with nuclear reactors and cell towers, this book conceptualizes the specificity of radiant infrastructures as a particular kind of infrastructure. Radiant infrastructures, like other infrastructures, provide structure to our lives. They organize our mobility (cell phones keep us connected as we move) and shape the way we use our electrical appliances (nuclear reactors produce electricity). Radiant infrastructures, more particularly, are associated with radiance, understood as fields of energy. The signals emitted by cell antennas move like waves across the city, determining which phones stay connected and which don't. These signals enter people's homes, disturbing erstwhile notions of public-private boundaries. Radioactive isotopes emitted by nuclear reactors also defy boundaries.

The environment around an atomic power plant could potentially include invisible radioactive isotopes of tritium, cesium, and iodine, which then find their way into water, soil, and human bodies. Such radioactive nuclides accumulate in animals and plants, resurfacing and concentrating as they go up the food chain.

Radiant infrastructures are leaky, susceptible to both radiation and information leaks that could cause bodily contaminations and affective contagions. Examining the results of bodily exposure to controlled emissions from radiant infrastructures and the performances of experts and policy makers who hide and reveal information about reactors and towers helps one grasp the reasons for the epistemic uncertainties and ontological indeterminacies surrounding these infrastructures. Media operates across scale—bridging the micro-level bodily encounters with infrastructures and the macro-level discourses circulating about them—and thus becomes central to representing and shaping political subjectivities associated with such infrastructures.

This book critically interrogates the role of the media in covering nuclear reactors and cell antennas, both of which promise development and simultaneously generate intense fears regarding radioactive emissions. The techno-political debates over threshold levels of radiation, the moving testimonies of cancer patients, the claims and counterclaims by experts of an absolute control over the atom and the cell antenna, and the uncertainities about the future expressed by concerned citizens get enacted in mediated arenas. Journalists brag about getting exclusive access to report from inside the reactor core of a nuclear power plant, lifestyle shows depict children playing under the shadow of a cell tower (with camera tilts to emphasize the tower's enormous height), and regulators organize press conferences to allay public apprehensions about an imminent catastrophe. This book traces these intercommunicating media events and practices as a way to understand the temporal fluctuations and geographic spread of environmental controversies. Various media programs help keep the issues and concerns related to the disruptive infrastructure in circulation, and this "discursive circularity" (Warner 2002) sustains the controversy.

In this book, I do not use "radiant infrastructures" as a mere descriptor for cell towers and nuclear reactors. Rather, I conceptualize radiant infrastructures through both their material properties and the work they do for different interests. "Radiant infrastructures" thereby becomes a heuristic that accretes the different ways people try to make sense of radiation-emitting technologies and their everyday encounters with them. The "radiance" of radiant infrastructures is a double-edged sword, because these infrastructures are at once harbingers of development and emitters of potentially carcinogenic radiations.

Radiance connotes the luster of hope about a nation's economic growth as well as the harmful radiations with carcinogenic effects. Mediation accentuates both aspects of radiance. The mediated radiance of radiant infrastructures as glistening objects of a nation's development is contaminated by the mediated uncertainties about the material effects of impalpable radiations on human bodies and citizens' well-being. Nuclear reactors as infrastructures of electrical illumination and cell towers as infrastructures of information communciation lend themselves well to metaphors and manifestations of radiance (glow, heat, spark, spread). However, for such demonstrations of radiance to occur, invisble processes involving scattering of radioactive particles and radial spreading of electromagnetic rays have to take place. Radiant infrastructures as a conceptual heuristic folds in both these glittering and impalpable aspects of radiance. Mediation of environmental controversies about radiant infrastructures also includes the role of media practices such as radiation detection and biomedical imaging that provide ordinary people the possibility of sensing their exposure to invisible radiant energies emitted by cell towers and nuclear reactors. The concept and phenomena of "radiance" in radiant infrastructures point to media's role in molding political imaginaries, bodily prehensions, and social aspirations about cell towers and nuclear reactors.

Radiance of Infrastructures

Infrastructures can be vast networks that connect and separate human and nonhuman entities. Media anthropologist Brian Larkin (2008) has often noted that infrastructures are both conceptual and technical objects. As such, infrastructures demonstrate material power and agency but also are imbued with social meanings. Infrastructures like nuclear reactors, electric lines, cell towers, sewage pipes, roads, railways, and hydroelectric dams consist of matter in the form of metals and minerals, and they have material effects on the people who build, maintain, and use them. These infrastructures are also associated with meanings beyond their instrumental functions. Nuclear reactors and hydroelectric dams provide electricity and can make a country energy self-sufficient, but they have also been labeled the "temples" and "cathedrals" of modern nation-states, promising a country the lofty goals of development and progress. Gyan Prakash (1999) and Itty Abraham (2009) have persuasively argued that mega-development projects, from big dams to monumental nuclear reactors, have been used by the postcolonial Indian governing institutions to gain political legitimacy in the name of science.[5] Thus, nuclear and dam technologies became material objects crucial for state imagination.

Soon after Indian independence, it was believed that the peaceful harnessing of the properties of the atom would produce abundant energy and end India's poverty and economic underdevelopment. While India has some coal, it has limited oil reserves; hence, the nuclear option, with its promise of boundless energy generation in the near future (pending some technical hurdles), has been attractive for bureaucrats and scientists alike (Mathai 2013). Both the nuclear weapons and atomic energy programs received tremendous backing from the government, which continued even after the international nuclear community boycotted the Indian nuclear establishment following the 1974 atomic tests. Domestic reaction to the atomic bomb tests conducted in Pokhran on May 18, 1974, painted it as a peaceful explosion, but international reaction suggested that India was accelerating its nuclear program, and with time, the international body of the Nuclear Suppliers Group (NSG) had ruled out nuclear exports to India. India pursued a self-reliant indigenous atomic power program and manufactured nuclear weapons. Within the Indian public discourse, nuclear weapons were championed as being essential for national security, and such discourses, referred to as "nuclear nationalism" (Bidwai and Vanaik 1999), rose to a pinnacle following the nuclear tests conducted by India (and then Pakistan) in 1998. Since signing the US-India Nuclear Nonproliferation Treaty in 2006 and befriending the global nuclear fraternity all over again (that is, nuclear trade with India blocked earlier by NSG resumed again), the Indian government has decided to gain energy security and minimize its carbon footprint through nuclear power plants. The unique selling point for nuclear reactors is that they emit zero greenhouse gases.[6]

In addition to dams and nuclear reactors, cellular infrastructures—enabling omniscience and connectivity—are also touted as the new temples (and cathedrals) of modern India. In August 1995, Jyoti Basu, at that time the chief minister of West Bengal, called Union Telecom minister Sukh Ram on a Nokia mobile phone, inaugurating the cell phone revolution in India. From that one cell phone subscriber to one billion subscribers as of January 2016, the Indian mobile phone market is the second largest in the world, surpassed only by China. With this exponential growth of cell phones, the cellular infrastructure to support them, particularly cell towers, has also had to grow at a breakneck pace. Indus Towers, the biggest tower company operating in fifteen circles in India, manages 116,454 towers.[7] Drawing a fascinating infrastructural analogy, Jeffrey and Doron (2013) note that towers are to cell phones what gas stations had been to automobiles.

Cell towers and nuclear reactors, like railways and hydroelectric dams, have often been associated with the symbolic glow of development and progress. This is one kind of radiance associated with many infrastructures. Media, too, has a crucial role to play in amplifying the discursive promises of infrastructures and publicizing the ceremonial events marking their inaugurations and anniversaries. So, if infrastructures other than radiant infrastructures have the symbolic radiance of development (and media is key to building such radiance), how are radiant infrastructures different from other infrastructures?

What differentiates cell towers and nuclear reactors from other infrastructures is their ability to emit radiant energies. Conceptualizing radiant infrastructures involves focusing on the electromagnetic fields and radiaoactive particles that such infrastructures emit. In order to explain the phenomena of radiance associated with these infrastructures, one would have to examine discourses surrounding radiant energies and the sociotechnical relations engendered by them. In a twenty-first-century world obsessed with digitality and information, the connections between energy and digital technology have created new conversations. The recent push toward grappling with climate change and the Anthropocene has renewed debates about energy and infrastructure, but energy considerations get eschewed as fascinations with screens, interfaces, and apps direct attention toward software. Contemporary digital life in India is made possible by cell antennas. But cell antenna signals don't just carry information; these signals are lightning-like pulses intensively drifting across electromagnetic frequencies. These electromagnetic waves were detected as part of highly publicized discoveries and inventions involving X-rays and wireless telegraphy in the late nineteenth century (Gabrys 2010; Thibault 2014).[8] In the Victorian period, before wireless science and capitalism bracketed and labeled the space through which these signals traveled as the "electromagnetic spectrum," the waves were intuited as radiant energies vibrating in the "luminiferous ether" (Clarke and Henderson 2002).

The discovery of X-rays, radio waves, and later microwaves—which constitute the electromagnetic spectrum—owed much to the early twentieth century's preoccupation with the science and technology of energy, which then led to the discovery of radioactivity.[9] Indeed, the media object "radio" and the element "radium" share not only etymological roots but also intersecting histories and cultures associated with luminescence, sparks, lightning, and glow. During the 1920s, cafés in Vienna advertised free radio using the image of a lightning bolt. This ideogram evoked the speed and power of electricity, as well as a visual translation of the sparks emitted from early radio devices or wireless transmitters (Born 2016). The element radium, discovered by Marie

Curie and later extracted for commercial purposes, gave off a wondrous glow when mixed with zinc sulphide. These properties of radium made it indispensable for watch dials that glowed in the night. In the 1920s in the United States, radium was dubbed "liquid sunshine."

Radiophones and cell phones emit radio waves. Radium and uranium are radioactive elements. Unlike the radiophones of the 1920s, cell phones of today do not spark, and unlike radium, uranium (used in nuclear reactors) does not render objects shiny. That said, cell antennas and nuclear reactors (like radio and radium) emit rays that seem to move in concentric circles. The radial spreading of particles and waves is thus a key characteristic of radiant infrastructures. These waves and particles, if considered harmful, make the radiant infrastructures disruptive in nature.

The word for "nuclear radiation" in Sanskrit, विकिरण (*vikiran*), connotes "scattering" and "strewing on," which captures perhaps the leaky quality of radiant infrastructures. Similar etymological understanding for "signal" or "wave," तरङ्ग (*tarang*), could mean "fly over" or "run over"—or तरङ्गिन् (*tarangin*), meaning "moving restlessly to and fro"—endowing radiant energies with atmospheric qualities, vibratory motions, and the ability to spread out.

All Radiations Are Not the Same!

Radiation is unstable matter continuously transforming (often decaying) to stable, and is better understood as "the sign of energy in the process of transformation" (DeLoughrey 2009, 471). Radiation permeates the atmosphere, pervades the body and soil, and suffuses even the cosmos. There are many kinds of radiation, and different radiant infrastructures emit rays with varying wavelengths and frequencies. All of them therefore should not be slotted together, and to understand the differences between them is a key part of theorizing radiant infrastructures. Nuclear radiation, especially gamma ray, is high-energy ionizing radiation that is carcinogenic and known to cause genetic mutation. Cell tower signals fall within low-energy nonionizing radiation, and their carcinogenic effects are yet to be fully established. That said, there continue to be debates both within the scientific community and beyond that suggest that cancer from long-term exposure to cell antenna signals cannot be ruled out.[10]

Even within nuclear radiation, there is a lot to differentiate. Gamma rays are one kind of ionizing radiation, the others being alpha and beta particles. Alpha particles, unlike gamma rays, do not travel long distances. While gamma rays can penetrate clothing and skin, alpha particles can be easily stopped by a sheet of paper. And yet, years of nuclear history warn us against underestimating the devastating power of alpha particles. In 1943, medical radiologists working on the Manhattan Project discovered the terrible consequences of plutonium, which emits primarily alpha particles (Brown 2013).[11]

In late 2011, when construction of the Koodankulam nuclear plant was stopped, NPCIL, in collaboration with Vigyan Prasar, the science publicity wing of the Indian government, placed a number of ads in leading newspapers. One of these read: "Radiation: A Constant Companion in Our Life." It contained statements like "The food that we eat, the water we drink and the houses in which we live also emit radiation continuously," "The medical examination like X-ray, CT-scan etc. exposes us to 15–20 times more radiation than the natural radiation," and "The radiation exposure received by population living nearby a nuclear power plant in 10 years is comparably less [than] that received in a single chest X-ray."[12]

Instead of presenting nuclear plants as threatening and the environment as threatened, this discourse merges technology and nature. In such a political ecology of "technonatures" (Escobar 1999; Masco 2004), the environment is seen as robust in the face of radioactive contaminants because radiation with atomic signatures is presented as insignificant compared with so many other sources of radiation: natural, biological, industrial, and medical. Radiation from these multiple sources blends together effortlessly.

Because NPCIL deals with nuclear radiation, which is ionizing and has proven carcinogenic effects, it produces a discourse where radiation remains undifferentiated and has so many sources (including the sun) as to effectively render radiation benign, mundane, and pervasive. In the past, nuclear scientists and organizations have drawn analogies between sun and nuclear radioactivity and have compared the light and heat emanating from atomic tests to the "radiance of a thousand suns."[13] Cell tower radiation is nonionizing, consisting of low-energy radio waves; hence the Telecom Regulatory Authority of India (TRAI) does differentiate cell antenna signals from the ionizing radiation of X-rays and nuclear reactors. In fact, in a "fact sheet" issued about "EMF radiation from mobile towers," TRAI asks a question: "Are all radiations the same?"[14] It then goes on to answer in the negative by differentiating between nonionizing and ionizing radiation, denoting nonionizing in green and marking ionizing in red. The nonionizing section of the electromagnetic spectrum is also labeled "No Harm Radiation." Based on this image, nuclear radiation in the form of gamma rays is harmful because it consists of high-energy waves (like X-rays) that can break molecular bonds, while nonionizing radiation of cell towers has low energy and "cannot break any chemical bond within the body."

Cell antenna signals "can warm cells, boil water and stimulate chemical reactions," but they cannot break molecular bonds or lead genes to mutate. Can something be a carcinogen without damaging the DNA? Nuclear radiation and X-rays can cause DNA to mutate, but cell antenna signals cannot. That, however, does not rule them out as potential carcinogens. Some carcinogens have the ability to chemically modify DNA without causing mutations.[15]

(Un)Controlled Emissions and Bodily Encounters

Radiant infrastructures are not random radiation-emitting machines. Any theorization of nuclear reactors and cell towers as radiant infrastructures will have to grapple with the fact that reactors and towers are controlled emitters. Nuclear reactors control the radioactive power of uranium atoms to harness electricity, and cell antennas modulate, filter, and process signals and direct them toward mobile phones. The duality of spread and containment is critical to both the materiality of radiant infrastructures and the discourses surrounding them. India's nuclear establishment and cellular operators want to control conversations about nuclear reactors and cell towers. The nuclear authorities and cellular operators do not want to share with ordinary Indian citizens their knowledge about a reactor's nuclide emissions or permitted threshold levels of cellular signals, beyond a certain extent. Some opacity is necessary; total transparency is just not possible. Spillage of such knowledge could lead to public anxiety and panic. It might affect state and corporate interests, as they would have to incur high mitigation costs in redressing affected citizens' compensation claims and building robust risk prevention programs. On television shows, experts try to frame and contain questions about reactors and towers within specific boundaries. Studying radiant infrastructures therefore requires that we carefully explore such strategies of containment, which involve containing both radiation and discourses about radiation.

The siting of radiant infrastructures is often prone to debates about exposure: contacts between radiation and human flesh. Even when experts pronounce particular distances from radiant infrastructures and specific threshold levels of radiation to be absolutely safe, the bodies of victims and survivors rebel. Different bodies demonstrate different sensitivities toward ionizing radiations and electromagnetic emissions. Therefore, many citizens question the wisdom of blanket threshold levels. On television, patients often offer testimonies next to the cell antenna near their house. Such mediations of uncertainty can be seen in the lifestyle show *Living It Up*.

On an episode of *Living It Up*, Rabani Garg offers a "situated testimony" from the place where and when she first recognized the deleterious effects of proximate cell towers (Walker 2010). By presenting Garg next to the tower, by using her embodied presence in a mobile tower's field of influence (the

FIGURE I.6 Garg in situated testimony with cell tower (*Living It Up*)

strength of a tower's signal is inversely proportional to the square of the distance from it), *Living It Up* wants to emplace the audience in that location, in that moment (figure I.6). The audience gets a sense of the affective intensity that would have oscillated between Garg and the mobile tower when her eyes became transfixed on it for the first time. Affect cannot be fixed; it circulates, and it operates not only through conscious emotions but also through unsayable feelings and molecular-level (not molar-level) impulses (Massumi 2002).

In some instances, the bodies of cancer patients—former workers in a rare earth minerals mine—testify. Radioactive minerals such as monazite have interred themselves in the bodies of these miners, leading to cancerous growths and contorted limbs. (The mined monazite is later used in nuclear reactors.) R. P. Amudhan's documentary *Radiation Stories* mediates such bodily testimonies.

Amudhan interviews a cheek cancer survivor who demonstrates her symptoms. She drinks quickly from a glass and then has to eject the excess water through her nose. Audiences see water oozing from her nose. Sometimes, people do not talk. They stare offscreen with sad smiles. A man at his doorstep is captured with a handheld camera; the camera moves down slowly, surveying him from head to toe, showing a bent arm and a tumid belly. Oral testimonies are at times no longer needed; the radioactive body testifies by itself.

Both *Radiation Stories* and *Living It Up* provide platforms for "lay" citizens to present anecdotal evidence about the hazards of nuclear energy and cell towers. Bodily encounters with radiant infrastructures happen at both the molar and the molecular level. At the molar level, we have visible bodies living close to conspicuous infrastructures such as cell towers and nuclear reactors. At the molecular level, imperceptible electromagnetic radiations interact with invisible neural impulses, and radioactive nuclides inconspicuously accumulate. Media remains important in putting the spotlight on the phenomenological encounters between human bodies and radiant infrastructures and in showing the possible dark outcomes of radiant energies on bodies.

Taking seriously the embodied sensitivities of humans living in unwanted intimacies with radiant energies is another way to understand wireless signals and radioactivity. During the late nineteenth century, the Indian biophysicist Jagdish Chandra Bose developed wireless signal-emitting devices in Calcutta (then part of British colonial India) before Marconi's radio (Shepherd 2012). Bose was less interested in commercial applications of wireless and more drawn toward using wireless devices to measure plant sensitivity to radiation exposure. Bose believed that plant, animal, and human matter were all powered by *mahashakti* (Sanskrit for "ultimate energy"), and that wireless signals were interfering with this mahashakti (a notion of energy similar to "ether" in its all-encompassing quality) (Shepherd 2012). Bose's wireless devices were later modified for use in radar technologies. More recently, the millimeter-wave band spanning from 30 to 300 GHz (which Bose's devices operated in) is being used in 5G (fifth generation) wireless networks. Yet again, like the late nineteenth-century debates regarding plant sensitivity to millimeter waves, the electro-sensitivity of today's human beings to waves emitted by 5G cellular antennas is a subject of controversy (Moskowitz 2019; Rappaport, Roh, and Cheun 2014).[16]

While occasionally gesturing to historical controversies surrounding radiant infrastructures like the one mentioned earlier, this book focuses on contemporary media debates about such technologies. Indeed, this coming together of what I call "environmental publics" around radiant infrastructures is not possible without a variety of connected media events and texts.

Environmental Publics

Radiant energies are the reason that radiant infrastructures are both useful and disruptive. When infrastructures get disrupted or cause actual or anticipated disruption, people are affected and, to deal with the issue at hand, they organize themselves into publics. I examine how such environmental controversies gather stakeholders such as scientists, activists, policy makers, and affected patients. These stakeholders compose an environmental public, which uses or interacts with the media to influence public opinion. The environmental public cannot be materialized or imagined without mediation. Thus, environmental publics and mediated publics intersect with and shape each other, and my book tracks the dynamic reconfigurations of such publics and the debates that ensue. I posit "environmental publics" as a key conceptual framework to examine the interactions between stakeholders during an environmental controversy. Many of such interactions occur in mediated venues.

Environmental publics gather around disruptive infrastructures because affected stakeholders realize they have to work together to adequately negotiate the consequences of the infrastructures' effects. John Dewey's contention that a public is invoked into being only when an issue at hand needs such a public is crucial for my conceptualization of an environmental public. In his key book on political theory, *The Public and Its Problems*, Dewey ([1927] 1991) notes, "The public consists of all those who are affected by the indirect consequences of transactions to such an extent that it is deemed necessary to have those consequences systematically cared for" (213). Thus, the specificity of the environmental public is that its emergence is sparked by an environmental issue, and the public consists of people who are implicated in the issue.[17]

When the cell tower panic erupted, cell tower operators, telecommunication regulators, radio-frequency scientists, and antiradiation activists responded. Cancer patients demanded that the towers be removed to protect their health, and telecom operators wanted them to remain in place to guarantee cell service. Radio-frequency scientists looked for ways to measure the signals from the antennas reliably. Oncologists tried to determine whether the signals were indeed carcinogenic. Tower builders attempted to convince apartment dwellers that the towers were not harmful. Regulators kept trying to come up with a safety standard for the emission of signals that could maintain network coverage and alleviate public apprehension. Journalists covering the controversy went around the city with radiation detectors and then published maps of radiation hot spots.

Even before the controversy erupted publicly, many of these actors had been involved with the infrastructure of cell towers. The radio-frequency scientists I talked with described how they made cell tower components such as filters in their laboratories. The tower builders rented space on rooftops of houses and apartments from the building owners, while cellular operators and tower builders worked together to ensure smooth cellular network coverage. Infrastructures, therefore, not only instigate new public actors but also serve as "crystallizations of institutional relations" (Dourish and Bell 2001) and manifestations of everyday cultural practices (see Star 1999). At the same time, disruptions bring new actors into contact with earlier players, generating new social arrangements.

In suggesting that environmental publics be explored as issue-based publics, I do not mean to adhere to a strictly Deweyian framework of understanding publics. Interpreted and championed by Bruno Latour and Noortje Marres, among others, John Dewey's model seems to suggest that *no issue* means *no politics* and *no publics*. As somebody who is committed to retheorizing publics based on grounded empirical investigations, I find it necessary to recalibrate such absolute object-oriented notions of publics. Publics are sparked and catalyzed by issues that have consequences for affected communities. Having said that, publics do not just appear because of issues. The form that publics take on has much to do with historical and cultural ways of gathering and prior ideas and practices of community making. Furthermore, an issue-based public does not mean an eschewal of other forms of political subjectivity realized through public spheres and public spaces: throughout my tracing of the trajectory of the cell tower radiation and nuclear radiation issues, the reader will encounter deliberative publics, publics realized through embodied experiences and contagious effects, and publics as displaceable populations because of sovereign exceptions. Beyond denoting the stakeholders as the environmental public's constituents, the term "publics" in "environmental publics" gestures toward the centrality of publicity to the formation of publics. Publicity should not be construed as just propaganda. Rather, publicity allows for mobilization of subjects at affective, performative, and cognitive registers.

The use of the word "environmental" in "environmental public" denotes not an imagined pristine nature *out there* but a political ecology of densely enmeshed human-nonhuman relations and interhuman social connections.[18] Indeed the "environment" cannot just be about human relations, and it cannot merely be about the "green" or "blue" wilderness. The environment includes the invisible radioactive isotopes of tritium, cesium, and iodine that are emitted by reactors and then find their way into water, soil, and human bodies. The human body is also part of the electromagnetic environment created by cell antenna signals, as the impulses within the body vibrate and interfere with the electromagnetic fields of antenna radiation. The environment imagined in the molecular-atomic level therefore becomes a "bioelectromagnetic terrain" (see Mitchell and Cambrosio 1997).

Why not call the environmental publics formed around disruptive infrastructures such as cell antennas and nuclear reactors simply "infrastructural publics"?[19] Why choose "environmental publics"? Susan Leigh Star (1999) has noted that infrastructures are best treated as socioeconomic, political, and technological arrangements; as such, they are simultaneously "ecological" and "relational." By mobilizing the term "environmental publics," I want to stress the ecological and relational characteristics of infrastructures. Furthermore, most of the book's focus is on the environmental effects of radiant infrastructures and how media shapes the environmental controversies that are activated by them.

During environmental controversies, the environmental public includes actors who debate and champion their positions in various mediated arenas, including newspaper columns, social media hashtags, and television studios. Newspaper readers, online activists, and television audiences may not be directly impacted by radiation, but they nonetheless take an interest in the issue through mediation, and some of them act on the views expressed in the article/hashtag/show. In so doing, they become part of the reconfiguring public.

One example of an environmental public formed around radiant infrastructures is the way different stakeholders debated the cell tower radiation issue on television. The television journalist Faye D'Souza hosts an issue-based show called *The Urban Debate*, which discusses issues affecting urban citizens such as crime, corruption, women's safety, and air pollution. The cell tower radiation hazard had concerned citizens expressing outrage over too many towers mushrooming across cities like Delhi and Mumbai with complete disregard for municipality regulations. On April 18, 2017, various stakeholders in the cell tower radiation issue assembled in Mirror Now's studio in Mumbai or joined the discussions via Skype. The issue that had brought them all together was the supreme court ruling to shut down a cell tower in the city of Gwalior. A domestic worker based there named Harish Chand Tiwari won the case. He and his attorney, Nivedita Sharma, had argued that Tiwari was suffering from Hodgkin's lymphoma, a form of cancer, because he had endured continuous and prolonged exposure to signals from the cell tower for the last fourteen years. This decision fueled the debate unfolding in Mirror Now's studio.

The televised debate in contemporary India is now part of most news channels' prime-time programming, with several shows like *The Urban Debate* across different channels that focus on particular issues of the day. This shared practice indicates the popularity of televised argumentation in the country and substantiates Nalin Mehta's (2008) claim that Indian television's basic feature is that it is "argumentative television." At one point in the *Mirror Now* show, the screen is divided into seven boxes, with different stakeholders occupying different sections (figure I.7). The split screen is a familiar device used in television news to depict often simultaneous action in two or more locations and dialogue between news makers and newscasters in disparate locations. The split screen emphasizes the *liveness* of the televisual medium and its ability to manage contingency. In transitioning from interrogating one expert to another, D'Souza gets an opportunity to shape the debate. The larger section she occupies emphasizes her centrality to the show and the conversation.

FIGURE 1.7 Split-screen debate (Screen grab from *Mirror Now*)

The chairman of the Cellular Operators Association of India, Rajan Matthews, spars with radio-frequency expert and dissident scientist Girish Kumar and concerned citizen Prakash Munshi about whether or not the currently mandated threshold levels in India are stringent enough when compared with those in other countries. Matthews maintains that the nonionizing radiation emitted by cell towers is not harmful, and he asserts that Kumar and Munshi are wrong about their facts, figures, and beliefs. The altercations continue. Kumar contends that the reduction in cell antenna signal limits prescribed by TRAI is insufficient, as it only takes into account acute exposure, not the chronic exposure that the people who live close to the towers are subjected to. Matthews disputes Kumar's claims, arguing that the reduction in the threshold prescribed by TRAI is substantial; it is one-tenth of the original electromagnetic field (EMF) value. He argues against further reduction of the threshold, which would affect the cellular network's ability to support calls. Furthermore, he does not want cell towers to be regarded negatively by the public. With such competing stakes, the cell tower has turned from a benign technology into a disruptive infrastructure, spawning both alliances and divisions.

It is this gathering of people in news studios and beyond—in rooftop meetings and tea stalls—to resolve issues sparked by disruptive infrastructures that I study through the concept of environmental publics. Environmental publics consist of both the stakeholders and the wider public that the stakeholders are trying to woo. Media forms a key arena for dialogue and debate among the stakeholders, and it serves as an important link between the interested parties and the general public of televisual audiences, newspaper readers, and Twitter users, among others. Girish Kumar and Rajan Matthews are using the platform of *The Urban Debate* to convince the public *out there*, the audience of the show, of their positions on the radiation controversy.

Intermediality

To trace the emergence and reconfiguration of environmental publics, it becomes crucial to track the intermedial connections: how one type of media coverage follows another, and how a news story develops as information and rumors flow across various news platforms. Media technologies transform publics by affording new spaces of sociality and novel forms of interaction across scales (Couldry and McCarthy 2004). The cell tower radiation or the nuclear radiation issue can be discussed on Twitter or a talk show, and each of these media venues forms one fragment of the public sphere. What we have here is what Axel Bruns and Jean Burgess (2011) call a "network of issue publics," some of which are formed at the moment of the controversy (ad hoc publics) and others that follow the controversy (post hoc publics). These media help connect disparate public spaces and events, leading to dynamically emerging issue-based publics. Since mediation and environmental publics are so entangled, it is important to discuss intermediality.

There is no one central, all-capturing (or all-conquering) medium capable of covering the entire environmental controversy around radiant infrastructures. Rather, media are dispersed across many forms, genres, and practices: documentary films, talk shows, and digital maps (of radiation hot spots). Intermediality allows for a capacious notion of media by enabling the mixing of different formats, platforms, and technologies and interlinking different media's discursive, materialist, sensory, and phenomenological dimensions (Parks 2018).[20] The concept of "intermediality" accounts for relations among media texts and forms covering a particular environmental controversy, as well as the interactions between the media technologies assembled to demonstrate radiation.

During the nuclear reactor controversy, the continuous ricochet of points and counterpoints between the nuclear establishment and the antinuke activists played out in diverse media forms: painting competitions, skits, advertisements, documentaries, amateur atomic superhero animations, protest pamphlets, blogs, and Twitter updates. These media texts seemed to be responding to one another, to the imminent crisis of electricity, and to the anticipated fear of nuclear fallout. Often, they followed one another as the controversy unfolded: a press release would be followed by an ad, an ad would be countered by a documentary film. As a researcher, I found myself moving from one media event to another while tracking the controversy. The concept of intermediality comes into play here, as media texts refer to one another, but intermediality is not just intertextuality. The practices of producing and consuming those texts are also entangled.

The concept of intermediality could mean many different things, depending on whether it is being discussed in an art history or a political communication context. However, both art historians like Jill Bennett (2007) and media studies scholars like Juha Herkman (2012) agree that "intermediality is not confined to semiotic or iconographic operations."[21] In addition, they agree that "instead of focusing on one medium alone, [intermediality] focuses on the interfaces and interrelationships between different media."[22] I shall now provide some examples of intermediality in the environmental controversies discussed in this book.

In February 2012, Prime Minister Manmohan Singh talked about a "foreign hand," alluding to US-based nongovernmental organizations (NGOs) involved in instigating protests in Koodankulam. In an interview with Pallava Bagla in the columns of *Science* magazine, Singh complained about this foreign involvement: "What's happening in Kudankulam . . . the atomic energy program has got into difficulties because these NGOs, mostly I think based in the United States, don't appreciate the need for our country to increase the energy supply."[23] According to Singh, external groups do not want India to achieve energy independence and would prefer an India unable to develop. The internal problem of energy security is externalized into a discourse about "national security."[24]

Following the prime minister's accusation, the international environmental organization Greenpeace published an ad in Indian newspapers countering Singh's charge by saying that it is not activists who are supported by foreigners, but rather it is the nuclear plant being built in collaboration with foreign players. Greenpeace gave the Indian government a taste of its own medicine by asking about the secret transactions between the government and foreign investors. To quote a passage from the ad: "If you're looking for it [foreign hand] in hunger strikes and protest marches, you're looking in all the wrong places. . . . So, where it is then? . . . *It is in the nuclear reactor on the horizon. It's in every nuclear reactor on the horizon. . . . The foreign hand is behind nuclear deals* that value Indian lives at Rs 1,500 crores, the amount said to be enough compensation if a nuclear reactor blows up somewhere near you."

The Greenpeace ad is both an expression of solidarity with the Koodankulam protesters and an appeal for greater regulation. The photograph is taken close

FIGURE I.8 Where is the "foreign hand," asks a Greenpeace newspaper ad with women protesters pointing to nuclear reactor

to the nuclear plant site in Koodankulam (figure I.8). It is not an omniscient view of the crowd of protesters from above but an embedded view from the margins toward the reactor, which appears on the horizon. The accusatory fingers point toward the foreign-built nuclear reactor, implying that the whole plan for atomic power plants is based on geopolitical negotiations between the Indian government and foreign countries. The nuclear liability bill has been a highly contentious document, with critics alleging that the government has been soft on foreign investors and equipment suppliers. Lacking indigenous expertise, the Indian government has been courting foreign investors (from the United States, Russia, and France), who have been reluctant to put their money into nuclear plants, particularly because the plants are expensive to build.[25]

Examining the claims made by the prime minister and the counterclaims voiced by Greenpeace is one way to think of intermediality in terms of texts and practices. Intermediality (and an intermedial approach) helps me understand the sociocultural relationships through which media shapes and is shaped by infrastructural power. For example, secrets about nuclear reactors were revealed through strategic access provided to select journalists. In contrast, the preferred media for exposing emissions from cell tower radiation were e-portals providing interfaces to radiation maps. The different ways of disclosing details about these infrastructures have as much to do with their material properties (their scale of operation and their method of emitting) as with the way such infrastructures are historically and politically governed. Thus, intermediality refers to the historically specific media assemblage that is in place in India, where discourse about particular infrastructures moves across distinct media systems, gathering and losing publics in the process. Another kind of intermediality involves relations between radiation-sensing technologies as part of a complex media system.

Some objects become media objects when placed in medial relation to other objects. It is important to focus on the medial (and not just media) portion of intermediality. The move from *media* to *medial* makes one more attuned to the connections, conjunctions, and intersections in drawings, diagrams, and flows, which are all aspects of the medial. For example, espousing a media ecology approach, Matthew Fuller (2005) demonstrates that if one moves away from thinking of "pirate radio" as one media form and instead considers it to be composed of elements of complex medial systems (from microphone to reception technologies to mixers), then one observes that what is produced from the cooperation of these different medialities is more than the sum of their parts. I found something similar during the radiation demonstrations being carried out in public meetings in Mumbai by concerned citizens as they campaigned for greater regulation of cell towers. Here, too, environmental publics are formed not by circulation of media content but as part of media events entangled with sociomaterial practices of making radiation visible.

On July 27, 2013, I accompanied Prakash Munshi, one such concerned citizen, to a presentation he was giving in the Meherabad building on Warden Road. We were met by our host Pravet Javeri, who lives in the building. We then made our way through the elevator to Javeri's apartment to collect a microwave oven before heading to the rooftop for a presentation. On the wall of the elevator, I saw a notice asking the residents to attend the meeting. The residents had received complaints from neighbors that the cell antennas in their building were spurring cancer cases in the buildings facing them, and they had been asked to remove the towers. The tower officials had also been invited to present their side of the story, and they came with a blackboard on which to draw figures. The officials wanted to retain their towers in these apartment buildings and did not want the residents to be persuaded by Munshi.

During the presentation, Munshi switched the microwave on and stood in front of it with the radiometer manufactured by Girish Kumar's company, NESA Solutions. The LED lights of the radiation detector glowed red. As soon as Munshi moved away from the microwave oven, the detector lights shifted to green (figure I.9). "Ladies should not stand in front of the microwave oven,"

FIGURE I.9 Munshi demonstrating with a microwave oven in an apartment
rooftop meeting

Munshi cautioned. The radiation detector also glowed red when cell phones
rang as they exchanged signals with cell antennas.

Here, detectors translate across different modes of perception. The similar heating effects of microwaves and cell tower signals can be perceived by
bringing radiation detectors close to microwave ovens. People begin to comprehend that microwave ovens might have properties similar to those of cell
towers when they become part of a medial configuration using radiation detectors. In order to understand how media works and how people use it, it is
important to attend to such intermedial relations, where "intermediality is a
concept that brings forth relations that cannot be defined in media as fixed
forms" (Krtilova 2012, 40). The concept of intermediality helps to ascertain
the ways in which the technological objects of media are related both to one
another and to human actors.

If we consider the intermedial relays in Munshi's experiment across cell
antennas, mobile phones, microwave ovens, and radiation detectors, we emerge
with a media assemblage for measuring radiant energies. Instead of a techno-
deterministic or media-centric approach that highlights the efficacy of radiation detectors and sensors, I am more interested in interpreting Munshi's

experiment as an exercise in lay citizen participation, where human capacities to apprehend radiation emerge through actual encounters with sensing technologies. Here, media becomes a complex assemblage or, still better, a "practice in the making," where particular radiation-monitoring technologies and environmental concerns, as well as bodies and politics, "concretize into specific occasions that can galvanize citizen sensing" (Gabrys 2018, 508). In stressing media relations, intermediality becomes a useful concept to foreground how media is part of sociomaterially situated practices of radiation detection and citizen participation.

And Then the Peacocks Came Back to the Garden: Public Cultures of Uncertainty

The environmental publics I study grow out of fears of carcinogenic nuclear fallout and cell tower radiation. One significant reason these issues have the kind of impact they do is the unpredictable behavior of technological objects such as atomic reactors and cell antennas. However, technologies by themselves cannot provoke sustained protests. Technologically caused disruption can only lead to advocacy or strict regulatory frameworks in the presence of other conditions, like people's capacity to organize, the perception of an affected community about their own vulnerability, and cultures of formal and informal regulation maintained by the state and other players.

In science and the sociology of science, "uncertainty" as a term is often distinguished from risk. The notion of risk is associated with a scenario where the potential dangers from a new technology can be predicted within a quantifiable probability. Unlike risk, uncertainty does not operate within the "scientific calculus" (Button 2010). Uncertainty, in the words of Callon, Lascoumes, and Barthe (2001), carries the weight of unknowability: "We know that we do not know, but that is almost all that we know, there is no better definition of uncertainty" (21). Through "public cultures of uncertainty," I want to consider not only technical uncertainty but also social uncertainty (Wynne and Dressel 2001). The volatile materialities of radiant infrastructures certainly cause uncertainty, and even scientists are unsure about the effects of radiation. However, this is not the whole story of uncertainty. Uncertainty is politically inflected and socially produced. The fishermen in Koodankulam are worried not only that the reactor will explode one day but also that, once the reactor spills radioactive waste, the local administration will ignore the fishing villages and rescue the upper-caste Nadar villages. These fishing communities suffered from the December 2004 tsunami, and at that time the local administration was not helpful. Social relations shape technical uncertainties, as has been described by scholars in science studies.

In this book, I endeavor to explain the role of media in such sociocultural production of uncertainties. Along with culture, sensory and bodily knowledges shape uncertainties. It also needs to be stressed that the literature on public cultures in India—whether discussing contemporary consumption patterns of the neoliberal Indian urban middle class (Appadurai and Breckenridge 1995) or religious practices of Indian villagers in the late twentieth century (Pinney 2004)—has contended that there is a strong relationship between the "corporeal/affective" and the "discursive/ideological" aspects of sociopolitical life (Mazzarella 2005). Therefore, cultural knowledges and bodily knowledges cannot be neatly separated when considering cultures of uncertainty within Indian environmental publics.

What does such a public culture of uncertainty look like, or rather feel like? What kind of cultural density do uncertainties about radiant infrastructures attain in particular Indian contexts? The following anecdote might help us comprehend how public perceptions about risky infrastructures get inflected by vernacular mythologies.

During my fieldwork in December 2012, Sudhir Kasliwal, the brother of a cancer patient in the city of Jaipur who resided close to a cluster of cell towers, spoke of his efforts to get the towers removed. Kasliwal was convinced that the signals emitted by cell towers were causing his brother's cancer. The municipal authorities and telecom operators resisted Kasliwal's efforts but reassured him that they would reduce the signal levels emitted by the towers. Kasliwal feared that they would trick him by suddenly deciding to increase the power density of the electromagnetic radiation. He regularly monitored the transmission power levels with a radiation detector. The radiation detector helped Kasliwal perceive the cell tower radiation—in the form of glowing LED lights—that he could not see, smell, or taste. However, this did not give him complete satisfaction. He was only convinced that the radiation levels had been truly reduced when he saw peacocks return to his garden nine years after the mobile towers had been erected. The return of the peacocks was a sign of things getting back to normal. He relied more on the peacocks' perception of radiation than on the readings of the radiation detector. If the peacocks did not feel the radiation signals to be oppressive, they must be below the norm, and Kasliwal could finally relax. A peacock's body here mediates the infrastructure of cell towers: at the molecular level, impulses in the peacock's body interact and interfere with electromagnetic signals of the towers.

This anecdote, one among many that people living close to cell towers shared with me, suggests that, in situations of uncertainty, perceptions of technology are articulated using vernacular mythologies of the everyday. In this story, we sense the merging of discourses, affects, and practices as relationships between human bodies and animal bodies continue to emerge. Here mediation takes an "inter-species" turn (see Haraway 2003), a turn that also has a cultural dimension.[26] Sensory experiences change with new technologies (detectors, antennas), and yet they are culturally situated: the peacock is India's national bird and particularly dear to the people in the state of Rajasthan, whose capital is Jaipur.

Uncertainty, unlike risk, is less inclined to quickly assign probabilities and numbers to future scenarios and outcomes. That said, uncertainty, with its discursive usage in environmental controversies, is not without its share of problems. While a focus on uncertainty helps to bring to the public sphere new questions that are often not taken up by narrowly defined, official, expert-driven risk discourses, it is also possible that uncertainty is devised by experts who want to continue to create ambiguities about the particular effects of electromagnetic radiation or radioactive chemicals. Any finding that would support the claim that there are carcinogenic effects associated with electromagnetic radiation can be challenged by pointing to another study that found no effects.

Perhaps an indication of the uncertainty that remains in linking wireless radiation to cancer or genetic damage can be seen in the publication of the results of the World Health Organization's (WHO) Interphone Study in the pages of the *International Journal of Epidemiology* in 2010. This international, population-based, case-control study across thirteen countries concluded that "there were suggestions of an increased risk of glioma at the highest exposure levels, but biases and error prevent a causal interpretation. The possible effects of long-term heavy use of mobile phones require further investigation" (Cardis and the Interphone Study Group 2010, 675). As a recent article in the *Nation* by environment correspondent Mark Hertsgaard argues, this part of the results was sidelined by the spin doctors at the US-based Cellular Telecommunications and Internet Association and Federal Communications Commission, who influenced mainstream media to concentrate on the other part of that paragraph: "Overall, no increase in risk of glioma or meningioma was observed with use of mobile phones" (Cardis and the Interphone Study Group 2010, 675). Hertsgaard and Dowie (2018) contend that the word "overall," often used by telecom industry professionals, helps ignore those papers that connect incidences of cancer with phone usage, because there are always other papers that assert there is no connection between them. The industry explicitly and implicitly finances studies (which lead to peer-reviewed papers) that contradict those articles finding statistically significant results about the health effects of cell phones (Huss et al. 2007). Hertsgaard and Dowie (2018) somewhat provocatively suggest that wireless industry officials have realized that they do not have to win the scientific argument; it is enough to actively create doubt because the apparent "lack of certainty helps to reassure customers," even as controversies drag on.

Michelle Murphy (2004), writing about sick building syndrome, discusses several cases of environmental toxicology and chemical sensitivity where competing agencies with different funding sources led to the "generation of uncertainty ad infinitum, helping to make regulation next to impossible" (274). One of the key public perceptions about the mobile phone and cell tower companies is that they are very rich and, in order to save their business, will work very hard to prevent information or research that harms their reputation. Like cigarette companies before them, some antiradiation activists allege, cellular operators will go to any extent to scuttle research that proves their product is harmful.

Some nuclear workers, especially migrant and temporary workers, laboring at India's NPCIL did not know for a long time that they could be exposed to harmful radiation. The company regularly recruits seasonal workers for its Rawatbhata reactor site in the state of Rajasthan. Agricultural labor tends to be seasonal in this area, and in lean seasons these people work in the atomic plant without dosimeters or safety helmets.[27] Information about dangerous areas and hazardous substances was not communicated to them. By willfully witholding information in order to distance itself from being held responsible for exposure-based illnesses, NPCIL creates what Scott Kirsch (2004) has called "geographies of unknowing." Such geographies of unknowing create a perpetual regime of imperceptibility and uncertainty, where nuclear workers continue to not even know that they are being exposed to nuclear radiation.

To comprehend more fully the relationship between media and public cultures of uncertainty, we have to understand the place of media in Indian public spheres. This more general sense of Indian media publics will help us, then, to focus on how media influences public perceptions about uncertain behaviors of radiant infrastructures. Fear or trust of any technology or infrastructure based on media-generated information or rumor depends on the audience's view of media itself. Therefore, media—depending on its form (Twitter, WhatsApp, television) and who is producing it (the state, a corporation, an activist)—carries its own uncertainty of circulation and reception. Publics are a culturally dense concept, and thus attending to differentiated publics based on caste, class, region, and gender is critical in the postcolonial cultural context of India.

Indian Media, Public Spheres, and Different Environmentalisms

The cultural assumptions (about health, purity, danger, and pollution) that influence everyday environmental practices of different social groups in India may not neatly overlap with Western notions of risk perception. That said, by situating the study of radiant infrastructures in India, my endeavor is not merely to add cultural specificity (and variation) to already existing studies of environmental controversies around such infrastructures. Upon reading this book, it should be evident that ideas about radiation, nuclear reactors, and cell towers are not confined to national boundaries but circulate globally through multiple media platforms amid diverse publics. In elaborating different forms of activism and advocacy that emerged within the historical context of environmental movements in postcolonial India, I will be demonstrating that there is no one kind of environmentalism in India. The different environmentalisms there are shaped as much by historical contexts as they are by contemporary transnational processes. Even as the choice of environmental movements I study is guided by my scholarly location in South Asian media studies, the theories of intermediality, radiance, and public cultures of uncertainty elaborated here are not limited to South Asian contexts. In this book, I have explained the many innovative ways that Indian environmental activists deploy media to spotlight the volatile materialities of radiant infrastructures. I ask readers to engage with these media practices in order to better comprehend the intricacies of media coverage of environmental movements unfolding at both local and global scales.

The construction of nuclear reactors is sanctioned in rural areas of India without fair public hearings. While the government is more agreeable to engage with urban elites, it often views rural farmers and fishermen as unscientific and illiterate people whose worldviews and knowledge systems need not be respected. They are at best "governed populations" of "political society" (Chatterjee 2004), not part of civil society, and can be displaced from their homes and livelihoods and placated by monetary compensations. The antinuke movement can be considered part of the long tradition of ecological movements in India and the Global South known as "environmentalism of the poor" (Guha and Martinez-Alier 1998). Subaltern classes waging such movements have pointed out that the ecological sustainability of their livelihoods has been threatened by resource extraction by the privileged classes and multinational companies. Cell towers are considered proximate and immobile encroachments, and this has made them the concern of "bourgeois environmentalism," which is often about an individual's immediate surroundings.[28] Both environmentalism of the poor and bourgeois environmentalism are part of Indian environmentalisms. If we are to understand how the different political and ecological claims of these environmentalisms are expressed through media and find themselves circulating in the Indian public spheres, we need to recognize the linguistic and cultural diversity of such publics.

With an ever-expanding media landscape marked by vernacular newspapers and niche television channels, it has become more and more difficult for any single organization or stakeholder to define or appropriate the public (see Punathambekar and Kumar 2012). How can a project on environmental publics in India both draw from and provide insights about the general transformations that different public spheres have undergone over the years?[29] How has environmental reporting changed with the recent trends in contemporary media publics? I shall mention my own interventions as I undertake a brief historical overview of publics and media in India.

To begin, one has to question whether avenues to participate in decision making about technologies and to deliberate the legitimacy of environmental and development projects even exist in India. At times, deliberative democracy becomes difficult to attain. For example, in Koodankulam, the nuclear science establishment refuses to deliberatively engage with the local fishing communities as citizens and instead considers them an unruly population that can be appropriated through either employment incentives or police brutality. The Indian government has been far more responsive to concerns raised by elite urbanites about cell antennas. Such examples suggest the need to empirically examine the relation of publics to state, citizenship, and civil societies in non-Western contexts through Partha Chatterjee's (2004) concept of "political society."

Chatterjee suggests that only a small elite group in India has access to civil society, and most population groups have a political relationship to the Indian state based on the distribution of welfare benefits.[30] Drawing on Chatterjee's work, Shiju Varughese (2012) categorizes "scientific-citizen publics" as constituted by those who are able to participate legitimately in civil society. He labels those publics that are formed by groups who belong to the political society as "quasi-publics," a sphere in which quasi-legal transactions and informal methods of seeking welfare benefits operate. As an example, Varughese points out that when former president of India and nuclear scientist Dr. A. P. J. Abdul Kalam visited the construction site of the nuclear reactor at Koodankulam, he had long discussions with the scientists at the plant but no meetings with local community members. Soon after his visit, Kalam addressed Indian civil society through a column in the widely read English newspaper *The Hindu*, where he endorsed nuclear energy, as opposed to fossil fuels, as the way for India to move forward. To placate the vulnerable fishing communities, the "quasi-publics," Kalam proposed welfare measures when the nuclear plant becomes operational (Varughese 2012, 248). Kalam's column, which appeared in an important newspaper full of copious endnotes, can be seen as a performance of expertise in a mediated arena. Even more important, it shows how experts publicly deal with different population groups.

The concept of political society as a macro perspective is helpful in explaining general trends. My effort has been to begin with this approach and then see how my ethnographic research on media practices can complicate the neat divides between civil society and political society. I have found instances where communities of fishermen, whom the Indian government refuses to treat as citizens, assemble with metropolitan antinuclear activists in order to build a charter against nuclear energy. Such activities demonstrate the possibility of mediations across civil society/political society binaries.[31]

During my fieldwork, another fruitful way of thinking about media and publics was to find out who the vernacular media and English mainstream media imagined their audiences, readers, and consumers—that is, their publics—to be. When it came to anticipated nuclear fallout and cell tower radiation, vernacular newspapers seemed more open than English-language dailies to carry stories that were critical of the scientific establishment. The English media seemed hesitant to criticize the scientific establishment when there were high levels of uncertainty about these infrastructures. Thus, they ended up opting for "objective" reports—quoting different sources but eschewing opinion.[32] The vernacular newspapers and regional television channels depicted the miseries of their local citizenry; they aired and published stories of city neighborhoods that were riddled with cancer cases, potentially caused by cell towers. Vernacular media did not wait for scientific uncertainties to become certain, for, as one editor of such a newspaper, *Rajasthan Patrika*, said to me, if members of the community are suffering, how can they be expected to keep quiet? To not criticize the scientific establishment would be tantamount to a conspiracy of silence. Another editor noted, "They [English media] write for the parliament; our [local Hindi newspaper] readers are our local community" (interview excerpt, Jaipur, December 19, 2012). The close association that local vernacular newspapers have with their readers is thus different from mainstream national English media.

Arvind Rajagopal (2001) describes a similar trend while evaluating the differences in the reporting by English and Hindi newspapers of the Ram Janmabhoomi movement in 1991. The movement consisted of right-wing fundamentalist Hindu organizations' efforts to tear down a mosque in Ayodhya and build a temple of Lord Rama in its place. The local Hindi newspapers,

FIGURE I.10
Patrika's spirited antiradiation campaign, *bhatti mein shahar* (May 16, 2012)

in Rajagopal's reading, demonstrated a significantly greater authentic involvement with the thoughts, practices, and ideas of the movement. The English dailies, on the other hand, appeared to suggest that Ayodhya and its values system were extremist and foreign to the sensibilities of its secular metropolitan readers. Rajagopal characterizes the distinct roles of vernacular and English-language newspapers as "split publics," for they seemed to be speaking to two very different audiences in India.

The way media imagines its audiences and readers also influences the modes of address it deploys to target such publics. The vernacular newspaper *Rajasthan Patrika*, operating in the city of Jaipur, launched a campaign called *bhatti mein shahar* (city inside the furnace) that aimed to regulate cell towers. The campaign logo depicted skulls and bones around cell antennas (figure I.10).

Patrika opened a forum for complaints and asked its readers, the denizens of the city of Jaipur, to respond with text messages, phone calls, and letters about the problems they were facing from mobile towers. The newspaper articles that followed aggregated anecdotes of people suffering from radiation in different neighborhoods of the city. *Patrika* claimed to speak on behalf of the oppressed collective of Jaipur's residents while placing demands before the government and criticizing the activities of cellular operators and tower builders. *Patrika* spoke of, and addressed, the readers as formal citizens of a general community and, at the same time, vulnerable and embodied members living precariously in a city that was being slowly baked by the heating effects of cell towers.

The split-publics thesis, just like the civil society/political society framework, needs to be problematized.[33] I have examined letters to the editor of *Patrika* from residents of Jaipur and tweets responding to *We the People*, a mainstream national talk show; both types of communication asked media organizations to help them evict cell towers. Therefore, even as *Patrika* and *We the People* practice different modes of journalism in different languages and on different scales, their audiences have similar ways of asking them to make regulators and experts accountable.[34] Obviously, interactive journalism has a long history and did not begin with the internet and Twitter, but attending to the medium-specific qualities of immediacy and the liveness of new media is also important. In the age of convergent media, Web 2.0 technologies work together with live television shows, providing new avenues of participation. The Indian Twittersphere is often polarized, favoring extreme positions over moderate ones and trolling journalists and politicians. Thus, when Twitter conversations become part of an ongoing news segment or chat show, they amplify the show's spectacular value (Arya 2013). At the same time, tweets are a way that audiences react immediately to controversial issues, and such reactions could shape the ongoing televised conversation.[35]

Scholars in both science studies and media studies have for many years been trying to understand the epistemic possibilities of participation. In television studies, the question has been whether an audience (or public) can benefit from interactive television show formats "to hold politicians and experts to account" (see Livingstone and Lunt 1994; Livingstone 2013). Science studies scholars have reconceptualized science as a social activity, where avenues such as "hybrid forums" are being formed to permit boundary crossings between science experts and nonexperts and to open the possibility of collective decision making on uncertain issues (see Callon, Lascoumes, and Barthe 2001; Rip 2003). Tracking various television shows where the same environmental issue was discussed, this book analyzes the scope for dialogue and participation amid epistemic hierarchies of experts and laypersons.[36]

Approaching Infrastructures

A key research question for this book is: How does considering radiation reconfigure the way we approach infrastructures? Radiant infrastructures are not spatially restricted to their tangible materialities; they in fact cast a wider net through the effects of their imperceptible emissions that scatter and spread. While conceptualizing the infra-ness of (radiant) infrastructures, scholars simply cannot confine themselves to studying the visibility and/or invisibility of cell towers and nuclear reactors; they must account for the invisible radiations. And yet, radiations by themselves are not enough to comprehend the epistemic and political orders governing such infrastructures. For that, one would have to study mediations of such radiant energies. Networked media systems shape uncertainties, citizenship claims, and different environmentalisms about radiation and radiant infrastructures, thereby gathering or forestalling publics around them. By foregrounding the critical terms—environmental publics and intermediality—in the various chapters, I want the readers of the book to carefully attend to the relationship between mediation and radiance of infrastructures.

Across the chapters of the book, the central argument remains that to comprehend how ordinary people make sense of radiant infrastructures and to understand specific material properties of these infrastructures like leaks and exposures, we need to map the diversity of media forms and practices through which radiant infrastructures and radiant energies are made both palpable and nebulous. In chapter after chapter, through sustained and grounded empirical research, I traverse multiple assemblages of media (from talk shows to documentary films, from radiation detectors to biomedical imaging techniques) to explore how they afford the different modes of communication required to render radiations intelligble to various publics.

If one has to study infrastructures, one needs to get close to them. During my project, I visited cell antenna sites and talked with network engineers who maintained base stations. I cannot say the same for nuclear reactors. I never got permission to go inside them because these structures are a matter of state security. I negotiated this limitation in my research by conversing with people who had been inside the atomic power plants. If one is to understand infrastructures, one has to comprehend how they are perceived by the people who engage with them. Research for the cell tower case studies in this book was conducted in three cities: Jaipur, Mumbai, and New Delhi. It included interviews with stakeholders affected by the radiation issue and visits to densely clustered cell antenna locations, media organizations, and public meetings organized by apartment residents to debate the impact of cell tower signals. Research for the nuclear reactor sections in the book was undertaken in Chennai, Koodankulam, Nagercoil, Ahmedabad, and Delhi. Interviews with members of the People's Movement against Nuclear Energy were conducted in Koodankulam and Nagercoil, places close to the southernmost tip of India in the state of Tamil Nadu. I chatted with documentarians and journalists who were covering the Koodankulam nuclear reactors in Chennai and Delhi. I spent about a month interning and doing participant observation at the Delhi office of *Down to Earth*, one of India's only science and environment magazines. Anti-nuke activists engaged in protesting nuclear reactors in different parts of India had gathered in Ahmedabad in July 2013, and I attended that conference.

Infrastructures, at times, are very noticeable, yet, at other times, they can seem hidden or "infra." Public displays of nuclear reactor domes in media coverage are a way of highlighting their radiance, their monumentality. While the exterior footage of nuclear reactors is made hypervisible to highlight India's energy might, very little attention is devoted to understanding the daily operational processes that occur at a reactor. Mundane operations inside the nuclear chamber and spectacular displays of domes from the outside are two very different orders of visibilities, not always comparable. Indeed, as Harvey, Jensen, and Morita (2016) note, "Regular operations of infrastructures might remain opaque even as the infrastructure is publically exhibited" (20).[37] This should not be meant to suggest that media cannot give us a tour of the operations happening inside the atomic power plant. In fact, I discuss several television features and newspaper articles that do precisely that. However, governing radiant infrastructures leads to calculated deployment of media to make visible only specific characteristics, so as to manage public perceptions about their environmental effects.

Environmental controversies are conjunctive moments that provide opportunities to reassess previously unquestioned narratives of techno-political development. I am deeply interested in comprehending how, during a controversy, media can potentially redefine the debate over the environmental footprints of nuclear energy and wireless communication.[38] In investigating mediation of infrastructures and people's phenomenological encounters with infrastructures in terms of public health, I draw from the emerging literature on "critical infrastructure studies," including the landmark anthology *Signal Traffic* by Lisa Parks and Nicole Starosielski (2015), in which the authors emphasize studying the materialities of the electronic distribution circuits that form the basis of screen-media content. Olga Kuchinskaya's monograph *The Politics of Invisibility* (2014) explains how the radiological violence of nuclear accidents can be made invisible through exertions of political and infrastructural power. I extend such approaches to further consider the influence of infrastructures on people's everyday lives in postcolonial democracies like India. In doing so, I am invested in not only thinking through the informality of politics in the Global South (Chatterjee 2004) but also exploring the technical and material aspects of infrastructures that can shape citizenship claims and political goals. This is something that Nikhil Anand (2017) and Antina Von Schnitzler (2016) have admirably demonstrated in relation to their projects about water pipes in Mumbai, India, and water meters in Soweto, South Africa, respectively.

The first chapter deals with heated arguments about cell antenna signals, and the second lays out the major debates concerning the construction of nuclear reactors. These chapters map out the infrastructures and their corresponding environmental publics, tracing and unraveling connections. In so doing, the major risks and benefits associated with these infrastructures come to the fore. The third, fourth, and fifth chapters zoom in on particular aspects of these infrastructures: the leakages of radiation and information, the unwanted bodily intimacies with such leaked radiation, and the political subjectivities and environmentalisms shaping and shaped by radiant infrastructures.

In the first chapter, "Debating Cell Towers," I track environmental publics of cell tower radiation controversy by examining the work of the dissident scientists and antiradiation activists who helped carry news stories from local vernacular newspapers to mainstream national talk shows. The talk show *We the People* brought the affected stakeholders, studio audience members, and television viewers together to interrogate expertise in a live assembly. The local newspaper *Rajasthan Patrika* highlighted complaints about cell towers and prioritized community interests over objective journalism. The inability to properly measure radiation and the uncertainty about the health effects of cell tower signals exacerbated the debate between cancer patients living close to mobile towers and cellular operators. After stricter regulations were placed on the permitted signal levels from cell antennas, a new problem—call drops—emerged. Cellular operators asked the state and public to help them set up more cell antenna sites to provide mobile connectivity. Two entwined issues, cell tower radiation and call drops, kept reconfiguring environmental publics.

The second chapter, "Contested Nuclear Imaginaries," investigates how various constituents of the environmental public formed around nuclear reactor controversies used diverse media forms. Following the Fukushima catastrophe, and amid protests by Koodankulam fishermen about the effects of increasing radiation levels on their lives and livelihood, construction work at the nuclear power plant in Tamil Nadu came to a halt in September 2011. The nuclear establishment faced a crisis of accountability, and in order to gain public acceptance for the project, it went on an aggressive publicity campaign about the virtues of nuclear power. These efforts were countered by antinuke activists who deployed their own mediations to shape public perception about the dangers posed by nuclear reactors. In helping to conjure an environmental public, mediation created contrasting visions of a future lived in the shadow of these reactors.

The third chapter is titled "Emissions," which refers to a characteristic of radiant infrastructures. In order to ensure smooth functioning, both radiation and information leaks from nuclear reactors have to be regulated. The NPCIL gave privileged access to chosen journalists to report from inside nuclear reactors and thereby claimed to be transparent about its operations. Similarly, telecom regulators and cellular operators argued that doing away with cell antenna signals would be tantamount to not having phone connectivity. However, to win back public trust, they created Tarang Sanchar, an e-portal to share information about cell antennas and their emission levels. In this chapter, I analyze NPCIL's and Indian telecom players' media practices of transparency, which seek to control the flow of both radiation and information. Radiation and information leaks are sometimes controlled and sometimes uncontained. "(Un)regulated emission" therefore becomes a heuristic to understand both the material properties of radiant infrastructures and the way information about them is being shared with lay publics.

The fourth chapter, "Exposures," portrays the efforts by media groups to depict communities exposed to radiations and affected by radiant infrastructures. Audiences listen to testimonies from cancer patients, whose proximity to radiant infrastructures is captured by lifestyle shows and documentary films. Such situated testimonies carry an affective charge, even as some scientists dismiss them as mere anecdotal evidence. At a molecular level, there is the imperceptible, almost extrasensory intimacy of the human body with radiant energies emitted by cell antennas and nuclear reactors. Various visualization techniques, from CT scans to electroencephalograms, have been used to probe the intimacies between radioactive isotopes and human bodies, as well as to demonstrate the molecular-level interactions unfolding between neural impulses and nonionizing electromagnetic fields. Such mediations of interactions and interferences between human bodies and radiant energies, I argue, help us to understand the environmental effects of radiant infrastructures.

The fifth chapter, "Styling Advocacy: Activism and Citizenship," elaborates on the contrasting styles of advocacy adopted by antinuke and anti–cell antenna activists. One of the reasons that the movement for greater regulation of cell towers gained popularity among urban middle-class publics was that famous cases involving Bollywood personalities, such as Juhi Chawla, were reported early on. The campaign has continued to be associated with celebrities. In contrast, the movement against nuclear power plants, led by committed Gandhian and Marxist activists, comes as the latest stage of a peace movement with a long history of activism in India. The people I met who were opposing the indiscriminate growth of cell towers were often corporate professionals and managers. In my interviews with them and in interviews with the media, these urbanites have refused to be labeled or addressed as activists. They see themselves as concerned citizens. Such labels matter because they influence the modes of media involved in public outreach, the forms of address, and what I call "styling advocacy."[39]

If the first two chapters describe the environmental controversies related to nuclear reactors and cell towers, the next three compare the radiant infrastructures in terms of (1) the radiant energies they emit and the regulation of such emissions, (2) exposure of human bodies to such emissions, and (3) the varied political subjectivities that the radiant infrastructures engender.[40]

During environmental controversies, experts, gatekeepers, filmmakers, hackers, and advertisers have a role to play in naming risk, covering up or revealing defects in infrastructures, and making sense of sociotechnical uncertainties. Throughout the book, I endeavor to work out the notion of "public cultures of uncertainty" by tying together examples across my case studies. Ordinary people use their experiences and their wide and deep backgrounds to think about uncertain futures: the community of *beedi* sellers, agriculturists, and fishermen in Koodankulam, or the brother of a cancer patient in Jaipur who gauged the level of cell tower radiation in his house based on the peacocks' return to his garden. My attempt is to locate an epistemically active conception of environmental publics that is phenomenologically complex enough to accommodate cultural imaginaries (even when they are castigated as "traditional" and "unscientific"), "to make room for the unknown along with the known" (Jasanoff 2007), and to emphasize actual experiences of uncertainty and shared coping with them.

Debating Cell Towers

The Bandra-Worli sea link is an infrastructural marvel. This eight-lane twin carriageway bridge connects western suburbs of Mumbai to South Mumbai. I had taken a taxi from the airport and was on my way to Colaba in South Mumbai through the sea link. On my left was the Mumbai skyline, and also cell antennas that were ensuring smooth connectivity for my taxi driver's phone conversation. He was talking in Bhojpuri with a relative of his in the city of Benares. The whole stretch of the bridge had cell antennas lined up on the left at periodic intervals. On my right, interspersed between streetlights on the bridge's median strip were boards advertising cellular operator Reliance Jio's 4G data services on mobile phones (figures 1.1 and 1.2). These boards continued their prominence on the median strip until Mumbai's famed Marine Drive beach.

In June 2017, the city of Mumbai seemed like a cellular city, with cell antennas, cell phones, and cell phone service advertisements very much a part of its streetscape and skyline. Though not visible, cell antenna signals enveloping the city's cluttered atmosphere were making their way through (un)planned congeries of things and people. Bouncing off buildings and permeating crowds, these signals were connecting millions of cell phones.

Seven years earlier, first reports of potentially carcinogenic cell tower radiation appeared in Mumbai's daily newspaper *Mid-Day*. Cell antenna signals were causing concern for some Mumbai residents who found their apartment balconies in the way of antenna beams. By mid-2012, India's telecom regulatory authorities had passed "stringent" laws restricting antenna emission levels and ordered evictions of cell antennas that flouted city construction rules. In early 2014, cellular operators were citing the removal of cell towers by the government and antiradiation activists as the reason behind the recurrent call drops experienced by India's mobile service customers. With the entry of

FIGURES 1.1 AND 1.2 Cell antennas at Bandra-Worli sea link and cellular operator Jio's ad boards on median strip (Photos by author)

Reliance Jio in 2015, there was suddenly a spurt in infrastructural investments as other telecom players like Airtel were also constructing cell towers on a massive scale in order to provide affordable digital data packages to the rising number of smartphone users. As I saw cell antennas on my left and Jio's boards on my right, I found myself tracing this recent history of ongoing change in the country's wireless industry and environment. By the time I reached Colaba that day, it was raining, marking the beginning of monsoon showers in India's financial capital.

What I have briefly recounted is indeed a history packed with many twists and turns. My approach to studying these signal troubles in India's cities from 2010 to 2017 is to track the interactions between different stakeholders of the cell antenna radiation controversy and the call drops controversy as part of an emerging and continuously reconfiguring environmental public.

As Stephen Graham (2010) has argued, it is often only when infrastructures fail or cause disruption that people take notice of them. Before the health effects of cell towers became news in India, if people were ever reminded of their presence, it was when they faced difficulty in conversing on the phone—that is, in the case of a disruption in the telecom service and in cellular mobility. The problem was attributed to the distance of the tower, or its location out of sight, or the obstruction of the signal by buildings. To sustain the signal and the architecture of mobility, more cell towers were established. Yet when cell towers were associated with cancer, they became disruptive for the Indian public in a different way.

Through their disruptive nature—in this case, their impact on the environment—cell towers call into action environmental publics. Such publics consist of a variety of stakeholders, including radio-frequency scientists, cellular operators, journalists, tower builders, municipal corporations, and building owners. These stakeholders are affected by the radiation issue and are compelled to act to address it. Studying environmental publics does not merely entail knowing each stakeholder's perspective or opinion, but analyzing how they interact/debate with one another on the issues that affect them. From September to December 2012 and then again in February and June 2017, I conducted fieldwork in the three cities of Jaipur, Mumbai, and New Delhi. This work included interviews with stakeholders affected by the radiation issue and visits to densely clustered cell antenna sites, media houses, and public meetings organized by apartment residents to debate the impact of cell tower signals. The fieldwork helped me to comprehend how different stakeholders use or interact with the media to influence public opinion about environmental issues like the cell tower radiation scare.

Environmental publics are never bounded; they are always-in-formation. In what follows, I track this always emerging public composed of varied stakeholders and their interactions, through the course of an environmental controversy. This environmental public is both constituted by media events and objects and also influenced by them; tracing the public entails tracing the relations between such events and objects. The concept of "intermediality" (elaborated in the introduction to this book), with its stress on examining such relations, will prove to be an essential critical framework as I track the shifting configurations of the public. Tracking the mediations of cell antennas also includes attending to dynamic *intermedial* relations set up among the nonhuman actors of the ontologically heterogeneous environmental public, which include radiation detectors, microwave ovens, aluminum foil, cell phones, and cell antennas. These diverse technologies have become part of the knowledge system that makes radiation visible and palpable in popular public demonstrations.

In this chapter, I discuss various public gatherings and media events, and the circulation of discourses and experiences across them. Such a circulation is critical to the emergence of environmental publics. The environmental public, initially shaped by local concerns in Mumbai and Jaipur about cell tower radiation, catapulted into a national event with national TV channels taking up the issue. The environmental public gathered around the cell tower radiation controversy was further reshaped by the call drops issue in 2015. Cellular operators argued that strict regulation of towers had affected their ability to provide network coverage, and mobile phone consumers were frustrated with the problems they were encountering with calls.[1]

In the next section, I provide more context for the controversy in terms of its beginnings. I follow with an elaboration of the sociotechnical entanglements of human and nonhuman actors in making visible radiation. Thereafter, as a way of tracking the environmental controversy, this chapter moves across a series of media events, texts, and assemblages: from a vernacular newspaper report to a talk show discussing the radiation issue, from a microwave demonstration rendering visible cell antenna signals to a public park in a residential locality that was abandoned because cell towers were erected there.

Beginnings

Since 2010, the Indian news media has been reporting on cancer cases among urban residents living close to mobile towers. In January of that year, *Mid-Day* reported that residents of a number of buildings in the plush Carmichael Road area of South Mumbai had appealed to the owners of Vijay Apartments, one of the residential communities in their locality, to remove the cell tower on top of their building. The tower was considered to be the source of cancer cases reported from the Usha Kiran building that faced it (Ashar 2010). From Mumbai now to Jaipur: in its local edition which covers Jaipur, the capital city of the province of Rajasthan, the Hindi newspaper *Rajasthan Patrika* published eighty stories in three months detailing the anxieties residents experienced concerning the mobile phone towers in their neighborhood. *Rajasthan Patrika*'s sustained campaign, which was called *bhatti mein shahar* (city inside the furnace), made the courts take notice and also encouraged mainstream newspapers and television channels, which earlier had been hesitant to cover the controversy, to take up the issue on a national scale. The heating effect of furnaces (*bhattis*) was equated to the impact of exposure to the nonionizing electromagnetic radiation of a cell tower antenna.

Indus Towers is India's largest mobile tower company, operating 112,144 towers in fifteen circles of India with 225,252 tenancies.[2] The sheer strength of these numbers testifies to the ubiquitous presence of mobile towers in India. The number of cell antennas at a particular location also at times seemed com-

FIGURE 1.3 Dense cluster of cell antennas at Haji Ali Juice Center, Mumbai (Photo by author)

pletely unregulated, such as one at Mumbai's Haji Ali Juice Center (figure 1.3). In January 2011, Rajan Matthews, head of the Cellular Operators Association of India, sought to contain the backlash against cell towers by presenting, during a press conference, a survey that found radiation from cell towers to be much lower than had been reported earlier. Addressing journalists, Matthews declared: "Let the headlines be that cell towers are safe" (cited in Varshney 2011).

A lot was at stake for both sides in this controversy. The continued existence of towers in the vicinity of their homes meant that affected communities felt perpetually vulnerable to radiation exposure. Telecom operators did not want the towers removed because they were a key part of the telecom infrastructure involved in amplifying, directing, and relaying signals; not having them would affect network coverage. The inability to properly measure radiation and the uncertainty about the health effects of the cell tower signals exacerbated the debate between cancer patients and cellular operators. The imperceptibility of cell antenna radiation to the human senses further complicated matters, and cell tower officials, telecommunication regulators, radio-frequency scientists, and antiradiation activists went about the work of measuring and making visible radiation, arguing with one other about what that "visibility" actually meant.

Sociotechnical Entanglements: Making Antenna Radiation Visible

Radiation is not perceptible to the human senses and thus requires measurement devices to be made visible. I devote this section to discussing radiation detectors and microwave ovens. These detectors and ovens can be understood as part of the environmental public of this cell tower radiation controversy if we consider their dynamic interactions with cell towers, cell phones, and the many experts and lay users who deployed them to measure radiation. To begin with, I need to discuss some technical specificities about cell tower radiation and the social contexts that mark perceptions of them in India.

Cell antenna signals take the form of waves, and this radiation is often called an electromagnetic field (EMF). Cell antenna radiation differs from nuclear radiation in that while cell tower signals are nonionizing EMF, nuclear radiation is ionizing. Mobile phones and cell towers are not the only emitters of EMFs. Electromagnetic fields are generated by many electrical devices such as vacuum cleaners, electric razors, computers, and hair dryers. Since the late seventies in Canada and Australia, EMF scares from high-voltage electricity transmission lines and electrical appliances resulted in a number of environmental controversies (Mitchell and Cambrosio 1997; Mercer 2002). More recently, there were fresh controversies in Northern California with regard to the installation of wireless smart meters (D. Hess and Coley 2014). Mobile phones and cell towers coordinate with each other so as to maintain cellular communication, and this leads to the emission of nonionizing electromagnetic radiations. Electromagnetic fields can be extremely low frequency (ELF) or radio frequency (RF) EMFs. The RF-EMFs, the ones exchanged between mobile phones and cell towers, have higher frequencies than ELF-EMFs; in this chapter, I discuss only RF-EMFs exchanged between cell phones and cell antennas.

During the controversy, the discussion about mobile towers shifted from their removal to the strength of the signals that the antennas housed in the towers were allowed to transmit. Cellular operators maintained that they were following the International Commission on Non-Ionizing Radiation Protection (ICNIRP) guidelines, which set the permissible limit of cell tower signals at 4.5 watts per square meter (W/m^2). As a matter of abundant precaution, the Indian Department of Telecommunications (DoT), following the suggestions of an interministerial committee, reduced the allowable EMF emission levels to one-tenth of the prevailing ICNIRP norms, that is, 0.45 W/m². However, dissident scientists and antiradiation activists spotlighted cancer cases close to towers where the measured EMF was as low as 0.001 W/m², suggesting that individuals respond differently to EMFs. Children and the elderly are the most vulnerable, and therefore there cannot be a blanket threshold level for every section of society.

Different experts in the cell tower radiation debate assumed different threshold values of radiation to be safe. This is often the case in radiation controversies that involve nuclear radiation. The threshold levels prescribed in many environmental debates reference acute exposure to toxicity and radiation, without taking into account the fact that radiation in small but regular doses could cause slow mutations in human bodies and have enduring effects. According to radio-frequency scientist Girish Kumar, people who lived close to cell towers were exposed to antenna signals over a prolonged period of time, and hence chronic exposure had to be considered. Accounting for the "slow violence" of chronic exposure could lead to setting the threshold at a lower level that would affect state and corporate interests, since they would have to incur higher mitigation costs (see Kuchinskaya 2012; Nixon 2011).

Before discussing how mobile tower signals were measured and threshold values were determined, it is important to understand why these signals are necessary in the first place. Mobile phones and mobile towers—also known as base stations—exchange signals. Base stations link one mobile phone to other mobile phones in the network. Each base station provides radio coverage to a geographic area, often called a "cell," serving mobile phones within that area. Depending on the density of mobile phones and the number of calls made at a particular time under their coverage, base station towers, or cell towers, tend to have more or fewer transmitter antennas. Although cell towers became a target of attack, it was actually the antennas in those towers that posed the threat. Even more specifically, it was the sector antennas that were deemed harmful and not the dish antennas, which were involved in benign point-to-point communication.[3]

While electromagnetic radiation might be an extreme form of matter, one imperceptible to human senses, the radiation detector transforms it into numbers and beeping LED lights. In this way, the detector changes our relationship with EMF. Scientists and experts are acutely aware of the transformative role of mediation. Kumar describes how the earlier measuring device he made showed readings only in decibel-milliwatts (dBm), but this was very confusing for laypeople. As the dBm values decreased, the power received increased.

FIGURE 1.4 Priti Kapoor traversing the house with beeping radiation detector (*Living It Up*/CNN-IBN)

The decreasing dBm that would indicate a rising power level was counterintuitive for many general public users, and hence radiation detectors with beeping lights became popular among the masses.

Using beeping radiation detectors became a way for urban citizens to demonstrate in front of television cameras that their homes were radiation zones. On the urban lifestyle health show *Living It Up*, Priti Kapoor walks through her bedroom with the radiation detector beeping and its LED lights flashing red (figure 1.4). The diegetic sounds produced from the measurement device become part of the sound track as Kapoor narrates the story of how her pregnant daughter, who used to sleep in the room, gave birth to a baby with an eye tumor.[4] The sounds and lights from the measurement device act as audiovisual evidence of the pervasiveness of cell tower radiation in the room, and a correlation is drawn between tumors and radiation.

While these aural and visual perceptual affordances of the device certainly increased its popularity among the general public, many specialist experts cried foul, claiming that this was a move away from scientific precision. The general public, including frightened residents, affected patients, antiradiation activists, and inquisitive journalists, started navigating cities with radiation detectors, marking those places where the detector beeped red near a cluster of cell antennas. In this process, they generated maps of affected regions.

Kumar made radiation perceptible in the form of beeping lights and amplified sound gradients instead of "numbers." The limit at which the red light started to flicker (i.e., the permissible limit of what counted as high EMF) was decided by Kumar. Thus, those people who began using the device without concerning themselves with the politics and knowledge of limits started becoming fearful the moment they saw a flickering red light on their radiation detectors. Kumar put the limit at −15 dBm based on the contentious BioInitiative Report 2007, which posits a much lower limit than both the ICNIRP standards and the new standards that were later applied in India (which were one-tenth of the earlier ICNIRP value). K. S. Parthasarathy (2013), former secretary of the Atomic Energy Regulatory Board, took issue with Kumar's reliance on the BioInitiative Report, which, he argued, was "an advocacy document roundly slammed as unscientific by responsible specialists." According to Parthasarathy, the BioInitiative Report was prepared by biased advocacy groups and thus could not be considered credible. Since Kumar relied on the report, his prescribed threshold value and radiation device could not be trusted.

Common people were able to get some sense of the threat that had been troubling them through radiation meters and EMF detectors, but their dependency on experts persisted. The various detectors were made by different experts, and if these experts did not concur about the minimum permissible level of radiation, how could their manufactured devices be expected to adhere to a common standard? Kumar's critics noted that he could not continue to profit from selling radiation detectors and at the same time claim to be an antiradiation activist. In a tweet directed toward Neha Kumar (Girish Kumar's daughter), Milind Deora, the minister of state for communications and information technology, wrote: "Does your family sell 'solutions' for cell tower radiation? If so, your advocacy is a major conflict of interest."[5] While the politics of knowledge can possibly undergo a decisive shift if people have access to such measurement devices (see Weston 2017), the lack of consensus within the expert community on threshold levels continued to generate uncertainty among common people.

Extended Media Ecologies: Microwave Ovens and Aluminum Foils

It is important to understand the interrelationships between different media objects in this controversy. Often, microwave ovens were used along with radiation detectors to demonstrate radiation. These ovens were supposed to emit radiation of similar wavelength as mobile phone communication. As elaborated in the introduction to this book, the conceptualization of "mediation," with its emphasis on "flows" and "cuts," helps me to devise a radically intermedial approach to studying media's role in this environmental controversy: the medial in intermedial becomes an approach to study relations across media, actors, and platforms (see Fuller 2005; Kember and Zylinska 2012). Further-

FIGURE 1.5 Munshi with microwave oven (Photo by author)

more, intermediality (unlike intertextuality) should not just be understood as connections between content/texts of newspapers and television shows; new media objects such as radiation detectors and microwave ovens enter the dynamically reconfiguring environmental public of the unfolding radiation controversy. These objects are used alongside cell phones and cell towers in rooftop apartment meetings to demonstrate the effects of wireless signals. In one such meeting that I attended on July 28, 2013, atop the Meherabad apartment on Warden Road (Mumbai), key antiradiation campaigner Prakash Munshi made arrangements to ensure that he had a microwave oven ready for demonstration during his presentation. During the presentation, the LED lights of the detector glowed red when Munshi turned the microwave on (figure 1.5).

While one can agree that it required the will of human beings to make radiation visible, such demonstrations could not have been carried out without nonhumans such as radiation detectors and microwave ovens. The "ontological heterogeneity" (Jane Bennett 2010) of the environmental publics arises from the inclusion of both human stakeholders and the entourage of nonhuman objects such as detectors and ovens.

I hasten to add here that the use of microwave ovens to demonstrate radiation is not particular to India but has also been done in places like Canada by antiradiation activists such as Magda Havas. Furthermore, several artists such as Luis Hernan and Timo Arnall have used LED lights and long-exposure photographs, respectively, to make Wi-Fi signals visible (see Hogan 2015a). Compared with these artistic interventions, the repeated use of microwave ovens in public demonstrations in India suggests that they became part of "lay"/popular expertise of making radiations palpable, a part of the general public culture of dealing with the uncertainties that surround radiation.

I continue listening to Munshi's presentation to this apartment association, which is contemplating removing the cell antennas that are present on the building's rooftop. This apartment complex has received letters of complaint from a number of its neighbors living in houses or flats of other apartments, asking to have the towers removed. The residents of the apartment with cell antennas receive considerable payment from the cell tower companies for renting out their terrace and, in the face of complaints, are weighing the pros and cons of removing them. Munshi demonstrates how aluminum shielding can block cell tower radiation and radio waves completely by wrapping a sheet of aluminum foil around a mobile phone and asking one of the flat residents who is attending the presentation to call that phone. While earlier the mobile phone could be reached from any other phone, now it is unreachable. After the demonstration, Munshi adds that aluminum shields can also reflect back the radiation.

Though there is no conclusive evidence that aluminum can completely block all kinds of nonionizing electromagnetic radiation, a number of demonstrations by citizens worldwide, some of which are on YouTube, have exhibited how mobile phones wrapped in aluminum foil lose their connectivity. The other promised action of reflecting back the EMF signals is not that easy to demonstrate, but again, it has its backers. Certainly Munshi's statement could make his audiences more nervous than usual. Prior to attending this rooftop meeting, they had been evaluating the ethics and morals of benefiting financially from a technology that is potentially harmful to their neighbors in the path of the sector antenna beams. Now they were learning that their own lives could be threatened from the same radiation if the residents of adjoining apartments started installing aluminum shields in their respective houses. The EMF signals emitted from cell antennas would then be reflected back, and the residents of the host buildings affected. Media here are not fixed objects but are part of medial events and processes dynamically constituted within emerging systems.

AbdouMaliq Simone (2014) writes that infrastructure concerns itself with the "in-between": the things that lie in between humans that are able to both draw humans together and, at other times, make them withdraw from one other. Infrastructures thus exert not only a material force but also a socializing force that is closely connected to their materiality. The telecom infrastructure would undergo a change with the addition of aluminum shields to its assemblage. The residents of apartments hosting cell towers, who had presumed themselves immune from the dangers of radiation, find themselves having to rethink the situation. The effect of aluminum shields is not certain, but then neither is the effect of nonionizing EMF emissions. Munshi, through his presentation, has shared some information that he himself qualifies as indeterminate, but which has generated new ripples of uncertainty about the future of cell towers. Simone's (2014) remarks on infrastructures are both pithy and evocative here: "People work on things to work on each other, as these things work on them." It is through the implicit hint of the possibility of aluminum shield deployment that Munshi stands a chance of influencing flat residents to consider dismantling the antennas. Like the radiation detector and microwave oven, the aluminum foil is a technology that becomes part of the extended media ecology of the cell towers—or, put another way, the aluminum foil is yet another nonhuman addition to the (ontologically) heterogeneous environmental public.

So far, I have been discussing how media objects like detectors, microwaves, and aluminum shields are part of the dynamically reconfiguring environmental public of the cell tower radiation controversy. Now I want to move to how a local newspaper covered the cell tower radiation controversy. Apartment rooftop meetings had become a trend in Mumbai, but not many newspapers in the city diligently covered cell antenna stories as the local newspaper *Rajasthan Patrika* did in the city of Jaipur. This particular Hindi newspaper did a lot to keep the issue in circulation in the city of Jaipur and built a public around it.

Vernacular Publics

Unlike the English dailies operating in Delhi and Mumbai, which initially hesitated to cover the controversy in great depth, *Rajasthan Patrika* opened a forum for complaints and asked its readers to send the paper text messages, phone calls, and letters about the problems they were facing from mobile towers. *Patrika* had printed a story from its local Raipur edition about the cell tower scare of November 2010. It followed that up with a more sustained campaign later in December 2011, when several members of the Kasliwal family

FIGURE 1.6 Cell towers near the Kasliwal house, Adinath Marg, Jaipur (Photo by author)

who lived near cell towers in Jaipur were found to be suffering from cancer (figure 1.6). Although the Kasliwals had no family history of cancer, two of the three Kasliwal brothers were diagnosed with malignant tumors. Their dog also died of cancer.

The genre of vernacular local news, prevalent since the late 1990s, not only covered a wider ambit of news but also created a novel set of news givers or news gatherers. The newspaper opened itself to all kinds of news sources, reducing its gatekeeping practices to a minimum. It is within this context that we need to understand *Patrika*'s coverage of the mobile tower radiation controversy, with the additional detail that the newspaper's own headquarters are in Jaipur (figure 1.7).

Several articles prominently feature the argument that mobile towers are a problem for the city of Jaipur. Reports proliferate about how the beautiful pink city of Jaipur, a major tourist center for international visitors, is burning under the low flame of a furnace. Radiation levels at various localities in Jaipur are recorded, and a map of the city marked with regions and the levels measured there is presented as part of the news story. Over a period of six months, the paper features follow-up events from the Kasliwal family's news story in December 2011. The actions of local municipality officials are kept under close watch, experts are followed as they measure the electromagnetic radiation at

FIGURE 1.7   Head office of *Rajasthan Patrika* in Kesargarh, Jaipur (Photo by author)

different locales, and new court rulings and bylaws are diligently reported and monitored. However, what really enabled *Patrika* to come up with these 110 stories was its commitment to entertaining news complaints from local denizens who said they or their "housing societies" were facing problems from the mobile towers in the neighborhood.

Patrika editors told me that they practiced such an "open-door policy" (Rao 2010) because theirs was a community newspaper. When Sudhir Kasliwal came to them with his family's problem and explained how many others in Jaipur were under the threat of cancer from radiation, the newspaper felt compelled to take it up. When I asked a number of science-beat journalists in Delhi, some of whom had also covered the Jaipur story, for their opinion about *Patrika*'s coverage, almost all of them asserted that *Patrika*'s coverage was very one-sided. On an issue where scientists and experts were deeply divided, how, they asked, could *Patrika* be so convinced to go ahead and launch a wholehearted campaign to evict cell towers from Jaipur's skyline? When I put this question to Shipra Mathur, the editor heading *Patrika*'s campaign, she explained how Jaipur's residents were facing the problem and the newspaper had to be in solidarity with the community in their fight. She also cited scientists and technical reports the newspaper had consulted which indicated that there was a strong chance that radiation did indeed cause cancer.

Arvind Rajagopal (2001), in his canonical analysis of the coverage of the Ramjanmabhoomi (Birthplace of Lord Ram) movement in English and Hindi newspapers, found that while English-language newspapers emphasized the truth value of facts and imagined their public to prefer informative rational-critical debate, Hindi-language newspapers favored a much more dramatic and subjective style of reporting and did not assume a value-neutral approach to news. My findings here substantiate Rajagopal's claims about a "split public" in India's newspaper production and reception, but I am particularly interested in how subjectivity is interpreted and exercised in reportage on science-related issues. The Ramjanmabhoomi movement originated from the Hindi belt, and local beat journalists were in a better position to "access [the movement's] inner modes and meanings" (Rajagopal 2001) in vernacular Hindi, than was the elitist English press, which chose to be indifferent to colloquial expressions the movement offered. My case study is different. The mobile tower radiation controversy emerges as an environmental question, and technical experts spar over it. The English-language press does not give the issue significant attention even though one would have expected otherwise considering English, as the colonial language of technocracy, overlaps neatly with the purported objectivity of science and, by association, the objectivity demanded from reporting scientific issues. Perhaps "objectivity" demanded that different positions of various stakeholders were stated as they were and left at that.

Elaborating on *Patrika*'s initiative, Govind Ji notes that members of their community were battling cancer and so the newspaper took this issue primarily as an emotional issue and not as a scientific one. The paper definitely did scientific reporting, but in this case, reporters wanted to fight this issue, not just as a scientific issue but as an emotional one: "bahut se jagah hain jahan scientific issue bana ke lade honge, par yahan emotional and by heart, dil ka issue bana kar lade. Jin taklifon ko humne [hamare Pathak ne] bhoga, un taklifon ko lekar aaye" (There are many places where we made it a scientific issue and fought, but here (the cell tower radiation issue), was an emotional issue ("and by heart"), we made it a heart issue and fought. The problems that we [our readers] suffered, we expressed them [in the newspaper]) (interview with Govind Ji, editor, *Rajasthan Patrika*, translation from Hindi by the author, December 19, 2012).

Patrika's idealistic and communitarian ethos is famous all over Rajasthan; at the same time, its stubborn insistence on such idealism was met with impatience by some of my interviewees who thought the paper could benefit from some pragmatism and compromise. I do not want to underplay Mathur and Govind's emphasis on *Patrika*'s commitment to the community, but alongside such a commitment functions a particular kind of media practice, a local news-making practice prevalent across the Hindi heartland in India that works according to, in Ursula Rao's (2010) words, an "open-door policy." Rao elaborates on such a policy, which structures editorial procedures to make "editorial teams working for the local pages open to the influx of concerns formulated by citizens of all strata." The urban dwellers use the channels made available to them by the newspapers extensively to "launch complaints, share grievances, express opinions, inform about their 'social work,' give identity to a local community, and compete for eminence" (Rao 2010, 155). Shipra Mathur, the editor of *Patrika* for social campaigns, stressed that opening a forum for complaints had been a productive way to invite and elicit views about cell towers from Jaipur's denizens. In the course of our conversation, she kept showing me emails and text messages on her smartphone that she had received from affected communities in Jaipur.

The democratization of access offered by *Patrika* makes it a public arena where there is an explosion (or implosion) of public concerns about mobile towers. A technoscience controversy thus became a sociotechnical controversy. Expert voices exist and are even conspicuously marked out in the articles, but they seem to lose their primacy and are drowned out in the cacophony (or "music," if you prefer) of public articulations of fears regarding mobile towers. A pattern of headlines and reports emerges: a certain number of towers are located a certain number of meters away from an apartment complex, and in a certain number of months, a certain number of people have died of cancer, and another certain number are affected. This pattern is apparent from the following headlines from one page of radiation news in *Patrika* published on May 17, 2012: "2 Saal, 8 tower, 7 maut" (2 years, 8 towers, 7 deaths), "Tower se Cancer, Chhin Li 6 zindagiyan" (Tower leads to cancer, snatches away 6 lives), and "20 meter mein ghar-ghar mein log bimaar" (Within the 20 meter radius, every house has sick people) (figure 1.8).

In elaborating on *Patrika*'s cultural proximity to its readers and its open-door policy, I do not want to suggest that the newspaper practiced an absolute democratization of access and provided a platform for all kinds of expression. People with clout, whether political or based on class or caste, or those with writing skills in Hindi, might have influenced these news stories. Therefore, it might be an exaggeration to say that *Patrika* was giving voice to the voiceless. *Patrika* was not radically reconfiguring the public sphere so as to include the participation of subaltern populations or the popular practices and performances of the marginals, what Appadurai and Breckenridge (1995) termed

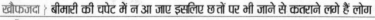

खौफजदा | बीमारी की चपेट में न आ जाए इसलिए छतों पर भी जाने से कतराने लगे हैं लोग

मौत तक पहुंचा रेडिएशन का दर्द

मो बाइल टावर से निकलने वाला रेडिएशन घर-घर में मौत बांट रहा है। राजधानी में जगह-जगह कैंसर, ब्रेन ट्यूमर-हेमरेज, रिस्टर्ट से जुड़े के पीड़ितों की संख्या में बढ़ोतरी हो रही है। इसके बावजूद प्रशासन और टेलीकॉम कंपनियां इस ओर ध्यान नहीं दे रही हैं। पत्रिका टीम ने शहर के कुछ इलाकों में जाने तो खौफनाक तस्वीरें सामने आईं....

2 साल, 8 टावर, 7 मौत

टावर से कैंसर, छीन ली 6 जिंदगियां

20 मीटर में घर-घर लोग बीमार

FIGURE 1.8 *Rajasthan Patrika* headline, May 17, 2012

"popular culture." Nevertheless, the public discourse generated by *Patrika* in the form of the demands it placed before the government and its criticism of the activities of cellular operators and tower builders was dramatic: *Patrika* claimed to speak on behalf of the oppressed collective of Jaipur's residents. It spoke of and addressed the readers as at once formal citizens of a general community and, at the same time, vulnerable and embodied members living precariously in a city that was being slowly baked.

Moreover, one needs to realize that the public expanded, created, and addressed by *Patrika* cannot be imagined as fostering a dialogue between individuals. The newspaper public, or the media public, we have here is performative in that expressive dimensions of idioms, stylistic markers, and speech genres matter. In its way of citing quotes from common people and opinion makers, in its interlocutory protocols, in its language of demanding action from the government, *Patrika* espouses an aggressive approach, at times almost a warning: "Government should awaken, otherwise the public [*Janata*] will take action," or sometimes, a categorically pithy assertion: "The tower is the one responsible for cancer." Such a manifestation of the public is closer to Michael Warner's (2002) articulation of a public as "a poetic world-making" (82). Warner argues that the erroneous idealization of "public discourse as conversation" fails to recognize its poetic function and hence its constitutive circularity. *Patrika*'s action-oriented journalism wants its addressed public to not just exist but to work toward realizing a certain kind of world, where affect, poesis, and expressivity matter because they influence the circulatory fate of the propelled discourse.

I shall now track how news flows across various media organizations and the key roles played by affected community members in such flows, with a particular focus on how Sudhir Kasliwal and his family played a key mediating role. How, indeed, did the radiation issue move to the national stage?

Mediated National Public

Studying interactions in the media landscape cannot be restricted to just communication between journalists but should take into account interactions between other stakeholders who are part of the environmental public. It is often stakeholders such as activists and affected community members who work very hard to get the media to report on an issue, and they can become key circulators of information across media organizations. Sudhir Kasliwal hails from a prominent family of jewelers in the city of Jaipur. His brother, Sanjay Kasliwal, died of cancer, and it was suspected that the cell tower cluster near their house was the culprit. In an effort to evict those cell towers, Sudhir Kasliwal met several senior bureaucrats and ministers in the state government of Rajasthan, who then rang up the cell tower officials. The cell tower people came to meet Kasliwal and complained that he should stop indulging in *Akhbarbaazi* (the Hindi word for "newspaper business" or "media shenanigans") about radiation. The tower officials were referring to Kasliwal's efforts to use the media to mar the reputation of mobile phone towers. In this long excerpt from an interview I conducted with Sudhir Kasliwal, he explains the interactions he had with various stakeholders, including newspaper journalists, during the controversy:

> Then after they [*Rajasthan Patrika*] took it up . . . much later, my daughter and son-in-law met an English newspaper editor [in Delhi] . . . and mentioned that [news about cell tower radiation] should appear on Sunday since your circulation is wider that day. . . . The result was that I received a phone call from a journalist of a rival newspaper. . . . I told her

that I had conversed with her six months back and had given her all the material. She told me she had prepared an article, but the Delhi editor said it would scare off advertisers and that they could not publish the story before. But now that their competing newspaper had published the story, they could not be left behind. . . . I sent *Rajasthan Patrika*'s clippings to every newspaper. So, they must have thought that if they are doing it, then we should not get behind. . . . Then, I talked to Barkha Dutt, who showed it on *We the People*. (interview with Sudhir Kasliwal, translation from Hindi by author, Jaipur, December 19, 2012)

Kasliwal notes that sending clippings of *Patrika* articles helped to convince other newspaper editors that the mobile tower radiation was serious and newsworthy. Members of the Kasliwal family wanted maximum information distribution and therefore asked the English newspaper editor to print the story in the Sunday edition. After publication, the rival newspaper did not want to be left behind in covering an important issue, one that it had earlier scuttled, fearing the wrath of the newspaper's prime advertisers—the telecom companies. Attempts by the Kasliwals and coverage in the national English daily newspaper finally convinced NDTV's Barkha Dutt to take up the radiation issue on Indian television's most successful talk show, *We the People*, thus making the issue known to a wider Indian population. As such, Kasliwal's *Akhbarbaazi*—his act of taking clippings from a vernacular newspaper to an English-language daily's editor or to a television show's anchor—is a media practice that allows for circulation of discourses about the harmful effects of cell tower radiation among a wider Indian national public. The environmental public is expanded by the mediating role played by affected community members like Kasliwal.

Kasliwal's comments also point to the hierarchies that mark the environmental public. The telecom networks were perceived as wielding too much influence on Indian media houses because they funded them. The media organizations thus were very careful to not present the cell tower radiation issue in a negative light. Finally, it seemed popular pressure prevailed. It is significant, though, that part of the reason that affected community members were able to get the media to cover the issue was because they too were upper middle-class elites like Kasliwal or Munshi, and thus could pursue high-level contacts.[6]

Mediated Publicness: Interrogating Expertise in Talk Shows

When NDTV's *We the People* talk show finally took up the issue of cell tower radiation on September 16, 2012, in its episode "Cell Phone Towers: India's Safety Check," the campaign against unregulated cell towers had reached its peak publicity point. Two weeks earlier, on September 1, 2012, the government had brought into effect new guidelines that reduced the upper limit of permitted radiation to one-tenth of its earlier value. The NDTV debate, ably moderated by Barkha Dutt, became an attempt to debate whether the new norms were safe enough, and to revisit the stories that had been surfacing since the beginnings of the controversy in January 2010. From that time, the issue involved many affected stakeholders who would either battle or express solidarity with each other in different public venues. They appeared in news programs and wrote newspaper columns supporting and contradicting one another. Some of the stakeholders would be summoned or invited by the Indian government's regulatory committees for consultations, and a few would hold press conferences. However, NDTV and Barkha Dutt's achievement was to assemble the whole cast of social actors from powerful experts to invited citizens related to the controversy in one studio at the same time. Concerned citizens like Sudhir Kasliwal, who were fighting cell tower radiation, had been instrumental in making the case to Barkha Dutt that a debate on the issue was necessary to create much-needed awareness.

Many of those present in the show—T. Chandrashekhar (secretary, DoT), Rajan Matthews (head, Cellular Operators Association of India), Girish Kumar (antenna scientist, Indian Institute of Technology, Powaii), Juhi Chawla (Bollywood celebrity), Sanjay Kasliwal (affected cancer patient), Prakash Munshi (antiradiation activist), Dr. Anand Gokani (diabetologist, Bombay Hospital), Anoop Kholi (neurologist, Apollo Hospital), Rabbani Garg (mother of a child suffering from cancer)—had been expressing their views on the controversy, but having them all together presented an opportunity to ask for crucial clarifications and to find out whether their views and arguments could withstand the test of questions from multiple actors and the assembled audience of the show.

The talk show format allows for experts and laypersons to come together and debate each other, but such a debate is often moderated and structured by the host of the show. Journalism scholar Radhika Parameswaran (2012) finds Barkha Dutt, the host of *We the People*, to be acting as a "performative vehicle for fostering argumentative television" (630) by seeking explanations and demanding accountability through animation and dialogue rendered in the idiom of liberal democracy. During the show, Dutt mediates between lay perspectives and expert commentaries.

In the show, Rabbani Garg gives a somber account of her unsuccessful attempts to understand what really caused her young daughter's malignant tumor. She ends with the question: "What is the appropriate distance? What is the distance the tower should be from your house?" When Dutt puts the same question to the regulator and policy maker T. Chandrashekhar, she is careful to maintain a calm atmosphere among audience members and participants for the telecom secretary to offer his answer. Chandrashekhar mentions how a number of other variables such as the height of buildings on the signal path and the direction of antennas play a role, making it difficult to give a universally applicable value for a safe distance from the tower. Chandrashekhar also speculates that a number of the "troublesome cases" occurred in sites where the towers were installed in violation of existing guidelines. He further remarks that the new stricter norms were set by the Central Government–run DoT, but the enforcement of norms and permission to set up towers was under the jurisdiction of the state governments. To this answer, Dutt replies: "Sir, these are lives, and if they are lost in the maze of bureaucracy between the center and state, I do not know whether this will comfort this mother of a seven-year-old battling cancer." In saying this, Dutt clearly positions herself with "the people," the vulnerable, and the affected. As a journalist hosting the show, she needs to be—and is—somewhat objective about managing her guests, but at times she has to make sure that lay voices are heard over those of experts.

Talk shows dealing with environmental issues might be the empirical sites where science studies and television studies scholars can traffic in ideas about expert-layperson dialogues. Sociologists of science like Callon, Lascoumes, and Barthe (2001, 127) argue for greater democratization of science by promoting deliberation (over delegation), where the gap between "laypersons" and "specialists" and that between "ordinary citizens" and "professional politicians" is reduced. Callon, Lascoumes, and Barthe (2001) propose "hybrid forums" as the place for dialogue among experts and laypersons, carefully laying out the rules of engagement to ensure that expert voices do not overpower common people's anxieties. Talk shows are precisely the places where television scholars find expert discourses negotiating the authentic experiences of common people. According to Livingstone and Lunt (1994), talk shows afford the opportunity for lay speakers to discuss their personal experiences, while experts end up regurgitating institutional discourse. Livingstone and Lunt argue that talk shows authenticate the subjective experiences of common people and challenge experts to translate their language of expertise into the language of lay experience in order to gain credibility for their expert knowledge.

We the People, as a talk show on cell tower radiation, brings together the affected stakeholders of the controversy, studio audience members, and television viewers of the show. The studio has arena seating, and the guests sit in a circle in the lower tier. Though Dutt acts as the key guide regulating the flow

CELL PHONE TOWERS: A SAFETY CHECK

FIGURE 1.9 *We the People* studio (Courtesy NDTV)

of arguments, moving energetically across the set with a microphone in her hand and seating herself next to different participants, nobody is spatially positioned in the center of the studio. The studio lighting is arranged in such a way that everybody, including the studio audience, is equally illuminated (figure 1.9).

Images captured from cameras located in various parts of the set as Dutt is talking with Chadrashekhar, the chief regulator, are arranged in an engagingly edited choreography. They spotlight the speaker Chandrashekhar with a medium close-up, and then we see the whole studio arena in a wide-angle establishing shot, followed by cutting back and forth between the speaker and the moderator, Dutt. Soon afterward, we find Prakash Munshi and Doctor Gokani taking copious notes, and other discussants and audience members listening as Chandrashekhar continues to speak. This editing of moving images from multiple camera locations is as much a representative strategy to showcase the studio as it is a performative practice of interacting with audiences outside the studio, who are tuning in to the discussion on their television sets; it is a way of making them a part of the discussion, and part of the dynamically emerging environmental public.

The assembled experts, patients, and advocates in *We the People* are not testifying or making demands in front of a judge or government officer; they are engaging in a conversation with one another. And yet, the discussants know that their comments are being carefully monitored not only by publics in the studio but also by the audiences (media publics) of the show outside the studio. The "talk" and the "show" in "talk show" are always in creative tension with one another.[7]

Thus, as the discussants are arguing with each other, they are also performing for the cameras in an attempt to reach expanded publics. The stakes are high. Girish Kumar is often quoted in papers saying that the international norms set by the ICNIRP are meant for short-term exposure and that this is mentioned in the guidelines themselves. For cellular operators and tower walas, this pronouncement carries enormous negative import, for it raises the suspicion of cancer patients who have lived in the vicinity of cell towers for five to ten years that the tower must have caused their suffering. When Kumar brings this up on *We the People*, Rajan Matthews does not even let him finish, arguing that Professor Kumar was falsifying the report. In this way, Matthews anticipates the danger of allowing Kumar's point to be left unchallenged.

The dramatic duel between Matthews and Kumar continued on *We the People*. The studio audience joined in vigorous clapping when Kumar declared, "If you say the ICNIRP guideline is safe for one year, two years, one hundred years, then please stand in front of your own tower where we do the measurement, and if you succeed without any problem for ten days, then this Professor Girish Kumar would never ever again talk about cell towers. So why don't they take the challenge?" (excerpt from "India's Safety Check" episode of *We the People*, NDTV). Should we construe this remark from a scientist as an attempt to play to the gallery? Kumar had also given this challenge to Matthews, when they were both called for consultation by Kapil Sibal, the Union minister of communications and information technology. However, by Kumar's own admission, he felt more agitated in the studio by Matthews's interruptions. Applause from the studio audience created a further affective layer over the "rational" and "scientific" arguments.

Talk and show were entangled in *We the People*: experts did not just offer cold, calculating analysis but expressed themselves emotionally in their conversations. The audience members gathered in the NDTV studio on the day of the cell tower episode also got a chance to interrogate the experts. Many of these members lived in residential colonies of Delhi and spoke about how they had initially been happy to have the towers installed above their houses, but now were encountering a lot of difficulty in having them removed. Some others contested Rajan Matthews's statement that without mobile phone towers, hospital emergency services would be disrupted. An audience member made a point about replacing mobile phones with landline telephone systems. When

Matthews began to hint that not everybody in India could afford landlines, the speaker became belligerent, got up, and gestured with his hands, asking Matthews to hear him out before replying. These clashes could be perceived as staging a spectacle to obtain higher ratings. The stakeholders wanted to rebut each other's arguments instantly, if not simultaneously.

These skirmishes convey a public mood that some citizens are fed up with towers. Different actors of the environmental public can be seen interacting as the talk show unfolds live: such altercations provide an occasion to analyze how the "lay" audiences in the studio might feel emboldened to argue freely with "experts," knowing that they were "live" on television, and this public visibility will deter the experts from harming them. According to Nalin Mehta (2008), this mediated publicness provides a protective environment for audiences to aggressively question politicians: "The publicness of the platform gives audiences agency" (43). The agency that Mehta attributes to the studio audience could be considered a dynamic property that emerges in the interactions of televisual practices of liveness, discursive practices of the gathered audiences (and participants) on the show's set, and the interpretive practices of audiences watching the show on television. If argumentative practices take on different modalities in mediated arenas, then affects and agencies need to be distributed across the mediated environmental public.[8]

The argumentative practices unleashed by the talk show format in India have implications for thinking about expert-layperson relationships within environmental publics. Experts cannot disregard lay arguments, at least not on the show. The voices of common people cannot be brushed aside, and experts are repeatedly asked for clarification; the simultaneous presence of a number of experts is expected to ensure that one expert's views are evaluated by other experts as well. This is of great significance in the cell tower radiation controversy because in order to understand its various dimensions, a single expert is not enough. While antenna specialists might be able to come up with accurate measurements of cell antenna signals, they may not be the best people to explain the effects of such measured signals on human bodies. For that, one would have to seek advice from a radiologist or an oncologist. But even these experts might disagree, as demonstrated in another episode of *We the People* on June 28, 2015, dedicated to the intertwined issues of call drops and cell tower radiation.

"Talk Back": Twitter Responses

One of the limitations of studying the mediated publicness of *We the People* is that I have been unable to study audiences in their homes and living rooms as they engaged with the talk show. I do not know how audiences outside the

NDTV studio "talk back" (Wood 2009) to the different positions on the cell tower radiation issue that were discussed in the talk show. However, I have researched the tweets posted during the show and the conversations that took place as people replied to questions posed by Barkha Dutt on Twitter.[9]

In some news shows, Twitter discussions do lead to anticipated or follow-up discussions within the show, but that does not seem to happen on *We the People*. Nevertheless, tracking Twitter activity does provide some ideas about how people were responding to the discussions happening in the talk show. Invoking the communications and information technology minister, Ravi Shankar Prasad, who had said that there were no scientific links between cell towers and cancer, Dutt had asked whether such an assurance is good enough for people who live close to towers. Responses to this question varied, with some asking for stricter regulation while others accused Dutt of promoting NIMBYism. Several responses suggested that the talk show was hyping the risks presented by towers: one tweet from Karishma (@its_rebel_time) humorously and "pragmatically" explained that if she lived opposite to the tower, she would get the SIM card of the company that rented/owned it. That would guarantee that she would receive good "net speed."

Some other audience members expressed their fear of living near cell towers by tweeting "live" pictures of those towers as the talk show proceeded. @Manikantan (name changed later to @cnm9888) posted a picture of a cell tower, mentioning that it was seventy-five meters away from his house, and that the tower was rented by the cell phone company Reliance. He added that he was afraid of the tower (figure 1.10). Another tweet from Renu Sharma involved posting a picture of a tower. Sharma also provided the address of the tower in the city of Bhopal and challenged Dutt to get it evicted. Some of these entreaties and provocations made by television audience members and Twitter followers suggest that citizens do feel media can/should intervene on their behalf to make the government politically responsive to their demands. Such Twitter responses to *We the People* are similar to the letters to the editor that *Patrika* received.

By closely analyzing media texts and practices, I have tried to understand how expertise and common sense are challenged and negotiated in public arenas such as talk shows. Examining Twitter responses to the discussion on *We the People* helps to shift the focus from texts and news to "texts-in-action" (Wood 2009) and news-in-the-making as a way to study practices alongside texts, and as a way to comprehend materiality and experience alongside discourse. Twitter publics were also part of the emerging environmental public and so were the call drops public.

FIGURE 1.10
We the People
Twitter feed
(Courtesy NDTV)

barkha dutt ✓ @BDUTT · 28 Jun 2015
On @WeThePeopleNDTV are Cell Towers (and our Mobile Phones) emitting
'danger' signals? Or is the Radiation-Cancer link alarmist?

○ 40   ⟲ 16   ♡ 24

Mani
@cmm9888   (Follow)

Replying to @BDUTT

@BDUTT @WeThePeopleNDTV here is one
just around 75mtrs from my house, Reliance
ka hai and I am afraid.

5:44 AM · 28 Jun 2015

○   ⟲   ♡

Call Drops

While mobile towers may not be environmentally sustainable, they do help to
sustain calls. Since late 2014, there has been fresh controversy over call drops.
Mobile phone users who subscribe to a number of different telecom companies were experiencing incomplete conversations. Other problems related to
connectivity, weak mobile signals, patchy mobile internet data services, and
busy networks have also been reported. When asked for explanations, cellular
companies pointed to the insufficient spectrum and a dearth of mobile towers. The Indian telecom minister stated that a larger portion of the spectrum
could not be allotted and the companies should undertake infrastructure upgrades and radio-frequency optimization of their networks to improve the

quality of service for their consumers. He declared that there was no conclusive evidence that mobile tower radiation was harmful, implicitly suggesting that more mobile towers could be constructed.

Since the cell tower health scare, with the attendant restrictions put in place by civic authorities and state governments, cellular operators have come to believe that the number of mobile towers has not grown sufficiently to keep pace with increasing demand for cell phone service, which includes supporting not only calls but also mobile internet. Between January 2014 and June 2015, sixteen thousand towers were added, but the tower companies felt that to support the 978 million mobile phone connections in India, fifty thousand to sixty thousand towers would be required (Ghosh 2015).

In September 2015, the telecom regulator TRAI observed that while on average the service providers were complying with the call drop benchmark of 2 percent, in some areas across India the call drop rates were very high. Consequently TRAI asked cellular operators to ready their systems to compensate mobile service customers for call drops. According to this penalty directive, telecom operators would have to compensate customers one rupee for every call drop (due to their particular faulty network) up to a maximum of three rupees per day. Cellular operators went to the Supreme Court to protest TRAI's decision and calling it both harsh and technically unfeasible.[10] By mid-2016, the court finally overturned TRAI's decision, declaring it "unreasonable and arbitrary."[11] Barring a few such instances, the regulatory body does not have a confrontational relationship with the telecom operators. At times, TRAI has tried to help the operators by having the urban development ministry allow installation of cell phone towers on government buildings and structures, including the post office (Sharma 2015). Along with government buildings, parks became another place where cell towers could be erected.

Since the intensity of cell tower signals decreases significantly with distance (it is inversely proportional to the square of distance), several urban development authority officials started relocating cell towers from residential houses to public parks. To ensure that there were no call drops, cell antennas had to be located somewhere close to where residents lived, and so parks were deemed to be the place. The erection of such sites has outraged residents again. Parks, the one place of refuge from all kinds of pollution that Indian cities suffer, have been defiled. Resident welfare associations in the posh Vasant Kunj area were up in arms when they learned that cell antennas were being set up in their neighborhood park, Vasant Vatika (Vasant Garden).[12]

I went to one such site in Greater Noida (near Delhi). This park was in the "Green Belt" area near the Army Welfare Housing Organization Society.

FIGURE 1.11
Cell tower in park
(Photo by author)

The cell tower there was a tall structure with a room for generators, filters, and coolers. The nonionizing EMF danger sign was there. My friend, the environmental activist from that locality, complained that nobody played cricket in the park anymore. The municipality officials have taken great pains to show just how much care has been taken to enclose the cell antenna structures to avoid "visual pollution" (figure 1.11). This approach to visual pollution is not so much about camouflaging antennas by disguising them as palm trees—as is the practice in several areas of the United States, including California—but hiding them in another way.[13] I observed that the giant structures by themselves were glaringly conspicuous, frightening away children who previously had their cricket pitch at that spot.

I must qualify that not all people are equally dismayed by antennas in parks. Some go about their jogging, walking, and playing without being concerned about cell sites. When I questioned one such park visitor in Ghatkopar, Mumbai, he mentioned that he is glad the antenna is now in the park and not on the rooftop of his apartment. This way, he can get quality signal reception but not have to worry about health effects. With the call drop issue now intertwined with the cell antenna issue, frustrated mobile phone users inhabiting dead network zones have become key constituents of environmental publics. Quite possibly, then, people facing call drops and connectivity problems might also have antiradiation activists among them.

Ecological Metaphors and Environmental Publics

As is apparent from this chapter, environmental publics are continuously being reconfigured at various scales. Environmental publics can manifest themselves in public spaces like the apartment rooftop meetings where tower builders and antiradiation activists are deploying media objects like radiation detectors, aluminum shields, and microwave ovens to influence new members to join the public by making them feel implicated in or concerned by the radiation issue.[14] Environmental publics include media publics: those participating in the talk show *We the People* (as well as the audiences of that show) and the readers of the local newspaper *Rajasthan Patrika* in Jaipur who mailed letters and sent emails and text messages to the newspaper's editor to tell her about how they were being negatively impacted by cell towers.

My discussion of this cell tower radiation controversy makes a case for studying the material properties of wireless telecom infrastructures—not just mobile phone apps and usage—in relation to human actions, as such infrastructures have potential environmental and health effects. While information and communication technologies (ICTs) are hailed as promoting horizontal interaction and environmental advocacy (even by premier network theorists like Manuel Castells), the fact is that ICTs are also contributing to ecological crises and environmental pollution (Maxwell and Miller 2012).[15]

The "infra-ness" of infrastructures is a reason that people often do not pay attention to them. For an individual using Facebook, the data server is very far away. That is not the case with the same individual using his or her cell phone because he or she would need to be close enough to the tower to be within its coverage area. Cell towers, like TV stations and telephone lines, are far more visible than server farms. While cell towers as (infra)structures are visible, the signals emitted by their antennas are invisible, unless humans start using radiometers. Thus, cell towers as radiant infrastructures are characterized by varying degrees of visibility.

As demonstrated through this process of tracking environmental publics, the invisibility of antenna signals produces competing expert discourses about ways of rendering signals visible. The environmental effects of cell towers insti-gate publics to emerge around them. Cell towers as infrastructures are neither just radiation-generating technologies nor mere machines that support mo-bile phone calls and mobile internet connectivity. Jumping to either of these conclusions would only prompt the reactionary moves of evicting towers or disproportionately constructing new ones. I have argued that an intermedial approach, with its stress on studying varied relations in which the cell tow-ers find themselves, will help in better comprehending their environmental effects. Put differently, thinking of the media infrastructure ecologically or environmentally—that is, as part of larger media systems and/or as connected with human and nonhuman actors of the public spawned by it—will help in addressing its environmental impacts in a more holistic way. Tracking environ-mental publics or approaching the study of cell towers from an intermedial framework is not just a prescription for methodological rigor in media studies scholarship. More important, this approach calls for taking the implications of mediation seriously. If and when telecom regulators understand the role played by microwave ovens and aluminum foil in this controversy, they might be able to think of the place of such objects in environmental policy making.

My use of ecological metaphors to describe the environmental public of the cell tower controversy should not be construed as suggesting that political and corporate power are not involved. Cellular operators are the key adver-tisers in both electronic and print media in India. Some of these operators even own shares of media organizations and pressured editors to not write anti–cell antenna pieces.[16] There is a political economy of media production. Though media ecology is one of the key methods for studying publics, the environmental public emerging around cell antenna debates does not a have a flat ecology. That said, debates related to cell towers were not a fight be-tween the powerful and the powerless. The people who started voicing their fears of cell tower radiation were not exactly without any means; they were powerful upper-middle-class elites based in the cities of Mumbai, Delhi, and Jaipur. These influential urban elites who donned the role of concerned citi-zens and asked for stricter regulation of cell towers exercised their power in a different way than the cellular companies. I have been investigating how such macrostructural aspects of power play out in specific mediated interactions and media practices operating across scales.

Cell antenna signals as nonionizing radiation are different from X-rays and nuclear radiation. The latter are ionizing radiation capable of breaking molecular bonds, and many studies have proved that such ionizing radiation causes cell mutation and cancer. There has been more research on the health effects of nuclear radiation than on the environmental impact of cell towers, though significant uncertainties remain about the exact spatiotemporal effects of exposure to radioactivity. What also becomes clear is that because in India the nuclear reactors were situated in villages rather than in cities, the agitation against them was channeled through different media outlets. The invisibility of nuclear radiation, just like that of cell tower radiation, turned media into powerful players in making sense of the uncanny qualities of radiation. The government was not as politically responsive in stopping the construction of nuclear reactors as it was with respect to evicting cell towers. Was it because elite urban middle-class people were agitators in the latter case? These and other questions are the topic of discussion in the next chapter dealing with environmental publics formed around nuclear reactors.

02

Contested Nuclear Imaginaries

As India undergoes rapid industrialization and population growth, the nation's hunger for energy is insatiable. The Indian nuclear establishment declares that its safety record is beyond reproach. And yet, shadows of suspicion loomed over such assurances when protests broke out in Southern India in 2011. For a while, the fishermen of the Idinthakarai village in the province of Tamil Nadu watched as the signature twin domes of the Koodankulam-based nuclear reactor were erected. In the midst of this construction project, they witnessed the tsunami-induced Fukushima catastrophe unfolding live on their television sets. That made them recall the tsunami that struck the southern Indian coast in 2004, bringing devastation to their village. Fukushima stirred anew the concerns these fishworkers had about the effects of increasing radiation levels on their lives and livelihoods. In September 2011, this anxiety reached a fever pitch, and the local community protested, bringing construction work at the Koodankulam nuclear power plant to a halt.

While the Fukushima disaster certainly catalyzed the protests, these villagers were not novices at opposing nuclear energy. In 1987, a year after the accident at the Chernobyl nuclear plant in Ukraine, the then Soviet Union proposed building an atomic plant in Koodankulam. The people of the region did not want a Chernobyl sprung on them, and there were agitations at the time, but the nuclear plant continued to be constructed. Twenty-four years later, the fishing communities were gripped by fear all over again, and this time, they undertook a sustained protest.

The villagers were skeptical of the Indian nuclear establishment's assurances that atomic plants posed minimal environmental risks. There were reported cases of human rights violations against protesters, which severely compromised the reputation of the Nuclear Power Corporation of India Limited. The nuclear establishment faced a crisis of accountability, and in order to gain public acceptance for the project, it initiated an aggressive publicity campaign promoting the virtues of nuclear power. These efforts were countered by antinuke activists who deployed their own mediations to shape public perception about the dangers associated with nuclear reactors.

Similar to tracing the process of mediation in the cell antenna radiation controversy, as a researcher, I find myself moving from one media event to another while tracking the controversy about nuclear energy. The concept of "intermediality" comes into play here again. Media texts certainly refer to one another, but as I have argued earlier, intermediality is not just intertextuality. The practices of producing and consuming those texts also become entangled with each other. Compared with the publics associated with the cell antenna radiation controversy, the environmental publics that emerge around nuclear reactor debates exhibit an even more stark expert-layperson split. Historically, a "powerful expert community" has dominated "representations of nuclear power in the [Indian] public sphere" (Abraham 2009, 13).

With a focus on media practices of publicity and access, I explore how media representations deployed by some stakeholders aided in building a nuclear imaginary of an energy-secure India on a path of green development; I also examine how media discourses by another set of stakeholders imagine an Indian nuclear future marked by nuclear accidents and environmental devastation. At the outset, I want to make clear that there are nuances to this dichotomous warfare over nuclear issues. Many pro-nuclear experts support India building nuclear energy but question the establishment's arrogant assertions of epistemic certainty about the risks posed by nuclear plants. Furthermore, some critics of the Indian nuclear establishment find the antinuke activist voices too confrontational, too unscientific, and therefore difficult to back.

The environmental public of affected stakeholders consists of not just the NPCIL, the antinuke activists, and the affected local communities. One needs to consider foreign nuclear equipment suppliers and investors as key actors of the environmental public because the NPCIL requires them to construct the giant power plants.[1] These investors know that the new plants are risky, and the more activists protest, the more they make investors nervous. Middle-class opinion matters for both the NPCIL and the activists because this is a class that loudly voices its views in public. The middle class and foreign investors are targeted by many ads and documentaries from both sides. The pro-nuclear camp aired ads that included aerial shots of children running across lush fields, implying that clean and green electricity from nuclear reactors is bringing agricultural prosperity. This ad was aimed not only at Indian farmers but also at the urban middle class who find such images exotic and, seeing them, feel proud to be Indian. Media produced by antinuclear activists portrayed a dystopian future of nuclear leaks and catastrophe, highlighting documentary evidence about the trials and tribulations of communities living close to atomic reactors and uranium mines, some of them lying prostrate, unable to walk or even urinate. The middle classes were asked to empathize with the conditions plaguing these affected communities.

All this being said, the middle class in India is not a monolith but is composed of a heterogeneous set of people who have different positions on the nuclear issue. I met a group of middle-class students who appreciated the films shown in the 2013 Traveling Uranium Festival (held in Mumbai). These films showcased the damages inflicted by uranium mining, and the students were enraged by the conduct of the nuclear establishment. At the same time, there is a subset of Indian youth who have a very different view on the Koodankulam protests. In this chapter I will be discussing a popular animated video made by a group of engineering students that criticizes the Koodankulam protesters for hindering the construction of the plant in the name of democracy, thus inhibiting the development of the country. These students felt the protesters were the reason that India could not catch up with developed nations. The middle class, with its aspirations and values, is conflicted and impressionable. The positions of the Indian youth are also in flux, with young people sometimes identifying with progressive grassroots initiatives critical of development projects, but at other times yearning for a better quality of life. The youth believe that the Americans and the French enjoy such "enriched" lives because they consume energy at a high rate. Such positions do not always have to be opposed to one another, but sometimes they indeed are.

Nuclear Imaginaries

In this chapter, I mobilize the term "nuclear imaginaries" to understand the affective and speculative work that mediation performs across the temporalities of past, present, and future. The philosopher Charles Taylor (2002) reminds us that imaginaries, in their orientation toward the future, are almost always drawn from historical experiences, geographic predicaments, and presently existing fields of social practice. Imaginaries stress shared understandings, and media helps to reconfigure them: shared interpretations of modernity, development, radiation, and nuclear power seem stubborn and deep-seated, but they can be molded through persuasive conversations, alternative visions, and affective resonances.[2]

Nuclear radiation, being odorless and invisible, has an estranging quality. What adds to radiation's uncanny quality is its ability to sneak up from out of nowhere and spread through air, water, river, and soil. Living next to an atomic test site or a nuclear reactor can totally disrupt a human being's sense of time and space. This quotidian nature, the everydayness with which tactile encounters with nuclear radiation sites unfold, an experience Joseph Masco (2006) calls "nuclear uncanny," weighs heavily in nuclear imaginaries. What I am interested in exploring through nuclear imaginaries is how media connects these individual (uncanny) encounters with an irradiated site to mega-discourses about nuclear reactors being national-cultural infrastructures. Nuclear imaginaries are in part constructed by cultures of uncertainty surrounding nuclear radiation, but imaginaries are not always dystopic future projections. That nuclear energy is key to India's development is equally powerful in exerting a hold on people's imaginations.

Imaginaries lie between the work of culture and the tasks of policy, and they thread together development priorities with lived realities. In using the term "nuclear imaginaries," I draw on Jasanoff and Kim's (2009) useful advice to consider "sociotechnical imaginaries" not as part of an individual scientist's or engineer's mind but as "promises, visions and expectations of future possibilities [that] are embedded in the social organization and practices of science and technology" (122). Projections of a nuclear future come from both the nuclear state and popular culture, and sometimes are coproduced by the state and the people.

Such a coproduction model necessitates that we account for the interactional dynamics between stakeholders (i.e., environmental publics, including state actors) and media professionals. The concepts of both imaginaries and intermediality are based on practice. Imaginaries are not just ideas, but practical templates. Similarly, with intermediality, the stress is on relations between media practices, and not merely media texts. Studying mediations of nuclear reactors cannot be limited to the effects of media framing but needs to account for the circulation of sounds, images, things, affect, and people in the wider societal realm. There has to be a focus on the production and reception contexts of media about nuclear issues and the practices involved in making pro-nuclear ads and antinuclear documentaries, including questions such as, What socialities and collaborations between various stakeholders are synergized in carrying out such publicity practices?

Some media practices, in unveiling a particular nuclear imaginary, veil information about nuclear risks. Studying the publicity of these nuclear imaginaries helps me explore how imagined nuclear futures are made present in the here and now of decision making. The half-lives of stored nuclear waste ask us to think about distant futures, but the decisions about reactors needs to be made now, for the crisis is "now." The Indian nuclear establishment found itself in one such crisis when the country experienced an acute energy shortage. Huge investments had already been made in the Koodankulam reactor, and many officials in the nuclear establishment were clamoring for it to be completed to resolve the energy crisis and recover the investments. However, the reactor's construction had to be put on hold because of the protests, at least temporarily.

The health effects caused by exposure to radiation from nuclear reactors remain uncertain, and in helping conjure an environmental public together, mediation works to create contending apprehensions and imaginaries about futures lived in the shadow of these reactors. Arguments have to be made about the future by both sides so that risk governance can happen in the present, and so that a decision can be made "right now" about whether or not to halt the construction of reactors. India's nuclear futures are related to a very contested nuclear present and a problematic nuclear past: a history of nuclear tests and remembered experiences of vulnerable communities living close to nuclear reactors and uranium mines. These connections across contested pasts, presents, and futures are represented and interpreted in a variety of media. I will begin with specific examples.

Cultivating Scientific Temper: Educating Budhiya about Nuclear Energy

Nuclear reactors are invariably being built in rural areas, and the nuclear establishment faces stiff resistance from villagers in these areas. For promoting nuclear energy, NPCIL's communication department and the Indian government's science publicity wing, Vigyan Prasar, pick up a country bumpkin, "Budhiya," and his atypical village whose illiterate residents engage in fishing and farming. These villagers are portrayed as being opposed to construction of nuclear reactors because of their superstitions and ignorance. This setting created for the animated cartoon series *Ek Tha Budhiya* could not have been a more stereotyped representation of the protesters that NPCIL is encountering.[3] In addition, NPCIL typecasts not only its adversaries but also itself. The supposedly hapless villagers convene to discuss the issue of atomic power plants (figure 2.1). The village head's son Samir, a young man who favors development, has returned from the city to educate the ignorant villagers. The cartoon animations serve a pedagogical purpose, with the easy availability of charts, figures, and images demonstrating varied energy infrastructures and the time-and-space scales of such infrastructures. Adhering to a perfect top-down model, Samir (standing in for NPCIL) lectures, as the villagers listen.

FIGURE 2.1 Villagers gather in *Ek Tha Budhiya*

Samir lays to rest Budhiya and his friends' apprehensions about the reactors. They ask Samir whether or not radiation is dangerous and also ask, can't India pursue solar and wind energy? Samir answers all such questions, sometimes laughing disparagingly at his friends' concerns and at other times condescendingly praising their questions. He emphasizes that nuclear reactors, like X-ray machines, are controlled emitters of radiation. Radiation in controlled doses is humans' friend, not their enemy. He notes how radiation is used for biomedical imaging, in cancer research, and in producing pest-resistant crops (figure 2.2). He lauds efforts at channeling solar energy and wind energy but contends that such renewable sources are not always available, whereas nuclear reactors produce green and clean energy around the clock in the most efficient way. Here NPCIL, epitomized and embodied in Samir, is intent on solving the environmental controversy around atomic reactors by reducing the knowledge gap between experts and lay villagers.

After the villagers listen to Samir, their questions remain: Can they not just continue farming and fishing? What really is the need for nuclear reactors and the new livelihoods they will generate? It is while answering this line of questioning that Samir is brutal about how this traditional mind-set of the villagers is the root cause of India's backwardness even sixty years after the country gained independence. He chides the villagers for not recognizing that if everybody thought

FIGURE 2.2 Samir lectures on productive uses of radiation (Screen grab from *Ek Tha Budhiya*)

the way they did, India would not have produced such great entrepreneurs, sportspeople, and scientists who have helped the country make great strides toward development. Even more important, Samir says that India needs development, that "only energy" can provide that development, and that nuclear energy is the most efficient and clean energy available right now. Here Samir's answer, and thereby NPCIL's answer, echoes the "need" for science-led development first espoused by Prime Minister Nehru from a very early stage of India's independence. Since then, the Indian government's Vigyan Prasar has continued to tout "scientific expertise" and "scientific temper" as key to India's development. While scientific expertise would involve devoted research on particular scientific topics, "scientific temper" or "temper of science" is an attitude toward development and science that needed to be cultivated by every citizen of India. Scientific temper was thus more of an outlook toward valuing scientific truths than a specialized body of expert knowledge (Roy 2007, 124). When Samir berates the villagers for being content with their backward lives, he is gesturing toward the lack of scientific temper among them as a result of which they are unable to foresee the virtues of nuclear science–led development.

Trumpeting of scientific temper by NPCIL and this organization's attitude of considering villagers who oppose nuclear plants as illiterate and

Are you listening to these uneducated villagers?

FIGURE 2.3 Villager posing as NPCIL official (Screen grab from *Nuclear Hallucinations*)

ignorant have come under severe criticism from documentary filmmakers such as Fathima Nizaruddin. In her performative documentary *Nuclear Hallucinations* (2016), Nizaruddin takes parody to a hyperbolic level by having antinuke protesters clustered in a tent in Idinthakarai enact the roles of both pro-nuclear experts and antinuke activists. To be clear, here her social actors, including affected fishworkers, are not reenacting their own lives but are acting out roles created for them by Nizaruddin. The marginalized villagers play out roles of other stakeholders: powerful ministers and senior nuclear scientists. At one point in the film, one of the actors sits on a chair inside the protest tent, with his hands placed on a table that holds a globe. Gesturing toward protesters, he declares that the world should not believe the assertions of uneducated people. A woman sitting on the ground rises up to contest this aspersion and says she can "teach" him. The smug man in the chair teasingly says, "Can you say ABCD upside down?" An altercation follows, and the woman finally reacts: "We have more knowledge than you." In this way, Nizaruddin stages the beginnings of a clash of knowledge systems (figures 2.3 and 2.4).

At other points in the documentary, Nizaruddin includes subvertisement-styled billboards that caricature official statements from NPCIL. One of these, with the words "India Is Electricity, Electricity in India," is foregrounded, with electric poles and wires in the background. A traffic police blockade is reappropriated with a sign that reads, "I love my India, I love my Radiation." The

You call us uneducated?
Come, we will teach you

FIGURE 2.4 Clash of knowledge systems (Screen grab from *Nuclear Hallucinations*)

choice of the police blockade board recalls the repressive hand of the state in coercing citizens to love nuclear energy. This is the documentarian's attempt to poke fun and express exasperation at *Ek Tha Budhiya* and other Vigyan Prasar and NPCIL-related promotional videos in which electricity and radiation are presented as essential to India's development. Even expressing reservations about nuclear energy is tantamount to being antinational. Parting with an observational documentary style and eschewing any presumption of documentary's claim on the real (see Winston 2000), Nizaruddin's strategy here is parody and hyperbole in a performative mode to make visible the absurdity of some of the official pronouncements about nuclear energy.

At another moment in the documentary, we hear about the Scientific Nuclear Temper Act, a new act passed by the Indian parliament, which stipulated that "no Indian adult or child will be permitted to have any apprehensions about safety arrangements in our nuclear plants." This indeed is an artistic attempt at extending both the concept of scientific temper and the safety assurances given by NPCIL to their absurd limits. To put it in Nizaruddin's words, in further stretching the clichéd set of statements from India's nuclear establishment, she "creates disturbance in the iterative networks of expertise" where statements about nuclear science and scientific temper carry an aura of truth by virtue of being repeated again and again. Nizaruddin wants to puncture the complacency of such official statements and contest the hierarchy of the knowledge systems they impose.

"Powerplant by Powerplayers"

From NPCIL's propaganda and its parodic retaliations/extensions by Niza-ruddin, let's move on to what the Indian science-educated middle class thinks about nuclear power. An amateur animation ("multimedia") video prepared by the students in the Department of Electrical and Electronics Engineering at Coimbatore Institute of Technology (CIT) in Tamil Nadu, not far from Koodankulam, was an entry into Interface T12, a tech-fest event that took place at CIT in 2012. The video begins with computers, cars, buses, and mobile phones not working due to a lack of electricity—robots have become useless. This is a nod to the robot Chiti, a character role played by southern cine-superstar Rajnikant in his latest film *Endhiran* (I-Robot), which was directed by Shankar. The background score is taken from the theme song "Stranger in Black" from *Aparachit* (The Stranger/Unknown/Aniyan), another of Shankar's films. We soon find out that the absence of power is due to a work stoppage at the Koodankulam nuclear power plant because of protests. A few people are shown to be protesting outside the plant.

And then, in the darkness, one encounters a subtitle that reads, "A stranger enters the plant." The stranger completes the construction and, in the process, electrifies the plant and the world outside. Modern technology is function-ing again, and life is normal thanks to the "Electrifier," who bears some re-semblance to Superman, Batman, and Shankar's "Aniyan"—the stranger. The commonality between these characters is that they are not only *superheroes* but also *citizen vigilantes*.

So far, the temporality of crisis engaged by this video is definitively the short term, the realm of the immediate. One will finally have to harness the boundless energy of the "Sun," something that the aging Electrifier realizes and does later. So, according to the powerplayers, the appropriate response to the present energy crisis is to restart work at the nuclear plant, and the prob-lem of long-term power needs shall be taken care of by capturing solar energy. The producers of the video present the "Stranger Electrifier" (like Shankar's *Aparachit* character) as a citizen vigilante who is able to circumvent the laws of the land (the stay order at the plant) and the supposedly "petty politics" of antinuke protesters to enable India to develop.

I am here compelled to read the engineering students' identification with the citizen vigilante, Electrifier, in light of what several scholars studying Indian nuclear nationalism have argued, namely, that the Indian middle class finds in techno-fetishism a way out of dealing with the anxiety of not having caught up with developed nations. Moreover, Sankaran Krishna (2009) finds the Indian middle class (with a few exceptions) has grown alienated from the Indian state (and the larger population) and is bent on retaining their technocratic elite positions by short-circuiting inept politics through supporting "technological solutions to socio-economic and political problems" (82). Krishna further argues, "The idea of governance by a supra-political scientific and technocratic elite is greatly appealing as it stands as a proof for what ordinary middle-class Indians can achieve if only they were unimpeded by the messy politics of Indian democracy and an inefficient state" (82).

The "animated" flying figure Electrifier embodies an Indian middle-class attitude that swiftly disembodies all repercussions of the setting up of the nuclear power plant felt by the people of Koodankulam—all this for the greater cause of larger national development. The frame of this energy requirement narrative—the spatiality of this crisis—is categorically *the national* (or, still better, *the global*); it is certainly not the local.

One other question is raised by this video: Why does one need the vigilante figure now? Vigilante figures in popular culture often tend to appear when the political establishment fails to check a crisis. The subgenre of vigilante films in Bombay cinema appeared during the 1970s, and their rise took place alongside a growing dissatisfaction with the breakdown of the legal system and the spread of state corruption. The appearance of this vigilante figure is also, therefore, a subtle hint that the Indian political and scientific establishment has failed to take decisions to effectively check the crisis (which is closure of the nuclear power plant) and has succumbed to the whims of a handful of protesters.

During the heyday of nuclear nationalism in 1998, India had its own atomic superhero Parmanu (atom), part of the Raj comic series, who would fight villains and supervillains in order to preserve a precarious present. Vinay, an ordinary cop, would be transformed into the hypermasculine Parmanu, who acquired atomic powers when he donned a suit. This vigilante would then protect the nation, something that the state apparatus (Vinay, the police) is unable to do within the ambit of existing laws. To legitimize their actions (the killing of people), the vigilantes need strong villains who have special powers. The villains in *Parmanu*, the comic series named after its hero, combine magic powers, yogic powers, and scientific powers and are capable of doing "absolute wrongs": they are often terrorists, monsters, dictators, and megalomaniac scientists (Kaur 2012). The twist in the tale brought by *Powerplant by Powerplayers* is that one cannot exactly identify the villain in this animated piece. The vigilante Electrifier does not seem to kill anybody; he just bypasses the obstacles put forward by the antinuke activists and local community protesters, as well as legal orders that barred entry into the plant.

The lack of villainous figures in this short speculative fiction carries an implicit suggestion that the local community's protests are not worth serious consideration, for they are preventing India from reaching its true development potential. One is not dealing with villains here but with people who are "nobodies" (no-bodies) or, at best, "collateral damage," in the eyes of the technocratic, elitist Indian middle class. The same rhetoric that postcolonial societies remain in the "waiting room of history" and hence need to catch up with the modern "West" (Chakrabarty 2000) operates in cases where the state, in connivance with multinational corporations, is building resource extraction enclaves in the form of mining activities in tribal areas or setting up industrial plants displacing local communities dependent on agriculture from their lands. This discourse paints the protesters (composed of marginal populations who find themselves in the least favorable position to be able to protect their rights to land, water, livelihood, and dignity) as unnecessary impediments. Such problematic Indians are seen as exploiting the nation's democratic ethos to keep India from catching up with the rest of the world.

The portrayal of the protesters in this video not as "villains" but as "sacrificial no-bodies" is symptomatic of the genocidal impulse in the Indian middle class that has come from a triangulation of the ideologies of development, science, and security. Social psychoanalyst Ashis Nandy (1998) articulates this triangulation in the following manner: "There are a lot of Indians now who are willing to sacrifice the unmanageable, chaotic real-life Indians for the sake of the idea of India" (293). This "idea of India" is an affective desire, which mobilizes symbolic resources in the form of media representations, and these representations compensate for gaps in knowledge. It is also this affective desire that prevents Indian nuclear scientists from conceding that there are epistemic uncertainties about the ontological (in)securities of nuclear radiation and radioactive waste.

While the atomic superhero Parmanu has come to embody India's nuclear nationalism around the atomic bomb by ensuring national security (Kaur 2012), the Stranger's efforts in *Powerplant by Powerplayers* are about meeting the country's energy needs and paving the way for national progress. Instead of securitizing against the threat of a possible nuclear disaster, the animation seeks to securitize a seamless future of continuously available energy. Such a discourse of "energy security" finds an obstacle in the form of protesters, but unlike terrorists who can easily be categorized as rank outsiders, local communities cannot be externalized as *noncitizens*, although they are certainly portrayed as *lesser citizens*.

I shall continue these debates about the topic of atomic energy by discussing how activist mediations critique nuclear reactors.

Activist Media Practices

Many activists who were supportive of the agitation against the Koodankulam nuclear plant told me that they felt the mainstream media (both print and electronic formats) had ignored the struggles of common people and their concerns about the atomic reactor. Some media (especially the English-language media from New Delhi) hardly came down south to Koodankulam, and when they did, simply got a sound bite from the government representative and then one more from S. P. Udayakumar, the leader of the People's Movement against Nuclear Energy (PMANE).[4] With journalists not well connected among themselves and with the difference in languages (Hindi and Tamil) creating a further barrier, there is bound to be biased and unverified coverage. With such a news practice protocol, one could not expect any detailed or nuanced reporting. Among local Tamil media, while the newspaper *Dinamalar* often printed negatively biased stories about PMANE, the Puthiya Thalaimurai TV channel, headquartered in Chennai, not only favorably covered the antinuke struggle but also stationed one of its correspondents in Koodankulam.

According to activists, there were live tweets coming from Koodankulam, but Facebook groups formed by PMANE were more active than Twitter. Facebook offered a wider space for local fishermen groups to express themselves in their language, Tamil, an affordance that was not available on Twitter. Another popular tactic for local community members in Koodankulam was texting metropolitan activists (in cities like Delhi and Chennai) about fasting events and police firing on protesters, which were then time-stamped and put on advocacy blogs and websites such as *Chai Kadai* and DiaNuke.[5] Sometimes this circulation of information on various social media platforms led to both established media houses as well as civil society members highlighting the issue and calling on administrators to take action. Several short time-stamped updates posted about events on the ground in Koodankulam can be found on the *Chai Kadai* blog. The snippet or the meme became a form that lent itself to intermedial circulation: texts, tweets, and Facebook status updates:

> 06.37 p.m.—Police on a rampage in Idinthakarai. They continue to attack, loot and destroy the Idinthakarai Tsunami Housing Colony. Amudhan R P status update

> 8.45 a.m. (fron [from] Nityanand)
> *I spoke to Sagaya Initha, a resident of Tsunami Colony, ward councillor and a prominent activist in the local anti-nuclear movement. This is what*

she had to say: "Last evening, I was at the Lourdu Matha church with the protest. The police entered Tsunami colony and went on a rampage. At least three houses have been badly damaged. Children's ear-rings and other small jewellery have been stolen. The window panes in at least 25 houses have been destroyed. They have been beating up just about any youth that walks by. Two people were arrested. The cycle parked in front of my house is broken. But now, looking around me and seeing the extent of damage to other people's property, I feel that my loss is not that significant. The police has opened cupboards and almirahs and pulled out people's clothes. Has the police department been instructed to loot our property? Are they police or dacoits?" (Chai Kadai blog)

During a conversation, Nityanand Jayaraman explained that time-stamped updates such as these were an initiative that the Chennai Solidarity Group for Koodankulam Struggle took upon itself to amplify news that the mainstream media would not cover. A need was felt to create one's own media. Incidents like houses being broken into, boys arrested by police on sedition charges, and protesters being *lathi*-charged (beaten by batons) became too mundane for national mainstream media to report. These blogs persisted with their efforts to chronicle each wrongdoing committed by the administration on a day-to-day basis. The blogs can now be read as collected archives of state oppression of local communities.[6]

St. Lourdes Mary Church of Idinthakarai served as the hub for the protesters. The parish is equipped with a robust internet connection and a functional computer from which press releases and Facebook updates, accompanied by pictures, were sent out.[7] Antony Kebiston Fernando, a grocery shop owner and local activist, has an internet connection in his store and periodically updated the Koodankulam page.[8] He was joined by photographers and documentarians from all around the state of Tamil Nadu, including Amritharaj Stephen and R. P. Amudhan. For some time, the electricity supply in the Koodankulam region was cut off, which hindered internet access and the charging of mobile phones.

Twitter seems to have currency among urban, middle-class, and English-using circulators, but it has yet to bridge the urban-rural divide in India. Facebook worked better for translocal/transnational collaborations among anti-nuke activist teams from Koodankulam, Chennai, and Delhi, as well as from Japan and Germany. Activists claimed that diasporic Tamilians living in the United States, Singapore, Malaysia, France, and the United Kingdom were following events through Facebook and social media because the mainstream media, even the Tamil-language media, was biased and politically motivated. Tamil newspapers like *Dinamalar* did cover the antinuclear agitations but were selective in their reporting. They hyped the spectacular aspects of the protests but failed to mention the level of police atrocity the fishermen were subjected to. Some antinuclear activists were even portrayed as antinationals who were being funded by foreign money to destabilize India. S. P. Udayakumar, the leader of PMANE, was maligned. His name Uday, meaning "kick" in Tamil, was deployed to suggest that he was fleeing the protests to avoid being kicked by the public. Numerous times, *Dinamalar* presumed that the protests would end soon, carrying a box item that read, "bussaanadhu porattam," meaning "the agitation has fizzled out" (N. Basu 2012).

One antinuclear organizer acknowledged Facebook as an invaluable tool for documenting and promoting the Koodankulam struggle but noted that the "me-centricity" of the Facebook interface for ordinary users was a limitation. Since the social media platform is geared toward personalization and customization, it makes publicizing issues challenging at times (also see Langlois et al. 2009). The Facebook posts of the Koodankulam struggle page would be visible to its followers for a short time and only if there was considerable interaction between the follower and the page. In addition to financial constraints and the me-centricity of certain social media platforms, these activists emphasize that they are not city-based NGOs working on urban issues that have social media–led public relations campaigns.[9] The antinuclear issue is not particularly an urban issue and thus does not have similar resonance on Twitter, which is popular with urban users. Thus, one activist reasoned, conversations about rural issues do not endure on Twitter: momentous spikes are possible, but steady circulation is difficult. With the government espousing discourses of nuclear nationalism and energy security, being antinuclear in India is sometimes considered antinational; hence some activists, fearing government surveillance, prefer to work anonymously on social media.

The on-the-ground movement at Koodankulam is being led by the PMANE, a movement that derives a certain autonomy precisely from its informal and local organizing methods. The PMANE had sustained a protest for a duration of about two years.[10] Along with an emphasis on sustenance, the protesters have also not shied away from manufacturing disruptions and spectacle. The Madras High Court decided to allow fuel loading in the Koodankulam nuclear plant on September 9, 2012. In response to the court's decision, the protesters squatted on the beach and then symbolically buried themselves in mass graves (figure 2.5). During the same time, anti-dam protestors were doing Jal Satyagrah in the province of Madhya Pradesh. Demand-

FIGURE 2.5 Mass graves in sand protests (Courtesy Countercurrents website)

ing land as compensation and reduction in water levels of the Omkareshwar Dam, they had immersed themselves in water and pledged to not come to land unless the government accepted their demands. Two days later, on September 14, 2012, taking a cue from villagers of Khandwa district in Madhya Pradesh, the Koodankulam protesters walked into the sea, threatening to drown themselves. On other occasions, they have blocked roads leading to the plant project site by lying down on them. They have laid siege to the Tuticorin port and blocked passage of ships to protest the police brutality meted out to residents of Koodankulam. These spectacles drew significant media attention.[11]

These are "image events" (Delicath and DeLuca 2003) that radical ecology groups stage for wider media distribution. The Koodankulam protesters were not getting sufficient national attention because of other citizens' indifference to this issue or their preoccupation with other issues. The beach graves and Jal Satyagrah made a lot of newspaper readers, web surfers, and television audiences take notice. These image events invite multiple interpretations and gesture toward several histories and arguments. These nonviolent acts of speaking truth to power (*Satyagrah*) have roots in India's freedom movement led by Mahatma Gandhi. Furthermore, these acts of immersing oneself in the ocean or emplacing oneself in the shore by digging a grave suggest that the protesters have an embodied relationship with the land and the sea, which they do not want to relinquish. Such tactics of Jal Satyagrah have been used earlier in prominent environmental movements in India such as the Narmada Bachao Andolan (Save the Narmada Struggle).[12]

The most comprehensive documentation of the antinuke protests in Koodankulam has been done by photojournalist Amirtharaj Stephen. Stephen grew up in Tuticorin (not far from Koodankulam) in an atomic township where his father worked at the heavy water plant.[13]

The atomic power plants in Koodankulam were literally being constructed in the backyard of his native village, Kavalkinaru, in the Tirunelveli district of Tamil Nadu. Stephen spent a lot of time with the villagers protesting the nuclear reactors and realized that the government was not answering the rather simple questions that these villagers were asking about the safety of their lives and the security of the plant.

The local Tamil media, the Indian national newspapers and television channels, and even international outlets such as the *Washington Post*, the *New York Times*, and Russia Today (RT) TV channel intermittently covered the antinuke protests in Koondakulam. Each of these major local, national, and international media houses depicted the subaltern struggles of the lungi-clad fishermen astride their *dinghies* and of the state police lathi-charging innocent women and children. But in doing so, they further deepened the subalternity of the struggle, exoticized popular democracy in India, and depicted nuclear politics in this country as a mad circus. One *New York Times* feature writer insinuated that the villagers were eating nutritional supplements to sustain themselves through the long duration of a protest fast, thereby questioning the authenticity of the subaltern (see Hayden 2012).

Amid all this, Amirtharaj Stephen remained the only photojournalist to document the struggle from the side of protesters; almost all other reportage was conducted by journalists with police protection on their side. One can find spectacle and affect in Stephen's pictures of the protest just as in *Dinamalar*, *The Hindu*, and the *New York Times*. But, along with that, Stephen shows the expressivity of the protesters and practices a form of activist witnessing that is only possible if one documents the struggle from the perspective of the beaten: as audiences, we are brought closer to the despair and anguish of the protesters. In his photographs, even as the protesters are being hit and are falling down, Stephen preserves the subject's humanity. Through an aesthetic strategy that relies on low-shot angles and shots of bodies in motion, he accords action (and a looming presence) to the social actors he photographs (figures 2.6–2.8). The antinuke protesters are not victimized individuals; they

FIGURES 2.6 AND 2.7 Photos of antinuke struggle by Amirtharaj Stephen (Published in *Galli* magazine, January 16, 2013)

FIGURE 2.8 Photo of antinuke struggle by Amirtharaj Stephen (Published in *Galli* magazine, January 16, 2013)

look distressed but are active, attentive, and sentient. Furthermore, Stephen shows the buildup to the protest and what transpires between one protest and the next: his photographs document children drawing postcards, mothers praying in church fearing a clampdown by local police officials, and women marching to protest through the narrow lanes of surrounding villages.

When I asked Stephen why his photographs are so markedly different from those appearing in other media outlets, he explained that he spent much more time in the villages than any journalist or photographer affiliated with a media outlet could.[14] The media vans of mainstream news outlets would leave by five in the evening, and thus the photographers were unable to show just how many fishermen slept on the beaches, the evening prayers in church, and the bonfire the protesters lit to stay warm late at night. Stephen also clarified that even the local newspaper photographer could only be on the protest site for two hours a day because the newspaper worked with minimum resources and the photographer's services were required in several other sites around the district headquarters of Tirunelveli. Having grown up in the area, Stephen knew the terrain well, and that helped. Finally, he was documenting the struggle from within: the children and women fighting the government trusted him as one of their own. I have delved into Stephen's photographic practices in granular detail to emphasize that media practices shape nuclear imaginaries. The media practices of local, national, and international media outlets need to be intermedially related to Stephen's photojournalism so as to comprehensively make sense of just how the media envelop the social.

The organizational strategies and tactics employed by the PMANE are connected to nuclear imaginaries. However, nuclear imaginaries in India are not—and cannot—just be about the technical aspects of nuclear energy and radioactivity.[15] As sociologist Shiv Visvanathan (2012) put it poignantly, "Koodankulam is about communities struggling with the nation state. A community as a local entity seeks its own interpretation of the future." In such an interpretation, the ecologies of sea and fishing and the idea of commons must be preserved. Such a sociotechnical imaginary is embodied in the protest practices of PMANE enacted in the present, whether it is the relay fast or Theripu, the graves in the beach or the capture of ports. This is one form of present-ing the nuclear imaginary. There was another imaginary that activists such as Jayaraman and Yasvir Arya sought to create, which challenged the exceptional status of nuclear science in India.

Soon after the police brutalities in Koodankulam, Jayaraman wrote an article in *Tehelka* magazine on September 22, which questioned the preparedness of the Indian government if a disaster like the one in Fukushima were to hit the southern coast of Tamil Nadu.[16] Jayaraman suggested that if a disaster were to occur, the nuclear establishment would be off the scene, and the responsibility for coordinating evacuation, relief efforts, and rehabilitation would fall to the local administration. Around the time Jayaraman was writing this article, an accident occurred in the Sivakasi fireworks factory (in the same state of Tamil Nadu), in which thirty-eight people were killed and many others injured.[17] Jayaraman argued that a local administration, which was incapable of controlling a fireworks factory accident, cannot possibly be relied on to handle the aftermath of a nuclear disaster. During our conversation, I mentioned to Jayaraman that in his piece he had effectively rendered banal the safety reports prepared by the nuclear establishment. Nuclear science alone could not help in case of leaks. Scientific experts could not fly high; they had to be brought down to encounter on-the-ground realities. When I asked Jayaraman to expand upon his argument made in the *Tehelka* article, he remarked that in India, there is a fundamental lack of "safety culture," which is reflected in small practices of everyday life. The effects of a nuclear accident cannot be restricted to nuclear science, since the shape the accident might take would also be influenced by the sociomaterial worlds of the populations inhabiting the region around the plant, including the categories and hierarchies that structure their lives. I am including here a lengthy excerpt of what Jayaraman very powerfully articulated:

> You cannot have a completely rotten system all over the country on every other aspect but you have a shining beacon, which is the nuclear power. That is somehow discordant—I cannot believe that. As I see it, it is true. A disaster from the nuclear plant will not be managed by nuclear machinima but the district administration. Once the radiation leaves the factory precincts, the problem is the district administration's. And we know what the district administration is all about. We know about their casteist tendencies. We know about their . . . revengeful mentalities. We have seen them in action after [the] tsunami. Why will they not come out now? . . . When I am having a disaster, I tend to evacuate or pay more attention to the Nadar villages than the fishing villages. It is there in my system. That's my culture. . . . I think if you are talking about a safety culture, it cannot start when you have built a nuclear plant. . . . And the manner in which they have dealt with people that you are not supposed to protest. You have jailed them, beaten them, told them they cannot speak out. (Nityanand Jayaraman, interview excerpt, Chennai, November 20, 2012)

The response to the disaster, according to Jayaraman, will be shaped by the relations between district administrators and villagers living around Koodankulam. This region had witnessed destruction from the 2004 tsunami, and the response from the local administration at the time had left much to be desired. Could it be relied on now, when the same people who are supposed to protect the protesting villagers have been oppressing them? The daily interactions between local officials and villagers have left a trust deficit on both sides. Jayaraman argues that this trust deficit will also have to find a place in the nuclear imaginary. Caste will not let risk be democratized; it will hierarchize risk. I found Yashvi Arya in a public gathering seven months later, making a similar point about such postapocalyptic scenarios. Arya, who has been campaigning against atomic power plants in Gorakhpur (in the state of Haryana), suggested that if a disaster were to occur, one could not expect the Indian people to be as disciplined as the Japanese. They would not be willing to settle into a queue to board the assigned evacuation bus. Along with the disaster, chaos would erupt, and India's defective safety culture would be found wanting.

Both the nuclear imaginaries presented in this section are indeed futuristic, but they are based on, to invoke Charles Taylor (2002), a "wide and deep" "background" (109). Such a background includes past experiences and an experiential feel of one's surroundings, revealing how people think of themselves in relation to others, how they find themselves fitting within a social collective (belonging to particular caste groups), and, at times, how they declare themselves unfit to handle particular situations (standing with discipline in a queue). What Arya and Jayaraman are suggesting is that the techno-politics of nuclear reactors cannot be about labeling nuclear technologies as exceptionally high-end. The environmental public around nuclear reactors is shaped by caste dynamics and quotidian safety cultures involving firecrackers. From such nuclear imaginaries of anticipating ruination, let us shift to NPCIL's nuclear imaginaries that promise dreams of boundless energies.

Securitizing against Financial Risks:
The National Geographic–NPCIL Ads

The NPCIL ads of 2012 were made in collaboration with the National Geographic channel. The vocabulary and tone adopted in these ads are at times preachy and pedantic, reminiscent of the Nehruvian-era documentaries praising dams. However, such an authoritative narratorial voice is couched under sleek visuals of the lush green fields of Indian villages and the bird sanctuaries adjacent to the Narora atomic power plant in the province of Uttar Pradesh. These images were exotic to the eyes of Indian urbanites and the foreign audiences who saw them on National Geographic.

The narrating voice-over in one of these ads commences: "We don't always understand some things right away, we try and stick to our old ways, and when things change, we are at a loss, we lament our faith and despair . . . but every once in a while, it takes just a little spark to bring back a smile . . . brightening millions of lives" (National Geographic–NPCIL ad, 2012).

The ad, which features a grandmother and two children, begins with the grandmother laboring hard to draw water from a well. The children run among the fields, find bamboo sticks, then cut them and tie them together with twine to build a makeshift aqueduct. The grandmother's attempts are unsuccessful, and her earthen pot crashes. This shot is then cut to a running generator and water flowing through the makeshift conduit, thanks to the efforts of the inventive children (figures 2.9–2.11). Electricity has reached the villages: NPCIL has provided India with "energy security." The semiotic material of the makeshift aqueduct stands in for the Indian state's electricity infrastructure, a mini-display of the giant electricity grid through which it hopes to make nuclear power reach the remotest villages.

The makeshift aqueduct is built by children, the future visionaries of India. In their relation to the aqueduct, the children become part of the performance

FIGURES 2.9 AND 2.10 National Geographic–NPCIL ad

FIGURE 2.11 National Geographic–NPCIL ad

of making electricity available, thus "brightening millions of lives," which is NPCIL's campaign slogan. The implicit hint in the pedantic message about "some people not understanding some things right away" is an allusion to protesters at Koodankulam and every other site where NPCIL wants to set up power plants. The grandmother embodying such attitudes is shot from above in deep consternation, looking at the sky and the failed pulley technology of drawing water from wells (see figure 2.10).

The ads surfaced during a time when the economic viability of manufacturing nuclear reactors in India was being questioned.[18] The German bank Commerzbank pulled out of the Jaitapur project in India, citing "sustainability and reputational risk" (Jayaraman 2012). The protests by local villagers in Jaitapur factored into the reputational risk, and environmental concerns regarding the plant being built in an earthquake-prone region added to sustainability worries. Given the context in which these ads surfaced, one cannot deny the need NPCIL feels to rebrand itself; there is an acknowledgment that NPCIL's financial dealings require consideration of interrelated reputations, investments, and interests. It tries to securitize its future (also possibly India's nuclear future), which depends on finding financial backers and equipment suppliers whose reputations now are also tied to NPCIL's credibility. Securitizing futures pertains here to securitizing against financial risks.

The earlier publicity strategies of NPCIL were different than the recent National Geographic–NPCIL ads. The early publicity materials seemed to be exercises in popularizing science and had a "public sector" air about them, which retained some of the puritanical features (might we say "virtues") of Nehruvian socialism—one just could not be too fancy or too sleek. There was a certain guilt attached to being overly suave because the public sector represented something that was untainted by excess, something that was moral and substantive, something that, for all its comparative deficiencies (like being inefficient and lazy) at least retained the nostalgic aura of being uncorrupted by (neoliberal) capital. There were spectacular displays about atomic might during the Republican Day and Independence Day parades, but such spectacles remained contained within military and bureaucratic rituals. The audiences for the new ads are not just agricultural workers and affected communities but the Indian middle class and the foreign investors who are (re)assured of NPCIL's clean and green image.

The Elephant in the Room: Specter of Bhopal and Political Cartoons

Since the landmark 2006 Indo-US nuclear deal, enabling the United States and other "developed" nuclear nations such as France and Russia to engage with India in civilian nuclear energy cooperation, many atomic power plants have been proposed for construction across India.[19] The nuclear liability bill, part of the Indo-US nuclear deal, in its initial form, included clauses that affixed the liability of future disasters on both foreign nuclear suppliers and domestic Indian nuclear operators. Over the years, in order to attract foreign investment in the nuclear sector, the government has tried to dilute the supplier liability provisions. Bhopal's legacy persists in the controversy surrounding the mushrooming of nuclear reactors in contemporary India, particularly regarding affixing liability on foreign equipment suppliers in case of nuclear accidents.

Bhopal, capital of the state of Madhya Pradesh, India, witnessed a methyl isocyanate leak from the pesticide plant of Union Carbide (now part of Dow Chemical) on December 3, 1984. The leak led to thousands of deaths and injuries and precipitated unimaginable long-term birth defects. The leak happened because of the double standard often applied by transnational corporations in their Third World outposts, where environmental, worker, and community safety issues are given less attention than they would be at home, in developed countries (see Dembo, Morehouse, and Wykle 1990). Opponents of this liability act pointed out that the Indian government has learned nothing from Bhopal, where Union Carbide and Dow Chemical were never held accountable. In the

FIGURE 2.12 Cartoon on nuclear liability by Keshav for *The Hindu*, March 16, 2010

Hindu, the cartoonist Keshav drew the figure of an Indian politician who carries the nuclear energy symbol in one hand, even after suffering wounds from Bhopal that remain bandaged on his other hand (figure 2.12). Entwining caricature and wit, Keshav seems to be interrogating the power of Prime Minister Singh (and his backers in the Indian National Congress Party–led government) who seemed obsessed with constructing more and more reactors.

Keshav's political cartoons in the left-leaning *Hindu* do not simply provide ancillary support for prose-heavy newspaper reportage. In India, since colonial times, newspaper cartoons have satirized the asymmetries of power and are considered a serious form of "political journalism" and "a special category of news" (Gairola Khanduri 2014, 2). Keshav has continued his political critique of successive regimes (whether led by the Congress Party or the Bharatiya Janata Party) that have sought to soften the nuclear liability bill. The Nuclear Liability Act had aroused concerns in foreign suppliers who were worried about the unlimited liability period. The Indian government tried to ameliorate some of the suppliers problems by creating the Convention on Supplementary Compensation for Nuclear Damage that had provisions to reduce the liability period to five years. Even then, the supplier liability

FIGURE 2.13 Elephant in the room by Keshav for *The Hindu*, September 20, 2013

seemed unreasonable to foreign nuclear companies because, unlike India, most countries simply do not hold nuclear suppliers liable. While the French and Russian nuclear corporations were partially funded by their respective governments, American nuclear companies like Westinghouse Electric Corporation had no such backing and thus found the supplier liability clause in India to be especially unfair.[20]

With India having 400 million dark homes, the need for electricity is dire, and international nuclear companies are desperate to construct reactors in the country and thereby capture the nuclear market. And yet, in these companies' negotiations with Indian government officials, the liability question generates a very awkward moment. Nobody wants to raise the liability issue in the international meetings, fearing all sides will hit a dead end in the dialogue process, and yet it looms large, like an elephant in the room.

Keshav, the witty cartoonist, literally gives form to this elephant in a depiction of a pub where nuclear suppliers are meeting over glasses of aphrodisiacs. On the television set, there is the familiar nuclear energy icon. The elephant takes a seat next to the nuclear suppliers, and its gargantuan stature is unmistakable. On its back is written: "Liability in case of an accident" (figure 2.13). By giving nuclear liability the form of an elephant, Keshav deforms the political and infrastructural power of nuclear reactors. The specter of Bhopal haunts the cultural memory of India, and the nuclear liability clause simply does not stop bothering foreign nuclear suppliers. Even in the earlier illustration (see figure 2.12), Keshav had depicted the nuclear liability bill as a thin knife that could have been the bridge to safety but unfortunately is not taken by the politician. The environmental consequences of the Indo-US nuclear deal should not be dismissed. By that same logic, the environmental immediacy of Keshav's political cartoons, interrogating such (international/geopolitical) nuclear deals, should also not be dismissed.

"My Films Are Like Their *Mela*": Documenting Disappearing Publics of Nuclear India

So far, I have been examining the voices and countervoices that shape nuclear imaginaries. There are still other voices, which are so very marginalized by the bulldozing development activities of the Indian state that they hardly get heard in the Indian public sphere. The documentaries of Shriprakash and R. P. Amudhan acutely gesture toward the problematic contracts between science and society in a disorderly democracy like India, where certain stakeholders might disappear before they are even allowed into the debate. While formalizing and conducting a debate on atomic power plants, science policy makers have knowingly failed to identify the people of Jadugoda and Manavalakurichi as publics to be engaged with, even though uranium and rare earth minerals from these places are used in the reactors. The work of documentary filmmakers like Shriprakash and Amudhan has been to go to Jadugoda and Manavalakurichi, respectively, and record the lives of people who have disappeared from the public imagination about nuclear energy. It bears repeating here that the "vocation of documentary is testimonial" (Chanan 1990, 40), and in combination, "the vocation of testimony is archival" and "the vocation of the archive is ethical" (Sarkar and Walker 2010, 5).

The documentarian R. P. Amudhan directed *Radiation Stories*, a trilogy of antinuclear films. The first film of the trilogy, which was completed in 2010, is set in Manavalakurichi and presents testimonies of people, mostly Indian Rare Earth Limited (IREL) workers, affected by various kinds of tumors and limb impediments. The IREL workers engage in sand mining monazite, which, after being processed, is used in the nuclear fuel cycle.[21]

The striking quality of the interviews Amudhan conducts in the villages of Medilam, Periyavilai, and Chinnavilai near the *panchayat* town of Manavalakurichi is the amount of time allotted for the fishing communities and former and present IREL workers to speak about their experiences. The pace of *Radiation Stories 1: Manavalakurichi* (and the pace of the documentary interviews) is invariably slow. At times, it is mellow like the waves on the shore of Manavalakurichi, embodying the rhythm of villagers going about their lives quietly, drawing water from the wells, drying the caught fishes, and making fishing nets. At other times, the film seems almost to pause so that audiences can wait to consider the sheer difficulty—of moving, of drinking water, of getting up, of living—for affected patients with breast cancer, contorted limbs, nerve problems, and tumors swelling up from various parts of their bodies. Many of these patients worked for IREL, procuring raw sand near the sea shore.

There are very few moments of exchange with experts and people occupying positions of power in Amudhan's documentaries. When I interviewed Amudhan in his Chennai apartment, which doubles as a studio for his media activism organization Marupakkam, he was categorical in admitting his selection of documentary subjects:

> I make heavily one-sided films. I have made eighteen films. I never show anybody from authority, . . . the perpetrator, the violator—they do not deserve to be in my film. They have every power to misuse. They can buy a TV channel. They can buy a journalist. . . . So, I never give them space in my films. My protagonists are ordinary people and they will never get a chance [anywhere else]. So, it is their *mela* [fair]. My films are like their *mela* . . . they can talk and share their stories. My film is a platform to share their stories. I also talk about their activities. They are heroes. (R. P. Amudhan, interview excerpt, Chennai, July 12, 2013)

This emphatic declaration from Amudhan about his film being a "fair" for "ordinary people" helps film critics situate him alongside other documentary filmmakers like Anand Patwardhan and Shriprakash, who have also made films on the subject of atomic India. These documentarians have continued to make politically charged films as an alternative to Griersonian or Indian state–sponsored documentaries. These creators of "committed documentary," as Thomas Waugh (1984) terms it, are devoted to sociopolitical transformation and believe their intervention through the process of documentary production and distribution will bring about social change.[22] Given the context, where the Indian nuclear establishment engages in unprecedented cover-ups, where thousands of lives are exposed to health risks (and categorized as collateral damage), and where the majority of the media houses hesitate to criticize the nuclear state beyond a point, it is not surprising that the documentary films become (and remain) a privileged medium to oppose the hegemony of the nuclear state.

The antinuke documentary films interrogate expertise, privilege lay knowledge and experience, and show their solidarity with antinuke protesters.[23] These documentarians hold similar ideological positions and deploy analogous aesthetic strategies, but they also differ in many respects. Amudhan prefers minimum interference while filming his documentary subjects. However, Shriprakash, another documentary filmmaker, is ambivalent about what to do during his encounters with his interview subjects.

Shriprakash talks candidly about the interviewing process during the making of *Buddha Weeps in Jadugoda* (1999). The documentary depicts the illnesses of tribal people living in Jadugoda (in the Jharkhand province), where unsafe uranium mining activities and poor management of tailing ponds by the Uranium Corporation of India Limited (UCIL) take place. Shriprakash became frustrated when, in spite of the fact that he found abundant cancer cases in Jadugoda, the UCIL continued to deny that its mining operations had any harmful effects. His frustration was aggravated by the euphoric celebrations of atomic tests conducted by India in 1998, which were drowning out the miseries of the people of Jadugoda. He was searching for something that would move his documentary audience, both emotionally and to act(ion). According to Shriprakash, he finally found that something in one of his interviews.

Many of the interviews in *Buddha Weeps in Jadugoda* continually switch between talking heads and "talking groups." That is, interviews are often conducted in public spaces where a number of people speak, sometimes one after another; at other times, their enunciations overlap over in consonance and dissonance.[24] Shriprakash tends to focus on a particular speaker expressing his or her views with a close-up or midshot, but he also periodically zooms in on the faces of other people in the gathering so as to register the emotions evoked in them by their fellow villagers' testimonies.

In one such instance, he is interviewing Manju Das, whose child is suffering from thalassemia (an inherited blood disorder), and a group of women have gathered in a courtyard to watch this exchange. They are listening to Das lament how it is not just old people but also young people who are dying in Jadugoda. There are medium close-ups of a number of women listeners in a sad, pensive state. Shriprakash asks, "With blood transfusion continuing, will

FIGURE 2.14
Close-up of Manju
Das in deep conster-
nation (Screen grab
from *Buddha Weeps
in Jadugoda*)

you be able to save your child?," while continuing to zoom in on Das's face (figure 2.14). Das shakes her head and then answers, "No." By this time, the camera has zoomed out and Das has broken into sobs (figure 2.15). The camera slowly zooms back out to a medium close-up as she says that she has already lost two of her children.

Shriprakash explains why he felt compelled to ask this "abject" provocative question about whether a mother thought her child would live:

> It is the worst interview of my life, but it is the most effective interview. I needed to show emotion to people, and I knew that the woman's child was going to die. She was very strong and I needed to break her. And this was circling in my mind. . . . After talking with her, I got it. That woman while talking about her child broke down. Because of my middle-class desire, my hand on the camera, subconsciously or unconsciously, started zooming-in further . . . if you see in that scene, the camera is zooming to capture the woman's emotion and then after a while, I realize, something wrong is also happening and it zooms out again . . . that shows out in the public inside that [film/scene]. (Shriprakash, lecture at AIDS conference, Boston, 2011)[25]

Shriprakash acknowledges the power of the camera, and of the documentary filmmaker using that camera, over the documentary subject who is answering questions. As a documentarian, he believes in the cinema verité mode of interviewing, where provocative questions are asked, but on this occasion he admits he crossed the line ethically. Zooming in conveys an opportunism to capture and use a woman's emotion, and not just logical, fact-based argu-

FIGURE 2.15
Resigned Manju
Das, with camera
zoomed out (Screen
grab from *Buddha
Weeps in Jadugoda*)

What can we do? Two of my children died earlier...

ments, to make audiences outside Jadugoda care about the condition of tribal populations near uranium mines. Zooming out conveys a certain sensitivity, perhaps a kind of empathetic identification, with the condition of the mother grieving her son's irreversible demise in the near future: zooming out is the reaction that Shriprakash semiconsciously offers after feeling guilty about his earlier zoom-in. But, the decision to keep this scene in the film demonstrates that he was ready to compromise ethical engagement for the effectiveness of communicated pathos.

The process of mediation in Shriprakash's documentary operates in the affective economy of images. *Buddha Weeps in Jadugoda*, by Shriprakash's own admission, can be seen at one level as a publicity strategy that banks on spectacular displays and affective modulations. By prompting the breakdown of a mother grieving her child's imminent death, Shriprakash attempts to publicize the disappearing publics of nuclear energy, the ones whose stories, as he has often said, no other media wants to tell. "Publicity" in these circumstances, as Mazzarella and Kaur (2009) put it beautifully, "touches upon the embodied and the intimate; its mode of persuasion is one of resonance rather than reason" (8). A practice-oriented approach to media studies shows that these moments were moments of unplanned originality, hesitancy, ambivalence, and undecidability and could potentially be moments of slippage and change. Had Manju Das not broken down, the public circulation of the antinuke documentary might have been impacted. Here, the documentary filmmaker's (im)mediate interactions with the affected community member as a stakeholder in the environmental public are shaped by his created text's (documentary's) imagined and anticipated encounter with urban middle-class audiences, who are also constituents of the (wider) mediated public of the nuclear debate in India.[26]

In this chapter, my goal has been to study mediated environmental publics with a particular emphasis on the interactions between stakeholders and affected communities. A focus on media practices has been useful to describe and interpret the social situatedness of mediation. Keeping this in mind, the interaction between documentarians and the filmed subjects is critical to examine. It was not easy for Shriprakash to film people who had too often been deceived by outside experts, and who believed they would be filmed by someone who would then go away, leaving them to suffer silently as usual. Amudhan faced resistance from residents in Manavalakurichi who were currently working for IREL and who suspected that Amudhan's films would bring disrepute to their company (and village). The ex-IREL workers and fishermen communities who were suffering from cancer in the same villages very much wanted to tell their stories. Some others had suffered too long, and their attitudes toward the documentary ranged from indifference to hesitancy.

Amudhan had to remain inconspicuous while shooting in the villages of Medilam, Periyavilai, and Chinnavilai. He explained to me that he would often take the bus (and not a car or taxi) from Tuticorin to these villages, and in order to avoid attracting attention, he had to keep his filmmaking equipment light. He often did not carry along a tripod, and hence the use of a handheld camera in most of the shots in the documentary. In many sequences in the film, we find Amudhan waiting in a public place and then somebody approaches him to talk. Other times, Amudhan would wait outside a home until someone ventured outside; Amudhan would begin a conversation and then be invited into the house. Villagers wanted to tell their stories but were afraid their neighbors would report them to IREL.

Restrictions on filming by outsiders were also imposed by NPCIL wherever there were local agitations against construction of reactors. At Koodankulam, the Oscar-nominated Australian documentarian David Bradbury, famous for his films like *Hard Rain* (2007) about the global nuclear industry and uranium mining, was stopped from entering the forbidden zone: it was feared that he would influence the minds of locals and also bring a bad reputation to NPCIL and India (see Bradbury 2013). Fathima Nizaruddin's native village is in the neighboring province of Kerala, which is close to Idinthakarai, and hence she used her local contacts to get past the security infrastructure of NPCIL. Nizaruddin added that NPCIL's gendered lenses proved to be an asset for her as she heard local policemen at Idinthakarai suggest that because Nizaruddin was a woman, she could not cause much harm.

To provide another instance, the two French documentary filmmakers Micha Patault and Sarah Irion, on tourist visas to India, could shoot for only four days at a stretch in the village of Sakhri-Nate in Jaitapur, Maharashtra, where the French multinational company Areva is building six third-generation European pressurized reactors (EPRs).[27] Patault and Irion had to make periodic trips to the village to complete the film shooting without attracting the attention of NPCIL authorities.

Mediations

Nuclear imaginaries and their mediations, as discussed in this chapter, have alternated between utopic visions of surplus energy and dystopic imaginations of radioactive catastrophe. The nuclear establishment has an opinion about the imaginaries of the Koodankulam fishing community. It believes the fishermen fear nuclear reactors out of their ignorance of science, and also believes that if only these local communities knew about nuclear technologies, they would consider an energy-secure nuclear India a desirable future. The nuclear establishment's understanding of the public is based on an epistemic deficit, a knowledge gap between itself and the local community. In the cartoons like *Ek Tha Budhiya* or the National Geographic–NPCIL ads, we see such a knowledge gap being explicitly or implicitly presented.

However, nuclear imaginaries are not just about nuclear science, for such imaginaries have to negotiate social thickness and shared meanings.[28] The sea and the marine life mean something for the fishermen, and these meanings have been troubled by the emergence of a new entity, an atomic reactor, in their midst. Nuclear imaginaries of these publics are not merely about carcinogenic radiation leaks but also about what nuclear technology is going to do to their land, their sea, and their livelihoods. Nuclear imaginaries of these publics are also about addressing the question of how casteist local authorities are going to treat Dalit fishermen in the event of a future scenario of radioactive fallout. The mediation of nuclear elites "forecloses engagement with broader public meanings" (Welsh and Wynne 2013, 540) raised by social movement actors and local communities, but activist mediations find a way to make lived ontologies of fishermen a part of nuclear imaginaries.

The cartoons and documentaries discussed in this chapter invite intermedial reflections. Both media can be used by pro-nuclear and antinuclear groups for pedagogical purposes, that is, spreading the knowledge about and radiance of nuclear reactors. Furthermore, both of these media can interrogate the infrastructural power of nuclear reactors: one by caricaturing (and thereby deforming) policies and politicians, and the other by capturing mimetically/

indexically the grounded realities of dark lives brought by radiant infrastructures. Accompanying newspaper reportage, political cartoons are ambiguous and uncertain cultural forms as they blur fact and fiction, evidential power and cultural power. Even as Keshav's political cartoons question the nuclear energy policies, the nuclear establishment draws on the cultural popularity in India of a similar media form—comic books and their digital extensions in animated cartoons (*Ek Tha Budhiya*)—to spread its message. Some nonfictional accounts like journalistic reportage and political documentaries can veer toward instrumental solution-oriented arguments. However, the documentaries discussed in this chapter contain expressive testimonies (*Buddha Weeps in Jadugoda*) and speculative tendencies (*Nuclear Hallucinations*) that tap into the political unconscious where lived realities, public discourses, and current fears and fascinations collide.[29]

The Indian nuclear establishment is plagued by insularity. Despite India being a democratic country, the decision making about nuclear matters is done by a select few experts who constitute the planning and energy elite. The ads produced by the NPCIL also are insular in that they avoid specificity and inject abstraction into the depictions: they promote the effortless harmony of technology and nature, and the images of nuclear plants look like picture postcards. The inner workings of the reactors are not shown. The antinuke documentary films detail the particular problems faced by local people living near the reactors. Such depictions highlight situated concerns. While the NPCIL ads, even when they depict a specific nuclear reactor, operate at a macro scale by abstracting particularities, the antinuke documentaries operate at the local level.

At the invitation of local protest leaders, Gandhian nuclear scientists Surendra and Sangahmitra Gadekar came to Madban near Jaitapur, where nuclear reactors designed by the French energy giant Areva are being constructed. The Gadekars started circulating CDs among locals as well as conducting workshops for them about cancer victims of uranium mining in North India (Bhadra 2012). The Gadekars' activities have been portrayed in documentaries by Shriprakash and Anand Patwardhan. Shriprakash has followed them as they conducted "epidemiological" studies in Jadugoda. The Gadekars carried out some of their epidemiological surveys by cycling from village to village and stopping at tea stalls to strike up *addas* (conversations). In one memorable scene from Anand Patwardhan's *Jung Aur Aman*, it is nighttime, and people of Khetolai (close to Pokhran, where nuclear testing was conducted) have gathered to witness a slide show run on a solar-powered slide projector. Sangahmitra Gadekar is displaying slides depicting early signs of skin cancer among communities living close to the Rawatbhatta atomic power plant. These grounded forms of image circulation create translocal connections and do not fit neatly into formal or informal media practices. They also suggest that the import of nuclear imaginaries cannot be comprehended just by studying disaster discourse, but by making connections between the textual politics and circulatory politics of disaster scripts. Attending to media forms and practices within an intermedial framework shows the emergent need to come up with new vocabularies of talking about nuclear technology's epistemic uncertainties and public engagement with science.

While this chapter and the previous one have focused on specific environmental publics that formed around cell towers and nuclear reactors, the next three chapters are comparative in scope. They compare how different radiant infrastructures emit radiation (chapter 3), the effects of such radiation exposure on human bodies (chapter 4), and the differing subjectivities activated or tempered by cell towers and nuclear reactors (chapter 5). In the next chapter, I will examine the processes and performances of environmental governance of radiant infrastructures by looking at both the regulation of emissions and the regulation of publicly available information about radiation. Indeed, publicity and secrecy are both key, even concomitant, to the constitution of environmental publics.

03

Emissions

This chapter tracks the various ways in which cellular operators purportedly attempt to keep signal emissions within threshold levels, and the Indian nuclear establishment desperately tries to contain the spread of radioactive nuclides from an atomic power plant. There is an appearance of control, but containment proves impossible. Along with limiting radiation emissions, these corporate and governmental players also tightly regulate the spread of information about any big radiation spills. This close-knit web of secrecy has a dialectical relationship with publicity about radiant infrastructures. Secrecy also shapes the public life of uncertainties about atomic power plants. However, the stakes of publicizing radiation leaks and disclosing information about radiation are immense for the health of the vulnerable affected communities. Governmental/corporate authorities enact staged presentations of disclosure, but such performative acts reveal less than they hide. While, in earlier chapters, the concept of environmental publics was conceptualized as the actors joining to constitute such publics through publicity drives, this chapter is a study of the practices of secrecy that shape the configurations of environmental publics.

In their article "Kudankulam Meltdown" (2012), journalist Latha Jishnu, Ankur Paliwal, and Arnab Pratim Dutta recounted how the nuclear reactor's "hot run" has become folklore in villages close to the power plant. Officials of the Nuclear Power Corporation of India Limited working at the Kudankulam Nuclear Power Plant failed to give advance warning to local villagers when they carried out a hot run test inside the reactor. The villagers had not been informed about the ramifications of the hot run, in which the primary coolant water was heated to the reactor's operating temperature of 280°C, resulting in the release of massive quantities of steam. The sound of the screaming valves in the middle of night startled villagers out of their sleep (see Jishnu, Paliwal, and Dutta 2012).

A nuclear reactor emits not only ionizing radiation but also steam, and operators can lose control of both types of emissions. If prior information is not shared with the public at large, it can lead to misgivings about the safety of an atomic power plant. Following the incident at Kudankulam, India's nuclear establishment realized it needed to contain the material spillage of both radiation and steam. At the same time, it also seemed necessary to share information with "lay" citizens, albeit in a controlled manner. Thus, leaks in both radiation and information from the reactor have to be regulated.

The same goes for cell tower radiation. One cannot do away with signals because that would result in losing phone connectivity. If citizens are scared about cell antenna signals, regulators and operators must share information with them to win their trust and allay their fears. How exactly do the NPCIL and Indian telecom players control the flow of radiation and information? The governance of radiant infrastructures leads to the strategic deployment of media to make visible only selected features of such infrastructures, in an attempt to manage uncertainties about their environmental impacts. That being said, neither radiation nor uncertainty can be fully contained or regulated. Leak detection systems fail, nuclear accidents happen, and during peak hours cell towers emit signal levels beyond threshold values to support cell phone calls and mobile data transactions. Journalists violate protocols of access laid out by officials governing nuclear reactors, and the affective contagion of fear about cell tower emissions spreads as rumors across urban India. These unregulated emissions (of information and radiation) are not aberrations but rather a systemic characteristic of radiant infrastructures. It appears that the emissions of radiant infrastructures are both regulated and unregulated at the same time.

Secrecy and Transparency

When the noted journalist Pallava Bagla, who has been covering strategic science stories in India for more than two decades, was reporting from a nuclear facility, he was told: "You are the first journalist and you are the last journalist who will ever come here. First and the last, that's a categorical distinction" (personal interview with Pallava Bagla, New Delhi, October 8, 2012). This particular space of reportage had never before been made accessible to journalists, and Bagla was the chosen one. It is this kind of secrecy that renders particular aspects of the infrastructure of nuclear reactors truly hidden, truly *infra*. While the spectacular domes of the Kudankulam nuclear reactor are hypermediated, only a handful of journalists are allowed to enter the plant to mediate its internal components.

Strategic sciences related to space research and nuclear technologies are often shrouded in secrecy. The Indian nuclear establishment, which consists of the Department of Atomic Energy, the Atomic Energy Regulatory Board, and the NPCIL, has employed secrecy not only with respect to the nuclear weaponization program but also in the arena of civilian nuclear energy, resulting in an epistemological vacuum that Itty Abraham (1992) and M. V. Ramana (2009) have described as a "nuclear enclave."[1] This strategic enclave encompasses sectors devoted to nuclear weapons, nuclear power, and space research (including intercontinental ballistic missiles [ICBMs]), with each of these sectors overlapping in terms of personnel and facilities. The culture of secrecy embedded in these sectors poses a seemingly insurmountable challenge for journalists, who, as a result, are forced to rely completely on official experts familiar with the nuclear world firsthand but conditioned to preserve its secrets.

Nevertheless, when the strategic sciences sector faces a crisis of legitimacy owing to public perceptions about the risks from nuclear reactors, or rising concerns over the disproportionately high funds allocated to the development of ICBMs, the establishment finds it necessary to provide only enough information to nudge public opinion back in its favor. The selective disclosure innate to this process of publicizing information involves both revealing and concealing, a contradiction Raminder Kaur (2009) has evocatively termed "measured revelation."

Secrecy is a key element to consider with regard to the mediation of nuclear reactors. Secrecy does not, however, exist in the same way with regard to cell towers. The physicality of infrastructures does affect the kind of secrecy. The strength of signals emitted by a cell tower can temporarily be kept a secret from reporters (before they start using radiometers), but access to a cell tower located in the heart of an urban area cannot be denied to journalists or curious citizens. This chapter will highlight the structural differences between these two radiant infrastructures: a nuclear reactor is like a factory and spans a large area, while the cell antenna is one node in a cellular network and thus is far more spatially constricted.

What has become abundantly clear is that cellular operators and telecom regulators have sometimes worked together to give an appearance of transparency to the general public while continuing to practice opacity. Girish Kumar, a radio frequency scientist, has argued that different companies have recorded different readings at different times, with measuring agencies deliberately controlling some of the emission variables in collusion with cellular operators. For example, in 2012 he visited the home of Bollywood actress Juhi Chawla to measure electromagnetic radiation and found the readings to be low. Chawla had initially obtained measurements taken by a private company, which found the electromagnetic field levels to be high. Soon after, the government agency Telecom Enforcement Resource and Monitoring (TERM) recorded much lower EMF levels at Chawla's house. Because those two readings were very different from one another, Chawla called Kumar to conduct tests for a third opinion. According to Kumar, his EMF measurements matched those of TERM, but only because cell tower officials had deliberately changed the direction of the antenna after the private agency took the first measurements—suggesting that the operators had been notified of TERM's plans to take a second reading. Kumar argued that, with the main beam of the antenna no longer directed toward Chawla's house, both his and TERM's instruments showed lower readings there. This was news to Chawla and her neighbors, and there was then a shift in the locus of panic, from Chawla's apartment to the one that now faced the main beam of the antenna.

During the late nineties, India's telecom revolution served as a signifier of neoliberal politics and global postmodernity. The mobile phone, the computer, and the internet—like international music videos and beauty pageants—were public-private partnerships in which the Indian state and Indian corporations collaborated to make the nation a global player (Shah 2007). Such technology-driven neoliberal consumerism ran parallel to e-governance projects promising transparency and efficiency (Mazzarella 2006). Given that the rise of Indian mobile phones was bolstered by a strategic partnership between the state and corporations, it is not surprising that the state has shown leniency toward telecom players. At the same time, the state as a regulator of the industry should be impartial and transparent in its dealings when it is interfacing between concerned citizens and allegedly deceptive cellular operators. The telecom players themselves tout the mobile phone as bringing transparency to governance, and thus their own products and services need to inspire transparency as well. It would hurt their image if they were found to be opaque. Both the Indian Department of Telecommunications and the cellular operator Airtel launched websites and applications with maps of cell towers and provided signal measurements to Indian citizens and consumers. But how effective are such visualizations of infrastructural and environmental data?

It is important to examine mediated arenas of interaction between scientists, activists, and journalists where nuclear secrets are performatively both hidden and revealed. The performance of transparency takes a different turn, however, when we are dealing with cell towers. In this case, e-portals provide maps to render cell towers and their signal strengths visible. Here, too, we have "measured revelations." The differences in each instance have as much to do with the material properties of the respective radiant infrastructures (their different ways of emitting) as with the ways in which such infrastructures are historically and politically governed.

The question of governing infrastructures is of utmost significance here. Nuclear reactors are publicly owned, while cell towers are in general privately owned. Unlike governance protocols in the United States and Japan, where major private corporations, including General Electric and the Tokyo Electric Power Company, respectively, run the atomic power plants, nuclear energy generation in India is centralized within the public sector. This makes the NPCIL answerable only to the government, and not to consumers, citizens, or users of electricity.[2] This further influences the amount of information that NPCIL does not share about reactors with the nation's citizens. The governance of infrastructures thus inevitably creates both infrastructural visibilities and infrastructural invisibilities.

Infrastructural (In)Visibilities

The question of the visibility and invisibility of infrastructures has preoccupied infrastructure studies scholars for several decades. Science studies scholars, including Geoffrey Bowker and Susan Leigh Star (1999) and anthropologists such as Casper Bruun Jensen (2017), have offered nuanced ways of appreciating the complexity of infrastructures in terms of their scale and daily operations, as well as the difficulty of making visible multiscalar infrastructural relations. Some of these same writers have also bemoaned the media's tendency to offer spectacular displays of infrastructures while doing little to further public understanding of what makes them work on a day-to-day basis. The ramifications of infrastructural (in)visibilities are even greater in the case of radiant infrastructures that *secrete* imperceptible radiation.

While I respect the concerns expressed by Jensen and others, I believe they generalize media representations or blackbox all media into a single category. Throughout this book, by analyzing a wide variety of media—including television shows, documentary films, microwave ovens, digital platforms of radiation maps, and Geiger counter measurements—I have resisted the blackboxing of media representations. Such mediational processes do much more than merely create spectacles out of infrastructures—that is, the result is not just an infatuation with aerial shots of twin domes of nuclear reactors. These mediational processes also render invisible radiation visible, allow lay publics to express their affective encounters with proximate infrastructures, show experts giving tours of a nuclear reactor's coolant channel, and help ordinary citizens monitor a cell antenna's signal levels. This does not mean that governments do not manipulate media to provide an appearance of transparency about radiant infrastructures. They most certainly do.

I argue that the revelation of a secret as an act of publicity is performative and that it involves an ensemble of journalists, nuclear science experts, and politicians. To that end, I focus on the minutiae of interactions in moments when access is granted to a strategic space, or a secret slips out, or when a situation is ripe with the possibilities of a revelation: in other words, I am attentive to structured protocols of access as well as possibilities of tactical trespass that could lead to unprepared and contingent revelations. Further, I investigate the repercussions of such regimes of secrecy on the visibility and invisibility of radiant infrastructures. I begin with two examples of journalists who were allowed to enter nuclear reactors. I then discuss the plans of the Indian government to roll out Tarang Sanchar, an e-portal that provides information about the signal levels emitted by cell antennas across India.

The regulation of radiant infrastructures involves control of their emissions, and a consideration of their infrastructural (in)visibilities certainly involves analysis of the (in)visibilities of radiation emanating from them. Thus, a discussion of the key material property of radiant infrastructures—that is, emissions—needs to be linked with infrastructural (in)visibilities and the governance of infrastructures, which are themselves inseparable from concerns regarding the proliferation of radiation and the public life of uncertainties about radiation.

Measured Revelations and Tactical Trespasses

After the 2011 Fukushima Daiichi nuclear fallout, the Indian nuclear establishment's plans to construct additional nuclear plants created concern in some sections of the Indian public sphere. The nuclear establishment undertook an aggressive advertising campaign to persuade the public that nuclear energy is safe, and, as discussed in chapter 2, these efforts faced resistance from antinuke activists who used their own media (in the form of documentary films) to counter the establishment's arguments. In association with Vigyan Prasar (the science publicity wing of the Indian state) and the National Geographic channel, the NPCIL has produced ads in praise of nuclear energy. Of course, ads about the safety of nuclear reactors do not necessarily provide the same reassurance for the Indian public as the reports of journalists. The latter are largely viewed as independent agents who can objectively report on nuclear reactors. Their favorable reports about the safety of nuclear reactors would certainly serve the nuclear establishment well, but the NPCIL nonetheless limits the flow of information to them. However, once the so-called independent media steps in, the arguments of experts belonging to the nuclear establishment are open to rigorous interrogation by journalists and experts. At the same time, the independence of media and journalists in this context is certainly questionable because they are dependent on in-house experts for access and information.

Pallava Bagla reports regularly on strategic science sectors and works across different media. He is the science editor of New Delhi Television (NDTV) and the South Asia chief correspondent for the well-respected *Science* magazine, for which he wrote a story on the Himalayan glaciers that won the David Perlman Award for Excellence in Science Journalism. Although Bagla began his professional career as an environmental activist, he told me that, as of the 1990s, "I am no longer an activist. I am no longer an ardent environmental reporter. I am more a *middle-of-the-road* science and technology person" (personal interview with Pallava Bagla, New Delhi, October 8, 2012, my emphasis).

Bagla is always able to obtain "exclusives," whether in reporting on Chandrayan, India's maiden mission to send a spacecraft to the moon from the Satish Dhawan Space Centre in Sriharikota, or accessing the test site of ICBMs that carry nuclear warheads, or gaining entry into the nuclear chamber of the Kudankulam atomic reactor. When I asked Bagla why he thinks he has been accorded this privilege, he says that is for others to explain, but he admits that the sectors he works on do not permit activist journalism. In his own words, "I cannot take a side. I have to report facts."

Following protests in the wake of the Fukushima catastrophe, construction work was suspended at the Kudankulam reactor from September 2011 to March 2012. The NPCIL faced a legitimacy crisis; it was accused of lacking transparency regarding its operations, and of not providing journalists access to nuclear reactors. To demonstrate its openness, the nuclear establishment decided to permit the latter. However, the timing of such gestures of openness raised suspicions of attempts to co-opt the media. As Elias Canetti (1984) once famously remarked, "Secrecy lies at the very core of power." Faced with protests at multiple nuclear reactor sites, the Indian nuclear establishment has found itself in a crisis. Part of the establishment's decision-making power comes from keeping impregnable secrets, but to hold on to power, it grants partial access, to share—selectively—some of its secrets.

In an NDTV television segment titled "Inside Kudankulam N-Plant: How Safe Are Our N-Reactors?," which first aired on November 13, 2011, Bagla arrives unannounced to the protest site in Kudankulam and finds the grounds

FIGURE 3.1 Bagla inside Koodankulam Nuclear Plant
(Screen grab from NDTV, November 13, 2011)

vacant, thus hinting that there is indeed no sustained or substantial resistance to the plant. Engaging in variants of immersive and investigative journalism, Bagla travels deep inside the nuclear plant and waxes eloquent about the safety systems, mentioning the thickness of hermetically sealed concrete walls that guarantee no radiation can escape (figure 3.1). Noting that the Fukushima disaster occurred because of a power failure, Bagla almost gifts a passing grade to the Kudankulam plant by explaining that a 400 percent backup has been provided by four diesel generator sets—"One would have been enough, but why take the risk?"

The security of an infrastructure is future-oriented. It is necessary to imagine foreseeable scenarios in which the infrastructure's ability to withstand difficult conditions may be tested. Fukushima presented one of these scenarios: How sturdy is the nuclear plant in the face of a tsunami and earthquake? Because the Kudankulam nuclear plant is located next to the ocean, the threat of tsunamis is always present; in fact, at the time of Bagla's visit, the southern coast of India had been ravaged by a tsunami as recently as 2004. With the sea waves and the domes of the Kudankulam nuclear reactor in the background, Pallava Bagla, holding his microphone, carefully spells out that the reactor is situated 6.5 meters higher than the highest wave seen in 2004. He also mentions that the reactor is situated in seismic zone 2, which is least prone to earthquakes.

In a report that simultaneously showcases the monumental nuclear reactor and the dryness of scientific facts, Bagla is shown standing above the container that will house 100 tons of enriched uranium, the nuclear fuel that will produce 1,000 megawatts of energy. In case of an emergency, this large quantity of potentially explosive material would need to be regulated. As Bagla elaborates on the security features, the camera tilts slowly to show the depth of the container vessel, and finally we see an array of control rods designed to stop the explosive fission reaction during an emergency.

In another NDTV segment, "Inside Protest Hit Kudankulam Nuclear Plant," Bagla interviews the scientist S. A. Bhardwaj, who was then second in command at the NPCIL, on November 9, 2011. Bhardwaj equates the insignificant effect of nuclear radiation generated by the plant to the negligible differences in temperature between various regions in India. Various nuclear scientists at NPCIL admit that, in retrospect, they should have done a better job of communicating the plant's safety features to citizens. The controversy and protests are explained as merely the results of a lack of effective communication, and the role of Bagla and NDTV is to transmit that official message.

The voice of the scientist is often privileged in news coverage because he or she represents the "expert" who presents the "facts," consequently setting the parameters within which discussion of the issue can take place and simultaneously eschewing alternative views (Hall 1978). Does not Bagla's dependence on the scientists who escorted him, in his own words, to "the heart of the nuclear plant" influence his favorable coverage of the plant? When I posed this question to Bagla, he acknowledged that it is indeed a challenge, but that "editorial control" has never been wrested from him. Pressing further, I asked whether his attempt to remain "middle-of-the-road" and his reliance on selected nuclear science experts for entry into strategic spaces made him, by default, a mere channel for their views. Bagla was quick to clarify: "It is very easy to fall in that trap. We need to have an extremely supportive editor who has a backbone. . . . You give access because you want the information put out. I get the access and I put out the information the way I want . . . that is the key point. . . . It is a very big challenge. . . . We dropped many stories because people have wanted editorial control" (personal interview with Pallava Bagla, New Delhi, October 8, 2012). Assuring me that journalistic dependency cannot compromise journalistic ethics, Bagla stressed the particular contingencies of live television reporting, which make it almost impossible for scientists to dictate terms. As an example, Bagla recounted how he and his television crew traversed the space of the Defense Research and Development Organization, where India's first ICBM, Agni-5, was being tested. Because this was a "national security issue," he and his team made compromises, but they did not give up editorial control:

> You may take us to a facility. You may want us to go blindfolded. We are willing to go blindfolded. But, end of the day, it is not my job to show you what I am going to write or what I am going to air. . . . On live television, there is no way you can control. There is no control on that. What I am saying live is what I am saying . . . I can't bounce it off anybody. But when I am being led into a facility, if I am told that "please, on the left side of the room we have stuff which we don't want to be shown, on the right side [stuff which] we want to be shown, so don't shoot left because left is national security issue," that boundary you respect, but editorial control . . . no way. (personal interview with Pallava Bagla, New Delhi, October 8, 2012)

The unwritten protocols of "national security" continue to guide the travel itinerary of Bagla and his crew, making "right sides" transparent and leaving "left sides" opaque. The movement of journalists inside the reactor, even though restricted, is key as it showcases the act of access. At one moment in the NDTV feature report, Bagla is shown climbing a ladder to enter the passive cooling system, a safety provision that makes the Kudankulam nuclear reactor unique: in the case of a loss of electricity at the plant, this system will release air to cool the generated steam and thereby prevent an explosion. Here, the movements of journalists and the spaces of the reactor are entangled in their performativity.

Not all journalists are like Bagla in following the codes of conduct set by the nuclear establishment. Latha Jishnu, a widely respected environmental journalist in India, has endured the risks of violating the limits imposed by the NPCIL. Jishnu's path to reporting on science issues was quite different from Bagla's. She wrote for financial newspapers, including the *Economic Times* and *Business Standard*, and the magazine *Business World*, before arriving at the science and environment magazine *Down to Earth*. She tells me that journalists at financial papers called her a "bleeding heart" because they felt she often took "the other's side." Her answer to them would always be "Do you take sides [in journalism]?" Jishnu simply believes that journalists should be inquisitive, and that means probing for more information, even from the most powerful.

In one of her earliest pieces on Kudankulam, "Running Out of Options" (2007), Jishnu began by stating: "The fact that the NPCIL is investing in both wind and hydropower is the most telling example of just where India's nuclear power programme is going." In this case, she effectively "trespassed" by referring to a slipup by a senior NPCIL official who had mentioned the NPCIL's investment in renewable energy (wind and hydropower)—thus suggesting that the Indian nuclear power sector might be vulnerable. The official's brief moment of carelessness within the structured conversational environment of the nuclear reactor became a moment of contingent opportunity for Jishnu. She then related the NPCIL's economic dependency on wind and hydropower to the aesthetic incongruity of nuclear reactors in an area that is dotted with windmills along the coast:

> Just a half-hour's drive up the Tamil Nadu coast from Kanyakumari, the twin domes of the Kudankulam nuclear reactors brood over the brown scrubland, dwarfing everything in sight—even the tallest of the windmills in the vicinity. This is essentially windmill country, with mile upon mile of tall white columns spiking the Tirunelveli landscape in a showy endorsement of renewable energy. Juxtaposed with the windmills, the 80-metre high domes—these contain what are among the largest reactors in the world—bring into sharp relief the disquieting issues about India's energy security and the role of nuclear power in it. (Jishnu 2007)

Acknowledging that the nuclear option is cleaner than coal in the short term, Jishnu's article highlights that nuclear power plants are nonetheless economically precarious. She faced repercussions from the nuclear establishment soon after publication. Scientists in India, Jishnu reflects, speak only to a select group of reporters. When she wrote neutral pieces, or what scientists thought to be neutral, she belonged to that exclusive list of pro-nuclear reporters who were asked to hold workshops for other journalists to train them on nuclear science. She was initially allowed to bring a camera, but once her stories started being considered antinuclear, she was asked not to use the pictures she had taken of the reactor site. In her own words:

> They actually took me on a special visit to Kudankulam in 2007 because, at that time, they thought it was going to generate power in December. So in June, they took me there. Showed me everything. I got to speak to Russian scientists, who were there . . . got to see everything. They even let me take pictures. Anyway, so after these stories came out on Kudankulam, which were critical of the delays and the costs, they were not happy. They

no longer responded to questions. It was very difficult to get an interview with the NPCIL chief. . . . They do not seem to understand the basics of journalism: that you will question, that you will be critical of something. But that does not make you . . . antinuclear. In fact, I have got rather an open mind on nuclear. (personal interview with Latha Jishnu, New Delhi, December 13, 2012)

Jishnu's predicament is that of a "middle-of-the-road" journalist who questions both scientists and activists and then has difficulty obtaining the interviews she needs for her reporting. She explains that speaking with activists alone is not sufficient for a proper science story—they say "the same thing again and again." She wants to understand the science, but scientists are reluctant to talk to her, since they view her coverage of them as negatively biased. According to Jishnu, several scientists are like "babus" (bureaucrats occupying high positions in India) who have a hierarchical mind-set—they need promotions, they do not want controversy, and they cannot tolerate criticism.

Communicating environmental risks to the general public occurs through a series of performative arenas, ranging from conversations at nuclear reactor sites to interactions inside television studios. My endeavor has been to ask journalists to reflect on their performances in particular contexts, to elaborate on their interactions with scientists, and to shed light on how they imagine their audiences. Media practices as well as communication sites are shaped by larger contexts: the politics of nuclear energy, the pragmatics of finding scientific experts to serve as news sources, and India's postcolonial condition.[3]

At the time of the Fukushima disaster, the Japanese mainstream media was under attack for being part of the exclusive press-club system and allegedly funneling information from government sources and the Tokyo Electric Power Company (the company that operated the Fukushima Daiichi nuclear reactors) to reassure Japanese citizens that there was no danger, rather than informing them about the potential risk of radiation exposure. Having a symbiotic relationship with official sources prevented influential Japanese journalists from carrying out independent reporting (McNeil 2012). Thus, providing journalists access to strategically selected nuclear secrets in moments of crisis raises suspicions of attempts to co-opt participating media, not only in India but also in Japan. My investigation extended beyond questions of whether Indian journalists compromised themselves to gain access to privileged information or resisted the Indian nuclear establishment's plans to appropriate them. I wanted to know what kinds of experiences journalists undergo while inside strategic technoscience sites, what decisions journalists make while spending time in such spaces, and what meanings they attach to those experiences and decisions. This has provided insight into how journalists bring their subjectivities to bear in reporting on practices of nuclear containment and spread.

Techno-politics of Mediating Nuclear Reactors

The Kudankulam reactor is not the only nuclear facility that journalist Pallava Bagla has visited. He was also granted access to a fully operational atomic power plant at Rawatbhata in the state of Rajasthan and was allowed to go deep inside the Jadugoda uranium mines. Moreover, Bagla is not alone among journalists in having been given permission to film inside nuclear reactors. Recently, the NPCIL has also given the National Geographic channel access to the Tarapur nuclear power plant. These are rare opportunities to mediate what really goes on inside an infrastructure like a nuclear reactor. The point raised by Bagla and the anchor of the National Geographic channel's *Inside* series "Tarapur Nuclear Power Plant: Unlock Power" episode is crucial. Both these journalists point out that while there is much talk about nuclear reactors in the public sphere, people rarely know what happens inside the walls of a reactor. The more secretive the nuclear establishment is, the more speculation there will be among the wider public that the NPCIL is hiding a deep secret. To win public hearts and to avoid proliferating conspiracy theories, nuclear reactors must be made open to media cameras.

The anchor of the National Geographic series, like Bagla, mentions that the access he has been given represents the "chance of a lifetime." He cannot help but emphasize the sheer magnitude of security that one must negotiate before being able to see the nuclear chamber or the control room. Checkpoints, the opening and closing of gates, barbed wire fences, and entry and exit signs are all highlighted in the choreography of exhibiting the reactor. This episode is part of the *Inside* series on the National Geographic channel, and this particular series is touted as the show that brings behind-the-scenes action and information from the most restricted of places in the world, whether it is an Indian nuclear reactor or the CIA's secret files or Russian prisons and security facilities.

Mediating a nuclear reactor from within the reactor is different than mediating it from a television studio: the latter provides more flexibility and power to control the flow of information. Thus, infrastructural properties and media practices of reporting on such infrastructures are mutually entangled. The need for secrecy while mediating a nuclear plant is due to the colossal monetary investments behind each, the great expectations of bringing energy security to India, and the confidential nature of nuclear technologies. Such a security regime furthers the invisibility of nuclear reactors. To reiterate, nuclear reactors as infrastructures are characterized by varying degrees of visibility. The most common mediated representations of nuclear reactors are their spectacular domes, but what about the complex interactions of the various parts inside those domes?

What are the challenges of mediating the nuclear reactor? It is a massive infrastructure, and one cannot help but talk about its individual, manageable parts: safety valves, the passive cooling system, control rods, and container vessels. The question remains: Who will connect the dots between them?

The NDTV coverage, through its camera angles and pans of the reactor, evoked the monumentality of the nuclear plant and the epic scale of construction, but it also succinctly focused on key safety features. The public watching the show may have been frustrated that the relations between components were not drawn out clearly, but they also may have been relieved that a number of security checks are in place to control nuclear fallout. The NDTV report also left the audience with a sense that there is no more to be done to address the complexity of nuclear reactors, and at the end of the day, members of the Indian public must remain passive spectators to this measured revelation.

The episode from the *Inside* series of National Geographic "Tarapur Nuclear Power Plant: Unlock Power" does an excellent job of systematically taking viewers through the different parts of the reactor. We first see the control room (where different factors/inputs are monitored to ensure they are within safety levels), the nuclear fuel loading area, the spent fuel storage tank, the turbine engine where electricity is produced, and the location where equipment maintenance is conducted. But this is not an innocent exercise in imparting infrastructural education. Other things are happening simultaneously.

In the show, the exquisite precision of nuclear technologies is demonstrated, and nuclear engineers' perfect control of the equipment in the plant is showcased. A certain kind of techno-politics is performed whereby nuclear technologies are made part of the politics of energy, and at the same time absolute control over the atom is asserted. At several points during the show, whether it is when he is handling the nuclear fuel bundle (wearing protective gear) or watching up close the robotic machine working on the coolant channel through a glass window, the show's anchor mentions that he has never seen or felt something so futuristic; it seems like something straight out of a science fiction film (figure 3.2). For the audience watching the episode, awe and wonder are evoked. The audience is made a subject of the infrastructure, a subject of the technoscientific leaps made by the Indian nation: the reactor

FIGURE 3.2 The anchor of *Inside* (National Geographic) looking at a coolant channel through a glass window

as the technological sublime is concretized in their imaginations. The monumentality of the Tarapur nuclear reactor is shown in many scenes, whether in aerial shots of its dome-like structure or in time-lapse photography of clouds moving across high-voltage transmission lines (shot from on-the-ground tilted cameras) that carry the electricity generated at the reactor (figure 3.3). These images seek to enchant audiences and suggest that infrastructures are not just "technical objects . . . but operate on the level of fantasy and desire" (Larkin 2013, 333).

Alongside an encounter with the technological sublime, journalists undergo a techno-struggle: they strive to know the truth of what is happening inside nuclear power plants and to speak confidently about technical systems operating in the plant. A guided tour in which nuclear scientists patiently answer a journalist's queries goes a long way to assure both the journalist and the audience that nuclear reactors are safe spaces.

It has been alleged that the NPCIL has opportunistically used seasonal/temporary/casual workers for maintenance labor in risky radiation environments without adequate protection. At the Rawatbhata reactor in August 2012, three contract workers were exposed to a tritium leak while performing repair work and received radiation doses above the annual regulatory limit of 15 millisieverts. Souwmya Sivakumar (2012) of the *Daily News and Analysis* reported that these casual workers were not given their medical reports. Typically,

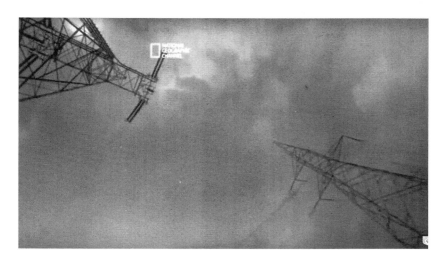

FIGURE 3.3 Time-lapse photography of clouds over transmission lines from *Inside* (National Geographic)

nuclear workers access information on their lifetime radiation doses through internal software at the plant by keying in their thermoluminescent dosimeter (TLD) number, but that software system had stopped working at the time of the leak. Furthermore, the affected workers were advised by plant management not to talk to the media. This is not the only incident in which safety and transparency protocols have allegedly been breached. In March 1993, two blades of a turbine in the heavy water reactor at Narora broke off, leading to vibrations in coolant pipes. These vibrations released liquid hydrogen that then caught fire (Ramana and Kumar 2013).

Given these instances, questions remain: Why do those journalists who are given access to the deep interiors of a plant come out praising the nuclear establishment? Why can they not ask tough questions of the so-called nucleocrats?

Exploring these issues is important, but what these mediated displays of the interior of nuclear reactors suggest is that when studying infrastructures, we cannot ignore the labor that is required to run and maintain them.[4] Nuclear engineers and contract workers are part of the nuclear workforce, and they are important constituents of the environmental public formed around atomic power plants, constituents whose voices we rarely hear in mainstream media. In terms of the different constituents of the environmental public, NDTV and the National Geographic channel show us confident, elite nuclear engineers who are emphatic that they love their jobs and find their working conditions to be very safe. But contract workers, the most vulnerable group in the nuclear industry, remain voiceless.[5]

Here again, we encounter the differentiated visibilities of nuclear reactors. For many people, nuclear reactors are hypervisible monumental domes that emit invisible radiation. But the interplay of seeing and not seeing does not end there. Many of us will never enter the domes of the reactor complex. We will only see the insides of reactors through the eyes of NDTV and the National Geographic channel, which will spotlight certain sections of reactors and obscure others. Media scholars and audiences need to be aware that such differentiated visibilities are not innocent exercises—they shape public uncertainties about nuclear reactors. Infrastructural (in)invisibilities, the governance of infrastructural emissions, and the management of uncertainty about radiation are all connected.

"Inki Jaanch Par Kaise Ho Vishwas"/How Can We Rely on Their Investigation?

Uncertainties about cell tower radiation have also arisen because some citizens distrusted the telecom regulatory agencies, as revealed by an anecdote I heard from Shipra Mathur in the offices of *Rajasthan Patrika*, the newspaper that she edits.

When the cell tower panic was at its peak, *Patrika* journalists traveled around the city with independent researchers from Rajasthan University who wielded microwave radiometers, recording high levels of EMF emissions and generating maps (figure 3.4). Later, when TERM officials arrived and conducted their own measurements at the same spots in the city, the radiation values were found to be lower. For example, when *Patrika* in association with university researchers made their survey on December 17, 2011, they recorded emission from the Gaurav tower in the Malviya Nagar region of Jaipur to be 4.4 mW/cm^2; two days later, on December 19, TERM officials found the radiation level at the same place to be 1.9 mW/cm^2.

This reiterative exercise made the *Patrika* team suspicious. After losing his confidence in local municipal authorities, Sudhir Kasliwal, belonging to the famed Jaipur jeweler family discussed earlier, wrote to TERM officials about conducting an independent inquiry, hoping their findings would result in the removal of three towers near his house. However, the next day, municipal authorities came to his home and said they knew he had written to TERM. Kasliwal concluded that the two groups (TERM and municipal authorities) were in collusion. When TERM officials venture out to measure a particular

FIGURE 3.4 Map of radiation hot spots published in *Rajasthan Patrika*, December 17, 2011

tower's radiation, they notify the tower companies and cellular operators in advance. Kasliwal and Mathur suspected that by the time TERM officials arrived at the specified sites to conduct their measurements, the tower operators would have already reduced the signal strength of the relevant mobile tower from the controlling base station.

Patrika published an article on December 20, 2011, asserting that TERM had no proper instruments to measure EMF radiation and had actually borrowed instruments from cellular operators to measure the radiation levels of their own towers. "Inki Jaanch Par Kaise Ho Vishwas" (How can we rely on their investigation?), the newspaper asked, when TERM takes money from cellular companies to measure their own towers and can only measure 10 percent of all towers under one cellular operator (figure 3.5). When another set of surveys was conducted by an interministerial committee that was designated to submit a report to the central government about adherence to regulation norms,

FIGURE 3.5 "How can we rely on their investigation?" (Headline in *Rajasthan Patrika*, December 20, 2011)

its members began to arrive inconspicuously at sites to take measurements without giving tower operators a chance to manipulate signal distribution.

"Tarang Sanchar"/Wave Transmission E-Portal

The Indian citizenry's trust in the ability of telecom regulators to enforce cellular operators' compliance with the new norms began to wane. The incidents of complicity between telecom regulators and cellular operators resulted in a further erosion of trust. In response, telecom regulators relied on the familiar device of embracing transparency, accountability, and efficiency: the e-portal Tarang Sanchar was to be their route to win back public trust. *Tarang* in Hindi means "waves," and *Sanchar* denotes "transmission" or "communication" (both of these words have been derived from Sanskrit). Tarang Sanchar, therefore, was literally designed to communicate information about waves—in this case, about electromagnetic fields, which are indeed waves or signals. Tarang Sanchar was launched on May 2, 2017, and offered an easy-to-use map-based feature for viewing mobile towers in the vicinity of any locality in India, and to ensure that cell antenna sites across the country were compliant with DoT guidelines.[6]

FIGURE 3.6 Tarang Sanchar's antenna site data

When a user specifies a region, the e-portal is designed to offer a map of cell antenna sites, with ground-based, wall-mounted, and rooftop sites differentiated by color. After clicking on an antenna site, a pop-up opens that indicates the different cellular operators (Idea Cellular, Airtel, Vodafone, Reliance Jio) whose antennas are located there, what technology they are using (2G, 3G, or 4G), and whether the site is EMF compliant (figure 3.6). If citizens want to know about the signal strengths of particular antenna sites in their locality, they must enter additional information on the Tarang Sanchar application and thereafter are sent an email with the details. If citizens require a particular location checked for signal strength, they can make a request through the portal, and for a nominal fee of 4,000 rupees, the local TERM unit of the DoT will come to their house or neighborhood, conduct the measurements, and provide a report.

Strikingly, while there is some discussion of the health effects of cell antenna signals on the Tarang Sanchar website, the e-portal was not framed as a source of environmental data or health information when it was launched. According to government ministers and regulators, it was designed to ensure compliance rather than environmental safety—because, in their view, there were no health or environmental effects from cell tower radiation. These politicians and officials related compliance to a vague notion of accountability: for them, emission compliance is not directly connected to environmental responsibility. Contrary to the positions espoused by regulators and politicians, my interest is in the intervention Tarang Sanchar performs in terms of environmental politics and citizenship by coupling issues of transparency in e-governance initiatives with environmental information systems. In other words, what kind of environmental action is envisaged by Tarang Sanchar when it makes information about antennas and antenna signal strengths visible and available?

Tarang Sanchar was touted as having data about 4.4 lakh towers and 14 lakh base stations (1 lakh is 100,000). Inaugurating the app, communications minister Manoj Sinha noted, "It will empower consumers to know—at the click of the mouse—about the towers in a particular area and whether they are compliant with the EMF emission norms as defined by the government."[7] The TRAI head R. S. Sharma spelled out a similar goal of empowering citizens and consumers through increased transparency, stating that the "portal will be a milestone for transparency, fair play, [and] citizen empowerment and will finally lead to a knowledge economy."[8] These euphoric pronouncements about Tarang Sanchar by Sinha and Sharma hark back to the late 1990s, when "e-governance" was espoused by successive administrations in India as a way of melding neoliberal high-tech consumerism and political administrative efficiency. Through the internet, it was believed, there would be efficient and transparent delivery of information and public services to citizen subjects, who were also marked as consumers. Later, with the advent of Web 2.0, e-governance discourse has shifted to a platform (app)–oriented fix, in which the solution to a problem is (partly) digital and takes the form of a platform or application.

The present government under Narendra Modi has placed tremendous emphasis on the need to go digital, and such a digitalization of governance has materialized in the form of e-portals. Between 2015 and 2018, the Modi government launched six major e-portals, including the well-known PayGov and Bharat Interface for Money, to promote cashless transactions, mobile banking, demonetization drives, and the online management and delivery of government documents. It is therefore not surprising that DoT secretary P. K. Pujari saw the launch of Tarang Sanchar not only as a landmark event in India's telecom history but also as a continuation of the efforts of the Modi government to ensure transparency and accountability. Pujari asserted that the "portal will make information available to all concerned" and then went on to underline that the "focus of the government in the last three years has been transparency, disclosures, and citizen-centric measures."[9]

I have explored the discourse of e-government initiatives to highlight the force of such an exercise in state legitimation predicated on extolling the right to information as a human right and showcasing the state's digital/technological prowess. The technology and aesthetics of information delivery are emphasized in such initiatives to such an extent that what is rendered invisible by these information visualization techniques is hardly broached.[10] I am certainly interested (as in the earlier case of opening nuclear reactors to journalists) to ascertain how this politics of transparency materialized in e-portals creates new opacities. I am even more intrigued by a somewhat different albeit related question.

What if Tarang Sanchar is considered an environmental information system? By mapping antenna signal strengths, Tarang Sanchar is a mobile/computer-based application that provides environmental data. If antenna signals are a public health hazard, and if they pollute the environment, data about their strength levels are environmental data, just like data on air quality, soil toxicity, carbon trading, and climate change. Indeed, Tarang Sanchar is not just a continuation of e-governance initiatives but also constitutes a trend by which informational technologies are increasingly used to address environmental problems, a procedure that science studies scholar Kim Fortun (2012) has called "informating environmentalism."

In June 2017, I started using the Tarang Sanchar portal along with other citizens in Mumbai who wanted to know more about how the app really worked. After orienting ourselves with the site and exchanging emails with telecom officials, we concluded that the app provided ambiguous and incomplete information: an aggregate reading at a single point from multiple antennas, and not specific signal readings from the individual antennas of each operator. Different antennas (depending on the operator and spectrum allocated to them) work on/at different frequencies, and each is associated with its own particular threshold level: for 900 MHz, the threshold level is 0.45 W/m^2; for 1,800 MHz, 0.9 W/m^2; for 2,000 MHz, 1 W/m^2. Therefore, we argued, it makes sense to have individual readings from individual antennas, which would make it possible to isolate a problematic antenna. For example, Tarang Sanchar indicated that Vodafone, Airtel, and Idea were operators with antennas—each of which operated at a different frequency—at a particular site, but the app provided data for a single overall signal strength (figures 3.7 and 3.8). The procedure to be followed for extracting aggregate readings was not outlined.

Another limitation of the e-portal is that it provides data for only one day. Thus, the readings of signal levels over the course of a year are not made available. Questions remain: Do the DoT and Tarang Sanchar have the capability to monitor cell antenna signals that could account for peak emissions? Can the DoT provide data for thirty continuous days of a month so that one can determine the peak hours? In other words, do signal levels fluctuate throughout the day in a specific pattern? Are there spikes in signal levels depending on cellular traffic density?

FIGURES 3.7 AND 3.8 Additional antenna EMF information provided by Tarang Sanchar via email

This e-mail is sent to you because you have requested additional information for the following site in Tarang Sanchar portal.

Site Details

Address:

Operators

Name of Operator	**Vodafone**
Frequency Bands	900, 2100 MHz
Technology	2G, 3G

Name of Operator	**Airtel**
Frequency Bands	1800, 2100 MHz
Technology	2G, 3G, 4G

Name of Operator	**Idea**
Frequency Bands	1800 MHz
Technology	2G

	EMF Exposure Status	
1	Compliant to Electromagnetic Field (EMF) Exposure Norms?	Yes
2	Latest Basis of Compliance	Operator Certified as per DoT Test Procedure
3	Certified on	12/03/2017
4	Latest certified EMF level (Watts per meter square) for the site	0.002145 (W/m²)
5	DoT prescribed EMF limit (Watts per meter square) for the site	0.4681 (W/m²)
6	Latest certified EMF level as a percentage of DoT prescribed EMF limit for the site	0.46 %

We also provide the facility to measure the EMF exposure at a particular location.

Would you like to request for a Public measurement?

This facility is available against a payment of **Rs. 4,000/-**

Thanks,
Tarang Sanchar Team

My interviewees felt that this kind of temporal monitoring of signal data was not carried by the DoT because its initiative was devoid of any environmental conscience. The DoT did not consider the lived experiences of those who had actual (and apprehensive) proximate encounters with towers every day while sitting on their apartment balconies drinking tea and reading the newspaper. Several people also mentioned the impossibility of comprehending signals as matter. Unlike lead particles in the air, cell antenna signals do not condense or settle. They flow and hence are ephemeral and fleeting, yet their effects can be cumulative and substantial. These facts present a dilemma for counting and calculating cell antenna signals, but at the same time they raise the stakes, making it necessary to take into account the different times at which measurements are made.

When I spoke with several citizens who had tried using Tarang Sanchar, they said that cell tower emissions are not measured by TERM unless someone comes to an individual's home to conduct measurements. The emissions provided through the app are those submitted to TERM by cellular operators. It can be argued that what the app hides is an exercise in transparency that is actually a continuation of the earlier flawed process whereby (as journalists and dissident scientists had objected) TERM lacked the instruments to measure antenna signals and thus depended on cellular operators for such information. In other words, TERM is not transparent about how the environmental data are collected.

Concerned citizens believed that the government should allow input on the design of the app, how the map should be represented, and how readings should be taken. They envisioned another mode of participation in which citizens themselves would enter their own radiation measurements onto a crowd-sourced map. The result would be a "citizen-sensing"/crowd-sensing project (Gabrys 2016) that would lead to both a democratization of environmental monitoring practices and a democratization of environmental data-gathering techniques. One problem with such an arrangement, however, would be the use of different measurement devices by various citizens, making it difficult to standardize across the collected readings. To address those concerns, a provision could be made within the app's map that would allow the addition of metadata details regarding different measurements taken from different devices.[11] Here, a particular constituent of environmental publics (concerned citizens) was attempting to negotiate the internal dynamics of such publics with respect to interaction and participation.

Open Network

Along with the controversy over cell tower radiation discussed earlier in this chapter, there also arose heated debates about an increase in dropped calls. This issue, if allowed to escalate, could lead to serious concerns regarding the credibility of telecom operators. In June 2016, Airtel began the Open Network initiative, which made available tower and signal visualization data regarding its network coverage and signal strengths.[12] This information is accessible via a platform/app on both laptops and mobile phones. Airtel, as a service provider, expressed the desire to share data with Indian consumers about where its network was strong and where it was weak (and thus needed work). Through this crowdsourcing/crowdmapping initiative, Airtel wanted those who were already its customers (and others who were potential customers) to provide the company with feedback and reviews about signal connectivity, network availability, and voice call quality in their respective local communities.

FIGURE 3.9 Walking to the parking level (Airtel's Open Network ad)

Like Tarang Sanchar, Open Network promises accountability, but in contrast to the former, the Open Network mapping platform was not designed to
give the illusion of ensuring public health or to enforce threshold standards.
Instead, it was tasked with ensuring that the signal levels from Airtel's cell towers were sufficient to maintain quality service for its customers. Open Network was designed to promote the efficiency of Airtel's cellular services.

Airtel also designed candid advertisement campaigns with punch lines
such as "Hum Aapse Kuch Nahin Chhupayenge" (We will not hide anything
from you) and "Kyunki Sahi Galat Samne Aane se Hi Banta Haye Sabse Best
Network" (Because only when right and wrong are foregrounded can we become the best network). In one such ad, a young man identifies himself as living in a zone with poor network service, where people constantly face erratic
shifts in signal level. A series of images show people going in and out of eleva-
tors and balconies to maintain signal levels. This leads the young man to joke
that he actually lives in "Island Colony" and not "Paradise Colony." When
he discovers Airtel's Open Network, he fills out a feedback form through the
mobile app, prompting Airtel officials to meet with people living in his neighborhood. Soon, a tower is erected and the neighborhood is no longer Island
Colony but becomes Paradise Colony once again.

Another ad is narrated by a group of young professionals who manage to
secure space in a basement for a start-up company they have launched. But
because the basement office does not receive network coverage, they are compelled to go to the parking level to get a signal (figure 3.9). They improvise
their working locations by turning the "watchman's cabin" (security booth)

FIGURE 3.10 Watchman's cabin converted to a conference room (Airtel's Open Network ad)

into a conference room, since their basement space is unsuitable for such a purpose (figure 3.10). As in the previous story line, these young professionals hear about Airtel's Open Network and contact the company. Airtel officials arrive and make signal adjustments, after which the young entrepreneurs enjoy excellent connectivity in their basement office.

It was in these ads that cellular infrastructures were first revealed to citizens. One saw telecom maintenance staff installing antennas and working on modulating signals (figure 3.11). Since the disruptive effects of cell antennas had caused the dropped-call issues, cellular operators found themselves compelled to make cell antennas a part of their advertisements. Such infrastructural visibility was a change from earlier advertising campaigns, which rarely foregrounded infrastructures. Airtel sought to retain irate customers by listening to their problems and admitting that there were gaps in its network, but also showing that it was determined to improve its infrastructure and serve its customers honestly.

The Open Network app maps cell tower locations and signal strengths, and works intermedially with the Open Network ads, to carry forward a new brand image of Airtel that cultivates trust, which in turn depends on infrastructural visibility. Trust in the network required transparency about network strengths and weaknesses. Airtel managed to improve its network performance by attracting the attention of its existing and potential customers, locating new geographic areas for building towers, increasing its bandwidth connectivity, and enhancing the quality of service for its consumers.

FIGURE 3.11 Cell tower (Airtel's Open Network ad)

How truly transparent Airtel's operations are remains debatable. Some media critics in India, such as the think tank Center for Internet and Society, have argued that the Open Network website contains merely the "visualization of data" but not actual data. The app has no provisions for customers to access "raw data" through application program interfaces.[13] Furthermore, even though the platform color-codes individual towers to indicate their signal strength, it remains unclear how the categories (no coverage, moderate, good, excellent) are arrived at, and the date/time stamp when each signal level was obtained is not indicated (figure 3.12). Customers are able to provide only minimal feedback. They can call a help center or submit an online form through the app, but they cannot insert signal levels or cell tower data directly onto the maps. Thus, customer participation is limited in this somewhat superficial crowdmapping or crowdsourcing effort.

In any crowdsourcing venture, control continually shifts between the organization and the public, between the strategic priorities of institutions and the benefits of the crowd. This is inevitable given that crowdsourcing is a shared process of devising ideas and solutions whereby both top-down management and bottom-up participation/creativity operate together (see Brabham 2013, xxi). Open Network was not meant as a citizen-sensing project in which people obtained measurement instruments to monitor antenna signal strengths and upload them on Airtel's network coverage map. Airtel retains its access and expertise to measure and upload data, and it permits a certain amount of feedback from its customers. Through its Open Network,

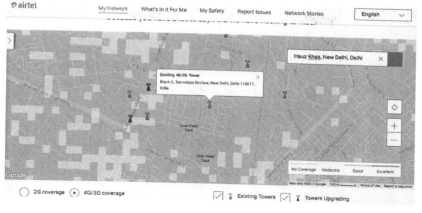

FIGURE 3.12 Towers are color-coded to indicate signal-strength levels in Open Network map

Airtel strategically hoped to appear transparent about its network capabilities and flaws in order to provide visibility to people who were suffering from call drops, but also to expand its network.

The Open Network initiative has helped Airtel to build cell antennas in places where earlier it had faced resistance because of panic over cell tower radiation. By its own admission, just two months after the launch of the initiative, Airtel had upgraded nine thousand cell antenna sites and optimized thirty thousand sites (Rathee 2016). It is true that Open Network has made cell antennas partially visible. This limited infrastructural visibility helped Airtel collect and make visible the diffuse incidents of call drops to an audience that became part of the continuously reconfiguring environmental public that had been activated by the cell tower radiation issue.

Intermediality and Infrastructural Governance

Throughout this chapter, I have tried to argue that (un)regulated emission is a characteristic of radiant infrastructures as well as a practice of governing such infrastructures. (Un)regulated emission therefore becomes a heuristic to understand both the material properties of radiant infrastructures (their capabilities to emit radiation and signals) and the ways in which information about the material qualities of such infrastructures is shared with "lay" publics. Inviting pro-nuclear journalists to enter atomic power plants and report on the "stellar record" of India's nuclear program is one way of managing the transparency and secrecy of nuclear reactors. Launching e-portals that promise to deliver extensive "environmental" data about cell towers and their emission levels, while hiding the procedures through which such data have been gathered, is another way of controlling the leakage of information about radiant infrastructures. While these are different performances of/in mediating radiant infrastructures, both are examples in which media plays a constitutive role in regulating emissions from such infrastructures.

Whether it is media coverage provided by journalists from inside a nuclear reactor, or data sets about cell tower radiation provided by a digital platform, infrastructural governance is enacted through representations of infrastructural systems.[14] Different environmental publics have different interests in mind while highlighting and/or obscuring particular aspects of radiant infrastructures. In thinking through the intermedial relays between crowdsourced radiation maps, telecom advertisements, and citizen-sensing technologies that lead to an understanding of radiant infrastructures (and, in this chapter, Airtel cell towers), what becomes apparent is that mediation needs to be more capaciously conceived as involving publicity, mapping, and monitoring. Intermediality recognizes the multiple assemblages of media that afford the different modes of communication required to make radiant infrastructures, and their emissions, intelligible to various publics.

The difference in the forms of media that are mobilized to manage secrets about leaky infrastructures owes much to the difference in governance protocols regulating them. Nuclear reactors and cell towers have had different histories in India. As has been discussed in earlier chapters, nuclear reactors were part of India's postindependence development vision, which was steered by the nation's first prime minister, Jawaharlal Nehru. Questioning nuclear energy was tantamount to questioning science, and simply could not be accommodated in a Nehruvian vision, which held that a "scientific temper" was the only way forward for the nation (Roy 2007). Nuclear technologies retain some of their original aura as symbols of India's progress in science, but also as the most secretive security infrastructures. Cell towers and other cellular technologies, in contrast, arrived with the burst of neoliberal reforms of the nineties that promised privatization, less government control, and more transparency.

Joseph Masco has written extensively about the historical relationship between atomic tests and official secrets in American society. Following the work of Émile Durkheim and Georg Simmel, Masco (2010) presciently explained that secrecy draws its power not just from the content of what is kept secret but also from the way in which the secret is managed and organized. Thus, the practice of secrecy matters as much as the content of the secret.

Media practices, I contend, are not just practices of publicity but also practices of secrecy. This is particularly the case for media coverage of strategic sciences, in which journalists pride themselves on their access to erstwhile secret spaces and at the same time must obey security protocols that limit their movement in those spaces. However, managing information leaks about nuclear reactors is not always possible. The stories broken by Latha Jishnu attest to the fact that sometimes there are contingent moments when opportunities for tactical trespasses do occur.

The phrase "(un)regulated emissions," more than any other concept (such as "measured revelations" [Kaur 2009], as discussed earlier), tries to capture empirically the entanglement of both kinds of emissions: radiation and information. There are too many incidents of atomic leaks not to conclude that the nuclear bubble created by the NPCIL is perforated rather than airtight. On the morning of March 11, 2016, exactly five years after the Fukushima fallout, Unit Number 1 of the 220-MW PHWR at Kakrapar (in the state of Gujarat) developed a heavy-water leak in its primary coolant channel, leading to a plant emergency. The combination of the chemical composition of the heavy water, the temperature, and the particular manufacturing process used to produce the pipes for that reactor resulted in the development of additional cracks in many other pipes in relatively quick succession. Following this episode, many recalled the chances of faulty equipment being supplied by Zio-Podolsk (the subsidiary of the Russian Atomic Energy Commission) to the NPCIL. Accidents were entangled with geopolitical negotiations and corrupt international deals.[15]

The act of regulating the emissions of a nuclear reactor takes place in the control room, where switches are pressed and knobs are turned. Like a ceiling fan's regulator, the control room literally sets the levels of emissions from a nuclear reactor to ensure that they remain below the threshold levels permitted. That being said, the software displays of a control room cannot guarantee the timely detection of a radioactive leak. Atomic Energy Regulatory Board chairman S. A. Bhardwaj himself confessed that cracks in the pipes at Kakrapar developed so suddenly that the electronic detection system failed to raise an alarm. Given the radioactivity concentrations at the reactor core, both the repair work and the investigation to ascertain why such a leak took place required considerable time. The initial probe, using a specially designed tool, revealed that four large cracks in a coolant tube had led to the massive leak. Absolute nuclear containment remains a fiction.

Furthermore, the techno-politics of mediating radiant infrastructures is a selective operation that an attentive audience will *figure out*. While the

National Geographic channel episode inside Indian nuclear reactors did much to stress the sublime qualities of such technologies, it was not attentive to representing the (often unheard) voices of nuclear workers (especially the precarious working conditions of casual workers), who are crucial actors in the environmental publics formed around disruptive atomic power plants. Seasonal workers are vulnerable because they are not trained to have a somatic understanding of occupational exposure levels. They also work with defective or no equipment at all, which suggests that the NPCIL maintains different standards for radiation protection for different people, thus redistributing radiogenic injuries and risks based on socioeconomic status rather than technical manuals.

Contemporary neoliberalism can sometimes reduce politics to an interplay of transparency and secrecy enabled by the techno-cultures of hacking, stinging, and surveillance/*sousveillance* (Birchall 2011; Dean 2002; Sundaram 2015). Visibility is critically important to a public understanding of radiant infrastructures, and thus infrastructural politics are especially vulnerable to fetishizing particular acts of transparency and revelation. The stakes of making radiation visible and disclosing information about radiation are immense for the health of vulnerable affected communities. What I hope to have demonstrated is that some acts of transparency may not actually make infrastructures more visible or perceptible. Even as some secrets about radiant infrastructures are secreted through e-portals and investigative journalists, they do not always change our knowledge of infrastructures or radiation. Digital data about cell tower emissions on e-portals might help track peak-hour emission patterns, and yet such overwhelming amounts of data (often termed "data overload") could make any intelligent interpretation of such data impossible. Regulating emissions, whether by inviting selected journalists or establishing e-portals, is also an act that tries to control public uncertainties about radiant infrastructures. While at times they appear transparent, such media practices produce new uncertainties when they are critiqued for providing inadequate information.

Developments in radiant infrastructures are matched by developments in measurement infrastructures that have made it easier to detect radiation. New citizen-sensing projects based on critical data design are popping up; thus, ordinary citizens are now able to use Web 2.0 platforms to gather crowdsourced radiation data that can be linked with other environmental and health statistics such as demographic data, cancer rates in a particular area, and air pollution data. These projects are new exercises in democratic participation with regard to environmental decision making; they rely on but also problematize the data analytics of Big Data. Environmental data, generally, are indeed large, but citizen science–based environmental data are collected using data sensors at a local level, and this particularity is important to consider (Gabrys 2016; Fortun et al. 2016). In the case of citizen science–based collection, Big Data is not being deployed by a security state to surveil citizens, but by lay publics who believe in the critical interpretation of such data, who want their beliefs about toxicity affirmed, and who desire to hold governments and corporations accountable. It remains to be seen if (and how) the Indian nuclear establishment and telecom regulators will make their emissions-sharing web platforms more transparent and democratic by eliminating ambiguous top-down data and instead facilitating the circulation of crowdsourced data from the bottom up.

Attending to emissions in this chapter has helped us conceptualize environmental publics in terms of secrecy protocols and crowdsourced radiation maps. The focal point of chapter 4 is human bodies and radiant infrastructures. After an examination of how various media map and monitor radiation leakage from nuclear reactors and cell towers in this chapter, readers will be presented with mediations of human exposure to radiation in the next chapter. By examining the relations between human bodies and radiant infrastructures (and radiant energies), chapter 4 puts forward pertinent questions: How can human bodies be considered part of environmental publics? If bodies and radiant technologies are coextensive, how do embodied sensitivities to radiation make us think of the body as consituting a kind of media in an intermedial circuit with other media forms? The next chapter continues discussion of environmental publics and intermediality, and, on this occasion, in the bodily register.

04

Exposures

This chapter examines another specific material aspect of radiant infrastructures—that is, exposure of human bodies to radiation. Two questions are critical here: How do various media portray the proximity of people living close to reactors and towers, and how do these media capture bodily exposure to emissions by such radiant infrastructures? While depicting the proximity of human bodies to hypervisible, and by now conspicuous, infrastructures such as cell towers and nuclear reactors is easy, making perceptible the intimacies shared with radioactive nuclides and cell antenna signals is difficult. It is important here to parse out the distinction between "proximity" and "intimacy." Proximity connotes spatial contiguity, and intimacy (while certainly folding in proximity) allows for suffusion and permeability. Thus, human bodies, in being tangibly and spatially proximate to nuclear reactors and cell antennas, end up sharing micro-level intimacies with radioactive nuclides and wireless signals.

In examining the mediated testimonies of cancer patients living close to radiant infrastructures, as well as the biomedical capturing of molecular-level interactions between signals and bodies, this chapter zooms in on the importance of feelings and bodily sensations (as opposed to just talk, speech, and discourse) for the formation of environmental publics. There is a less known but equally important area of literature from the Frankfurt School by Alexander Kluge and others that, contra Jürgen Habermas, privileges experience over discourse in constituting publics (Negt and Kluge [1972] 1993). Building on this literature, I will further develop the concept of environmental publics discussed in the introduction and the earlier chapters, which in this chapter will gain a far more embodied and experiential character.

Post-Fukushima, when the protests against construction of new nuclear plants intensified in India, the nuclear establishment decided to rebrand itself. In collaboration with the National Geographic channel, the Nuclear Power

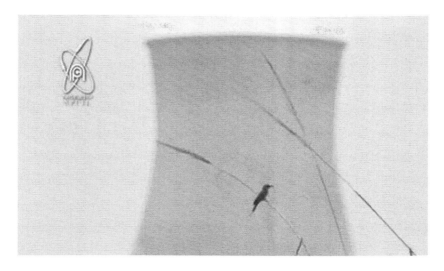

FIGURE 4.1 National Geographic–NPCIL ad

Corporation of India Limited launched a series of advertisements, some of these which I have discussed in an earlier chapter. One particular ad, however, goes beyond framing nuclear energy as illuminating lives through the power of the atom. It portrays the proximate encounters between living beings and nuclear reactors as benign, thus promoting the reactors as safe technologies producing clean and green energy.

In this ad, there are zoom-ins and extreme close-ups of butterflies sucking nectar, animals emerging from burrows, and a number of rare bird species going about their everyday lives. We seem to have entered a wildlife sanctuary, and, as in so many other National Geographic shows, we are asked to emplace ourselves within it. The voice-over tells us: "Some animals march ahead and others stand tall. In the end, they have to make it work; after all, it is their family." We see a bird perching on a slender twig in the foreground as clean white smoke comes out of NPCIL furnaces in the background (figure 4.1). The ad sells nuclear as clean energy and espouses corporate social responsibility tactics, all while blurring the boundaries between nature and nuclear technology. Here, they not only coexist but also share a kinship; they form what Arturo Escobar (1999) and Joseph Masco (2004) have called "techno-natures." The ad emphasizes the idea that a nuclear plant as nature reserve is not a paradox. Nuclear plants do not threaten the environment; rather, technology and nature seamlessly blend together.

FIGURE 4.2 A woman feeds a goat, with reactor domes in the background (from *Radiation Stories 3*)

This sleek ad targets the Indian urban middle class, for whom such ads carry not just the assurance that nuclear energy is safe and clean but also an exotic value. Additionally, it addresses foreign investors who, having seen the large-scale demonstrations against atomic power plants in India, had for some time been hesitant to fund the construction of the reactors. Most important, the ad asserts that the intimacy between birds and nuclear reactors is perfectly plausible. An oppositional reading of the NPCIL ad, instead of seeing a seamless blending of technology and nature, argues for the precarious existence of a bird so close to a reactor.

This perspective was recently demonstrated by the antinuke documentary filmmaker R. P. Amudhan, whose documentary *Radiation Stories 3: Koodankulam* portrays communities living close to the Koodankulam nuclear reactor in southern India and was made in solidarity with the protests against it. In one scene, Amudhan shows a woman feeding a goat in the same line of vision as the nuclear reactor (figure 4.2). When I interviewed Amudhan, he mentioned that, unlike the National Geographic–NPCIL ad, he wanted to juxtapose "life (women and goat)" and "death (nuclear reactor)." There is no blend of technology and nature here. Rather, there is a dissonance. The nuclear reactor will soon displace the woman and the goat and thus expel the woman from both her place and her livelihood. Amudhan's documentary has been widely shown in the alternative public spheres of the antinuke struggle in

India (press clubs, civic associations, universities). However, the film also addresses the urban Indian middle class, the same target group that is courted by the NPCIL ads. In this case, the documentary hopes to create empathy among the middle-class audience for the struggles of local communities fighting to keep reactors out of their neighborhoods.

In July 2013, I was present at a convention in Ahmedabad, where the people's charter against nuclear energy was to be drafted. There, I heard Xavieramma, a member of the affected community in the Idinthakarai village whose house was close to the reactor. A staunch critic of nuclear energy, Xavieramma asked why, if the nuclear reactor is really as safe as NPCIL claims, it is not being built close to the parliament of India or then prime minister Manmohan Singh's house. In a similar vein, Yashvir Arya, who lives close to the Gorakhpur village in Haryana, where another nuclear reactor is being built, asked why an atomic power plant is not being erected next to President Pranab Mukherjee's house in New Delhi. He sarcastically reasoned that the electricity produced by the plant could help light up all 340 rooms of the *rashtrapati bhavan* (presidential palace).

This rhetoric aimed at the Indian government's hypocrisy suggests that some lives in India are considered less privileged and less valuable. One could even say that the government creates a perpetually long-lasting *exception* around the energy security issue and uses its sovereign powers to decide who to protect and who to let die. The sovereign nuclear state turns potentially "necropolitical" (Mbembe 2001), deciding the locations of dangerous nuclear projects. The urban elite who seem so anxious about cell towers (which need to be in the city for them to have cellular coverage) are not that bothered about nuclear reactors because they are built away from the city.

The material properties of these radiant infrastructures alter the nature of the unwanted proximities involved. The field of influence of a cell tower antenna is about fifty to one hundred meters, while a nuclear reactor, if there is fallout, can affect populations living as far as fifty miles away, depending on wind speed and direction. The notion of what is proximate changes, and with it changes the socialization of fear with regard to the technology. To consider a well-known example, soon after the Chernobyl nuclear meltdown, radioactive ash spread across the European continent. Cumbrian and Welsh sheep farms were affected, and, until 2012, twenty-six years after the Chernobyl disaster, livestock from these farms had to be monitored for radiation levels before they could be sold.[1] Thus, the scale of the Chernobyl nuclear disaster is not contained in Ukraine but extends to Cumbria and Wales, where plumes of radioactive poison spewed by the reactor landed and then slowly decayed.

While the spatial scales can be ascertained in terms of the spread of radioactive materials, the time scales of radiation extend to several hundred years as many radioactive isotopes tend to have long half-lives and decay very slowly. The time scale of the Chernobyl reactor in Cumbria, the most northwesterly county of England, is twenty-six years; time in that landscape has not been the same, at least for the first twenty-six years since the wind blew radioactive ash there. Speaking of the "spacetimemattering-scape" of nuclear radioactivity, Karen Barad (2017) has evocatively remarked: "The whole world is downwind" (G106).

In comparison, the signals from a cell antenna are far more directed and targeted than nuclear radiation. In the case of nonionizing electromagnetic radiation, much depends on the direction of the main beam and the angle at which the apartment and antenna face each other. Ionizing radiation from nuclear reactors, in contrast, is seen to spread indiscriminately in a concentric circle around the reactor. Despite these differences, unwanted intimacies with (and considerations of distance from) these infrastructures have remained a point of concern and debate in both environmental controversies.

Documentary filmmakers took up the plight of rural fishermen affected by nuclear reactors, and lifestyle shows depicted elite urbanites concerned about cell antennas near their houses. Even though the preferred channel of mediation was different in the two controversies, both types framed the affected populations and the radiant infrastructures in one single image or shot. Understanding the specifics of mediation processes will help in deciphering just how media modulates risk perceptions among vulnerable communities and audience members. There is much here to discuss about the televisual and documentary testimonies of communities living close to reactors and towers.

Over the course of this chapter, I explain how mediating radiant infrastructures also involves mediating the radiant energies they emit. Measuring radiation levels in particular areas using Geiger counters, dosimeters, and radiation detectors is one aspect of such an exercise. The other aspect is understanding the entanglements of such emissions with our bodies—in other words, exposure.

Measuring and understanding exposure can lead to holding governments and corporations accountable for radiation-related illnesses. That being said, radiogenic injury is difficult to ascertain because it can take decades to manifest, and such a "latency period," as Shannon Cram (2016) has argued in regard to workers at the United States' Hanford nuclear site, "introduces doubt about the source of cancer, mutation, and birth defects" (524). Some documentarians in India have taken up this challenge by obsessively showing the very visible effects of invisible radiation on human bodies and therefore damning the government for unleashing violence on its own citizens. However, many devastating effects of radiation simply cannot be seen on the surface of human bodies. Other mediational strategies have included looking for traces of such "unwanted intimacies" (Weston 2017) in biomedical imaging of human bodies, through X-ray plates and CT scans of radioactive signatures on bodies and electroencephalogram (EEG) tests inscribing the interactions of neural impulses with cell antenna signals.[2]

While discussing mediated testimonies of cancer patients and communities living in proximity to radiant infrastructures, I deploy the terms "affect"/"affective" to include both subjective emotions (Staiger, Cvetkovich, and Reynolds 2010) and the corporeal dimension of sensations (Massumi 2002). While some readers might find this to be too expansive a usage of "affect," I believe it is generative as the two aspects of affect are linked in my case studies. Here, we have the subjective emotions of affected communities who believe that their feelings about cell towers and complaints of cancer are being pathologized and prevented from being expressed in the public spheres. At the same time, electromagnetic signals are noncognitively acting on the patients' bodies (without them consciously registering it) and thereby shaping larger political debates about radiant infrastructures.

Staiger, Cvetkovich, and Reynolds (2010) explain how certain groups and communities (women, queer, disabled, racial and ethnic minorities) have found it difficult to express their feelings in public, and hence the public sphere has been built up through a systematic exclusion of particular experiences. In my case studies, televisual and documentary testimonies of cancer patients suffering from radiogenic injury suggest their difficulty in having their experiences of encountering radiation be recognized by the wider public. Beyond this notion of public feelings and subjective/political emotions, I also want to hold on to affect as something that connects the body and the social, bypassing cognition, and is a part of the larger ontological reality (Massumi 2002), which includes signals and radioactive isotopes in intimate contact with vibrant human bodies.

I will be discussing many of these mediational strategies, but let me not get ahead of myself. In the next section, I begin with examples from the lifestyle show *Living It Up* and articles in *Rajasthan Patrika* that dealt with the cell tower radiation controversy.

Situated Testimony and Anecdotal Evidence

The television channel CNN-IBN presents *Living It Up*, a show dedicated to urban lifestyle and health problems, on Saturdays, and retelecasts it on Sundays. Targeted toward an urban middle-class and upper-middle-class audience,

FIGURE 4.3 Tilted cameras with silhouettes of towers and children (Screen grab from *Living It Up*)

Living It Up highlights the pros and cons of city life by exhibiting a cocktail of health issues and self-care practices, from fitness exercises to healthy food. An arbitrary sample of episode titles from the show: "Breast Cancer: India's Silent Plague," "Junk Food and Your Kids," and "Work Pains and How to Deal with Them." Instead of offering medical diagnoses, the show aims to find the behavioral symptoms of deficiencies, disorders, and diseases that urbanites may be suffering from by offering stories of people who have had similar problems.

Living It Up took on the cell tower scare issue in an episode that aired on October 6, 2012, and sought to represent the affective encounters between cell towers and human bodies. This episode presents carefully staged shots of children walking in a line with a tower looming over them. A dusky color palette provides expressiveness to this scene, which is shot from a low angle with the camera tilted up, emphasizing the height of the tower (figure 4.3). A sound track of metallic percussion instruments, electronic disturbance, and ringing phones accompanies scenes throughout the show, often layered over the narrational voices and patient testimonies. The sound design helps to create a sense of dread. The phrase "fear psychosis" is used repeatedly in the episode to describe the shared experience of people living close to mobile towers, but representing the current state of fear psychosis cannot be dissociated from spreading it further: the televisual images could panic viewers who live close to towers but have not heard of this issue before.

The show conveys a shared mood of restlessness and frustration among urban residents. In one scene, Karmel Nair complains of severe headaches, hair loss, nausea, and sleeplessness. She moved to her new apartment in Mum-

FIGURE 4.4 Karmel Nair on the window and the cell antenna outside (*Living It Up*)

bai when she was five months pregnant. There is anguish in Nair's account when she likens the experience of living close to cell towers as being X-ray scanned perpetually: "A pregnant woman taking an X-ray shot, that itself is considered so harmful that doctors do not prescribe an X-ray to a pregnant woman.... I have been living under this X-ray shot twenty-four by seven, under this radiation shot, which is as good as taking an X-ray every second. So how comfortable, how safe is it going to be for my child?" (Karmel Nair, *Living It Up*, October 6, 2012).

X-rays are ionizing radiation, which has the ability to disrupt molecular bonds and hence cause cancer. Cell antenna signals are different from X-rays in that they are nonionizing, and so Nair's comparisons might seem technically imprecise. That being said, she rightly implies that scientific experts have not sufficiently considered the effects of chronic exposure to electromagnetic fields. Through her testimony, the banality of this fear psychosis becomes apparent. It is not about a sudden pang of fear that erupts with the first recognition of the cell tower's effects and then leaves the body forever. Instead, there are small eruptions for Nair every single day. Nair's worry leads to premonitions about the future of her unborn child.

Nair would like to get up one morning, look out her window, and find the tower gone, but it obdurately remains, dangerously proximate (figure 4.4). In this unwanted proximity, in the energy spent worrying, and in the fear psychosis might lie the seeds of a political critique of the telecom infrastructure and its environmental effects (see Stewart 2007). Following Purnima Mankekar (2012), who contends that lifestyle-show images open up viewers' bodies to be influenced by television, I suggest that Nair's premonitions depicted in *Living*

It Up are another portal for affective flows between cell towers and televisual audiences.

Despite their emotional and affective charge, could situated testimonies—that is, testimonies like Nair's, delivered at the sight of an event or problem—count as evidence? During the cell tower radiation controversy, the term "anecdotal evidence" was invoked by a particular group of experts to question public claims of symptoms such as sleeplessness, depression, and cancer due to living in proximity to cell towers and/or overuse of mobile phones. Eminent physicist Vasant Natarajan, who conducts research at the Indian Institute of Science in Bangalore, strongly disparaged sellers of radiation filters for circulating the story of a person who developed brain cancer from talking on a cell phone, describing it as "anecdotal evidence" (Natrajan 2013). K. S. Parthasarathy, former secretary of the Atomic Energy Regulatory Board, criticized the Indian government–appointed interministerial committee for lowering the threshold of antenna radiation based on "anecdotal evidence" presented by "scare-mongers" who cite "vague symptoms such as joint pains, sleeplessness, and cancer among those who resided near cell towers" (Parthasarathy 2013).

Moore and Stilgoe (2009) write about a similar discourse of anecdotal evidence in relation to mobile phone radiation in the United Kingdom during the late nineties. They argue that "anecdotal evidence" in such cases "became a term that served as a focus for doubts and suspicions about the very existence of the syndromes in question, as well as their possible environmental risk factors" (55). Natarajan and Parthasarathy also question both the symptoms and the correlation between symptoms and cell towers. Parthasarathy argues for maintaining the boundary between the "scientific evidence" gathered from epidemiological studies and the "anecdotal evidence" procured by stitching together a couple of newspaper articles.

Such epistemological boundary making, such as by Parthasarathy and Natarajan, can prove difficult in cases where scientists are no longer in a position to envision all possible scenarios of toxic exposure. In the cell tower radiation controversy—where experts confess to not knowing the long-term effects and are unable to arrive at a consensus about the permissible level of radiation—anecdotal evidence attains particular salience in shaping public perception and making the state more responsive to the needs of citizens. We can observe instances of the presentation of anecdotal evidence in the newspaper *Rajasthan Patrika*.

Several images of concerned citizens in Jaipur appeared as part of *Patrika*'s coverage of the radiation story. These citizens, who were affected patients or relatives of sick people, appeared in the foreground, either wielding measure-

FIGURE 4.5 Maniram Ji and a couple hold radiation detectors in *Rajasthan Patrika* (May 5, 2012)

ment devices or pointing an accusatory finger at the set of mobile towers in the background. Such photographs almost give the impression that people like to see themselves in the newspapers. In the pictures, the tower was always nearby—just across the street or on the terrace of the adjoining house—looming, an ominous shadow set to engulf the city. Consider this example: Maniram Ji is shown standing on the terrace of his bungalow. He is holding the signal measuring instrument with LEDs on his right hand, and his index finger is pointing to the red light, conveying that radiation levels are dangerous. He is framed against the backdrop of the tower that is responsible for harmful radiation. It is a self-consciously staged image. Another image in the same article shows a couple wielding the radiation detector as three towers loom behind them (figure 4.5).

Patrika journalists went to many neighborhoods in Jaipur, responding to complaint letters from their readers, and were able to portray the individual experiences of the residents. Such a door-to-door—or rather rooftop-to-rooftop—campaign highlighted the "situated knowledges" (see Haraway 1998) of the locals suffering from the deleterious effects of nearby towers. Some of these stories mention how a family member in a particular room was more affected because that room intersected with the main beam of the cell antenna. Thus, *Patrika*'s hyperlocalized campaign emphasized that people have knowledge of their living situation and of their body, and that they feel the bodily sensations resonating with antenna frequencies. Such portrayals encouraged other Jaipur denizens to tell their stories and allowed some of them to stop worrying about the stigma of being recognized as a cancer patient. Being in the papers and telling their stories was akin to taking part in a community initiative. More stories meant more anecdotal evidence, but it remained uncertain whether this would lead to raising the epistemic status of anecdotal evidence to that of scientific evidence.

Dosage: Radiated Body Testifies

The problem of what counts as evidence is equally pervasive in the nuclear radiation controversies. Whether in a uranium mine or a nuclear reactor, the "scientific" way of ascertaining radioactivity inside nuclear bodies, of calculating radiation exposure, is determining dosage.[3] External radiation for uranium miners involves exposure to gamma rays from radioactive rocks. Miners also inhale alpha particles released from uranium and radon decay, and these particles continue to spit nuclides inside the miners' bodies. This is what is called "internal radiation."[4]

Uranium miners intricately encounter radiation, both internal and external, and the alpha particles inside their bodies produce varying inscriptions on their skin: lumps, moles, swollen limbs. Documentarian Shriprakash, in *Buddha Weeps in Jadugoda*, depicts these irradiated bodies. In the face of an agonizing lack of epidemiological studies on the effects of uranium mining, Shriprakash films antinuclear activists carrying out an informal survey in Jadugoda. As the activists go about the village selecting bodies to exhibit as examples of specific diseases, these ailing bodies undergo categorization: children with malformed torsos, children with deformed heads and the wrong number of fingers, children with hyperkeratosis ("toad skin"), children and the elderly suffering from blood cancer (figure 4.6). The body testifies all by itself.

Cinema is a play of surfaces. While one is viewing, cinema is experienced as a surface in the form of the screen. The filmic camera, even as it wants to illuminate all parts of the human body, can only show us the outside, the skin. Shriprakash would like to depict what the radioactive nuclides are doing in

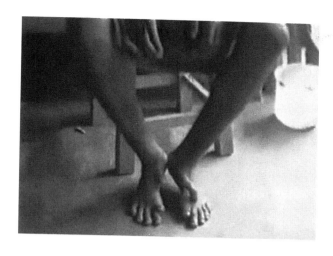

FIGURE 4.6
Body testifies
(From *Buddha
Weeps in Jadugoda*)

the depths of the interior human body, but the filmic medium restricts him. He deploys screen charts, animations, and X-ray reports to help us visualize intimate body-radiation encounters, circulation and accumulation of radiation through the food chain, and the traces of radiation stored inside the human body. This is as much he can do to excavate the "phenomenologies of the inside" (Lippit 2005).[5] The indexical facticity of the documentary image is restricted to recording the marks of radiation on the surface of bodies.

Beyond cinema, in what ways can one depict radiation inside a body? The dosimeter attached to a nuclear worker's body gives an indication of the radioactive dose imbibed. Workers who spend many years at nuclear reactors are trained to perceive (through their dosimeter readings) the shifts in radiation level as they move across different zones: from the nuclear fuel loading area to the spent fuel storage tank, from the turbine engine to the control room. The environment keeps changing, and the medium of perception is the dosimeter. Checking radiation doses of each worker is a pragmatic exercise and also an exercise of asserting control: control over the atom, control over emissions, control over radiogenic injury.

As discussed in chapter 3, the *Inside* series of National Geographic involved journalists touring an Indian nuclear reactor in one episode titled "Tarapur Nuclear Power Plant: Unlock Power." In one scene of this particular episode, the anchor comes from a zone of high radiation intensity and is inspected by other nuclear workers to check whether he is within the prescribed radiation limits. The anchor is depicted wearing a thermoluminescent dosimeter (TLD) badge and carrying another direct-reading dosimeter (DRD)

FIGURE 4.7 The anchor of "Tarapur Nuclear Power Plant: Unlock Power" with two dosimeters

(figure 4.7). The health physicist explains that the DRD is used to ascertain the immediate dosage the journalist has received, then the cumulative radiation is recorded in the TLD, which is sent to the plant's computer records. But is the security system really that compact? Is not the determination of the permissible radiation dose a somewhat arbitrary exercise?

Shannon Cram (2016), writing about the Hanford nuclear site in the state of Washington, traces the bureaucratic translation of exposure standards to the embodied practice of safe radiation dose. The term "nuclear body" is used by the Atomic Bomb Survivor Study to identify a statistically calculated human template, "a Reference Man/Standard Man," who can withstand a controlled dose of radiation and who accounts for collective variety across gender and race. (In most cases, considerations of race and gender are elided.) The "Reference Man" pushes for a universal notion of permissible dose. However, such a universal standard is simply not possible, and therefore it not only makes up an impossible "nuclear body" but also accuses workers (especially seasonal or temporary workers) who suffer radiogenic injury as being careless in their movements across different radioactive zones inside the nuclear plant. Some documentaries resist such a politics around the nuclear body.

Two documentaries—R. P. Amudhan's *Radiation Stories 1: Manavalaku-richi*, about former Indian Rare Earth Limited workers who had sand mined monazite (which is used to extract thorium, a speculated nuclear fuel), and

Shriprakash's *Buddha Weeps in Jadugoda*—unflinchingly and somewhat obsessively portray the tumors and limb impediments of miners.[6] In the testimonies recorded by Amudhan, the standard talking heads format seems unreasonable as an interview strategy, for the whole debilitated body needs to speak. Throughout one interview, one side of the interviewee's body keeps shaking. Amudhan's camera slowly moves from showing the man's bandaged leg, to his shaking arms, and then to his face as he describes the symptoms of a nerve problem that began with a shaking finger and skin peeling away from one leg. These bodies have become the storehouse for radioactive chemicals, a site for radioactive decay. The decaying chemicals mutate inside bodies, shaping their fate. Amudhan and Shriprakash demonstrate that each "exposed body (and each exposed part of the body) is a different expression of nuclear contact."[7] In other words, a generalizable *nuclear body* (cobbled together from dosage data) is simply a fiction. No body experiences the accumulation of nuclear radiation in the same way.

A man suffering from bowel cancer (piles) is shot lying on his side, his head resting on a pillow. He is shot at an angle so that his whole body is in the frame. At the beginning of the interview, the man talks but does not face the camera (figures 4.8 and 4.9). He seems to be conversing with a person who is either sitting or standing above and beside the camera. His answers to Amudhan's questions seem absentminded. He yawns, and at times gets lost in his own thoughts.

Amudhan does not edit out these silences. He waits and then gently prods: "Do you have to always lie down like this?" The cancer patient replies, "Yes, I need help to get up or lie down." He blows a leaf on the floor and then resumes, "If a person commits small mistakes, he should be pardoned. If he is penalized like this, he feels frustrated. What is God? If a man is not able to earn and support his family, he hates himself and his family. Is it not true?" Amudhan zooms in for a tight close-up of the old man's countenance when he reminiscences about his daughter who lost her life to blood cancer, perhaps to capture the full import of his sadness. Amudhan continues to frame the patient in this close-up as the man utters, "It was wrong on God's part to create man in this world in the first place. If a man commits small mistakes, he should be pardoned. He can improve on this life then. Where will he go if he is punished straightaway?" The patient's repetition of "If a man commits small mistakes, he should be pardoned" conveys the difficulty of reconciling himself to his condition. If the initial onset of cancer had brought intense rage and frustration, over the years those emotions have transformed into crippling depression.

FIGURES 4.8 AND
4.9 Zooming
in and zoom-
ing out (From
*Radiation Stories 1:
Manavalakurichi*)

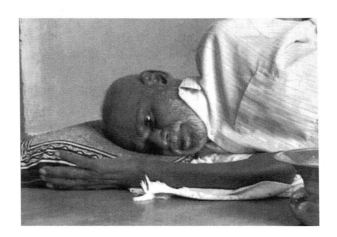

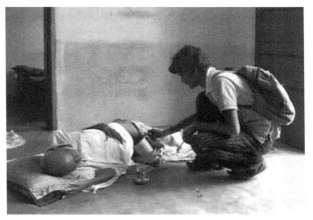

Later in the interview, Amudhan asks, "So many people are affected here like this. Why is it so?" The man replies, "Yes, so many people are affected. The reason behind that is . . . ," and then he seems to lose his train of thought, experiencing some discomfort. We find out that he needs to urinate, and he asks for help. Amudhan switches from close-up to long shot, showing us how the man struggles to drag a mug close to his penis. There is an awkward silence here, but Amudhan persists with his camerawork (figure 4.10).

The old man does not answer Amudhan's questions directly, but his deviations suggest that the stories people tell about themselves cannot be read merely as case studies appearing in health reports or viewed only through a sociological lens. The bowel cancer patient's testimony demonstrates Amudhan's ability to acknowledge his documentary subjects' "right to complex person-

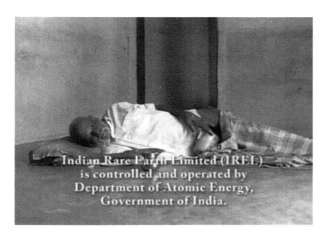

FIGURE 4.10
Camera persists
(From *Radiation
Stories 1:
Manavalakurichi*)

Indian Rare Parth Limited (IREL)
is controlled and operated by
Department of Atomic Energy,
Government of India.

hood." He knows that his subjects' stories about social problems are "entangled and weave between what is available as story and what their imaginations are reaching toward" (Gordon 2008, 4), and that these imaginations could very well involve getting stuck in the symptoms of their troubles.

This interview and several others that Amudhan conducts in the film highlight exactly what is missing in the pedestrian and easily digestible television network interviews. It is the "spaces of reticence," those "uneasy silences, ignored questions, vacuous smiles or blank stares" (Alley 2011) that lay open the testimonial/documentary apparatus of knowledge production and contest the notion that local experiences and knowledges can be easily grasped by elites, or even documentary audiences, from the outside. The testifiers demonstrate through their bodies and behaviors what they cannot articulate through language. The bodily experiences of pain and illness suffered by radiated testifiers will perhaps always defy language, but such experiences also form the "potential for humane community" (B. Taylor 1997, 306; see also Scarry 1985).[8] Amudhan's unhurried camera movements and slow pacing stitch together their bodily sensations and unsayable feelings, producing a shared sense-making of the effects of nuclearization. From what is made sensible and visible about these situated and expressive nuclear bodies, we know there is much more that we do not yet understand.

Interference: Electromagnetic Body and Energetic Environments

If the human body can be nuclear—storing radioactive wastes and forming the mutagenic theater for chromosomal transgressions—it can also be electromagnetic. Electromagnetic waves inside the body interfere with cell antenna

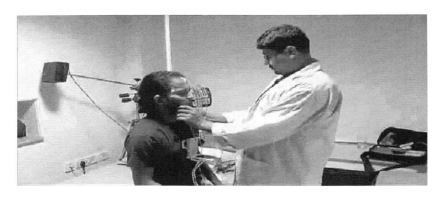

FIGURE 4.11 Mandal gets wired in a sleep lab (Screen grab from *Living It Up*)

signals. To fully grasp the idea of exposure to radiant energies, along with dosage, one needs to understand "interference."

The episode "Are Mobile Towers a Health Hazard?" of *Living It Up* begins with hosts Tridip Mandal in Delhi and Urmi Sahni in Mumbai reflecting on their own relationship to their mobiles. Are we addicted to cell phones? Can we live without them? A cell phone has a radio transmitter and receiver, which enable it to exchange signals with the base station at regular intervals so that the station knows that the phone is within its coverage area. The exchange of signals intensifies when the cell phone rings and calls take place. The mobile user's ears, cheeks, hands, and body are exposed to these signals.

In the episode, Mandal subjects himself to a sleep test and gets wired to sensors in a sleep lab (figure 4.11). His mobile phone keeps buzzing all through the night, and he has a restless sleep. This part of the episode is shot in night vision mode with little light, which helps the audience relate to Mandal's disconcerted feeling. The sleep specialist mentions in her observations that Mandal had fragmented sleep and delayed sleep onset.

The sleep test maps waves of activity in the brain and heart to graphical waves on electrocardiogram (EKG or EEG) monitors. These graphs are inscriptions of electromagnetic phenomena happening inside the human body. The electrodes and sensors placed on different parts of Mandal's body and head pick up voltage fluctuations generated by neural impulses deep inside. Such mediations of the human body transcend its flesh to place it in the context of electromagnetics. Writing about the possibility of electromagnetic pollution interfering with brain waves, the anthropologist Stefan Helmreich (2015) notes, "Where there are electromagnetic waves, interference is never far behind, and this is the case when it comes to thinking with and through

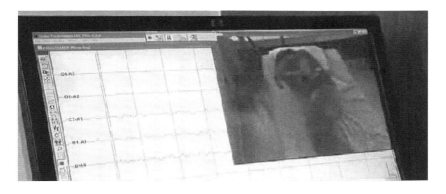

FIGURE 4.12 Graphical display on the sleep monitor (Screen grab from *Living It Up*)

brains, too" (s146). Monitoring Mandal's sleep becomes a biopolitical process of checking for any harmful interference between cell antenna signals and Mandal's cardiac and neural functions. Here, the body as media, the body as technology, the body as electrical impulses interacts with the electromagnetic environment, an environment of which the body is very much a part. The waves on the sleep monitor are a record of such interactions and interferences (figure 4.12). These graphs also register the affective modulations and sensations of an electric body.

When I asked Mandal about his decision to become an experimental subject, he replied, "It always works best if the reporter goes through the experience himself. That way, audience can find the whole show more believable." According to Mandal, including the personal self in the process of testing is a sign of legitimacy. In this scenario, there is both the affect of Mandal being put through a test and the affect of viewers seeing Mandal's sensations inscribed in the form of graphs.

I have already described several televised testimonies of Indian citizens affected by the presence of cell towers near their homes. These people not only argue that they got cancer from exposure to nonionizing electromagnetic radiation but also report symptoms such as dizziness, memory loss, sleeplessness, irritability, and muscular pain. Similarly, these symptoms have been reported by electro-sensitives in many "developed" countries such as the United Kingdom, the United States, Canada, and Sweden. These people are hypersensitive to the frequencies of EMFs produced by cell phones, cell towers, and Wi-Fi routers.

Discussions about electro-sensitivity are to some extent a part of popular media and cultural discourse in the United Kingdom and the United States.

However, in India, electro-sensitivity has never been picked up by concerned citizens agitating to evict cell towers. One of the reasons could be that the citizens feel that pointing out the electro-sensitives among them might weaken their overall struggle against cell towers. It could, after all, help the cellular operators claim that the illnesses were being imagined by people living close to cell towers. As is the case with multiple chemical sensitivity, people with electro-sensitivity, even in places like North America and Europe, are seen as paranoid and socially maladjusted. They are often accused of feigning the symptoms of their purported illness (see Murphy 2004; Mitchell and Cambrosio 1997). A relative of a cancer patient living close to a cell tower told me that in India people feel shy and stigmatized about even visiting a psychotherapist; such patients cannot be expected to say they suffer from a condition like electro-sensitivity. Perhaps, in the years to come, this may change.

Jeromy Johnson, an electro-sensitive, declared in a TEDx Talk that "your body is electric," stressing the electro-vitalism of the human body. Prevailing biomedical knowledge sometimes refuses to own up to the idea that electro-sensitivity is not an "impossible bodily state" (Murphy 2000) but an "undone science" (Hess 2016).[9] Electro-sensitives in the United States have sought refuge in the remote mountainous town of Green Bank, West Virginia, because it is a national radio quiet zone: in order to protect the highly sensitive astronomical radiotelescopes in Green Bank, no cell phone towers are allowed there.

The BBC medical drama *Holby City* (1999–) narrativizes the trauma experienced by electro-sensitives and depicts the interference of electromagnetic waves. In season eighteen, episode forty-three of the program, aired on August 22, 2016, a patient arrives on the doorstep of the hospital vomiting profusely, complaining of headaches, nausea, and palpitations. The doctors order a series of tests to check his pulse and blood pressure, and then an EKG, but they find no abnormal results. The patient continues to believe he is plagued by something mysterious, perhaps a "camouflaged brain tumor," and feels helpless that he has gone to three hospitals and none of them have been able to figure out what exactly is happening to him. The neurosurgeon Guy Self (played by John Michie) is called upon to take a look, and he orders an MRI. Magnetic resonance imaging, or MRI, technology produces still pictures (resembling X-rays) of the body's interior by coupling together electromagnetic and digital technologies: the electromagnetism measures the interior of the body, and the digital technology creates the visuals (Hastie 2009).

The patient, dressed in a hospital gown, is pushed into the glowing MRI machine. As a halo develops around the upper part of his body, the *Holby City* doctors peer at the digital images of his brain on the computer screen

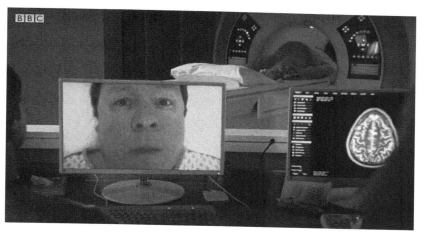

FIGURE 4.13 MRI exam in *Holby City* (Screen grab from *Holby City*)

(figure 4.13). Television audiences are treated to multiple perspectives at the same time: our perceptual possibilities expand as we see the MRI machine, the patient's face, and the biomedical image of his brain. (Indeed, for the audience, it is a TV encounter with the brain, as Amelie Hastie [2009] would put it.) An MRI exam is long and could last an hour, but the patient is unable to withstand the test for very long. He feels increasingly sick, and the upper part of his body, which was under the glow of the MRI scanner, has to be taken out from the contraption.

The MRI test does not produce any new leads (except to show that there is no tumor), and the consultant general surgeon Serena Campbell (played by Catherine Russell) is ready to dismiss this erratic behavior of the patient as psychotic, but the spirited consultant trauma surgeon Bernie Wolfe (played by Jemma Redgrave) disagrees. Wolfe has heard that the patient's job is to set up broadband connections for the elderly. She connects the patient's profession with his inability to withstand an MRI. Wolfe reasons that the patient has developed a hypersensitivity to EMFs because of his long-term exposure to broadband communications. This has to be the reason his body reacted negatively to the electromagnetic signals of the MRI machine, which were trying to probe for aberrations but were actually the cause of his discomfort. Wolfe's hypothesis is proved correct when the patient begins to return to a normal condition once he is isolated in a room that does not have any Wi-Fi.

Electro-sensitives bring attention to the soaked-up environmental milieu of radiant energies in addition to solid radiant infrastructures. If we are to comprehend the environmental effects of radiant infrastructures, we have to think more ecologically and relationally about their emissions. This means not only relating one radiant technology to another (like the MRI machine to cell towers or broadband) but also considering the interference of radiant energies produced by human bodies, MRI technologies, and cell antennas—that is, moving from the mediatic level to the signaletic level. Paying attention to wavy and fluid radiant energies rather than solid radiant infrastructures makes us notice "the intervening medium of the air" (Gabrys 2010, 46). The concept of intermediality as something that emphasizes the "inter" as the "in-between-ness" of media gets further buttressed as we think of the atmosphere between solid media objects and infrastructures as a medium as well.

Radiant energies point to shifting contact zones where the boundaries between bodies, infrastructures, and environments do not lie only at the skin or the metallic exterior. Such a theorization of "energetic environments," composed of ionizing and nonionizing radiation, helps to theorize radiant infrastructures and media technologies in environmental terms and address the environmental issues sparked by them.

Embodied Publics

Readers have encountered documentary filmmakers perusing X-ray reports of uranium miners' bodies and lifestyle show (*Living It Up*) hosts subjecting themselves to sleep tests that graphically trace electromagnetic interferences. On such occasions, we not only see the irradiated body under medical gaze but also witness the irradiated body as part of the public culture of visualizing the effects of radiant infrastructures (and radiant energies).[10] This submission of the human body to radiography and imaging techniques is necessitated by the need to make epistemological claims about the proximity and intimacy of bodily exposures to radiation. In order to make sense of the varying radiological and biomedical imaging techniques that are reconfiguring the irradiated body, whether they be the dosimeter readings of a National Geographic TV anchor being carefully monitored as he moves across the different sections of a nuclear reactor or an electro-sensitive character in a TV medical drama (*Holby City*) undergoing a painful MRI scanning, we need an embodied sense of environmental publics and mediation.

In this chapter, I have contended that the public fear and uncertainty about radiation in India are not just the result of biased media coverage; they arise from bodily sensations in relation to media infrastructures and affective modulations of mediated images. Thus, one needs to understand mediation not as some discrete media object or media text but as an envelope around the social, where matters of experience are as critical as matters of deliberation and discourse. If we, as scholars and audiences, pay attention to radioactive dosage and electromagnetic interference, we realize that molecular-level mediations of infrastructures help us to engage with cell antennas and nuclear reactors within a regime of sensation that is felt by human beings but evades conscious perception. The goal of this chapter, thus, has been to make the particular experiences and feelings of affected patients—as well as the micro-level intimacies the patients' bodies share with wireless signals and radioactive isotopes—come to matter in environmental public discourse.

Here my work is in dialogue with that of Linda Soneryd (2007), who argues that public protests against 3G cell phones in Sweden arose not only because of a lack of knowledge about invisible radiation but also due to bodily interactions between humans and mobile phone infrastructure. Soneryd explains that the reasons for public fear have as much to do with comprehension (conscious knowledge) as with prehension (bodily sensations).[11] Some other researchers—such as Adam Burgess (2004), who has examined the mobile phone radiation and cell-mast siting controversies in the United Kingdom—tend to view media as only capable of promoting fear. Burgess seems preoccupied with media effects (and especially the headlines of newspapers, in contrast to taking media genre or format into account) and fails to sufficiently consider the affective dimension of mediation: the ability of media coverage (talk shows and documentary interviews), media objects (cell phones), and media infrastructures (cell towers) to modulate bodily sensations. As a result, Burgess remains within the evidentiary and epidemiological paradigm of a certain kind of sociology-of-risk literature (the social amplification of risk framework), which tends to link scientific knowledge with experts and "objective" risk and then contrast it with the lay public's perceptions, which are considered subjective emotions fanned by the media. I have, in contrast, tried to engage with a popular, speculative, and affective paradigm of mediation.

In this chapter, we have witnessed efforts by media groups to depict proximities of affected communities to radiant infrastructures. Various visualization techniques have been used to probe the intimacies between radioactive isotopes and human bodies, as well as to show the molecular-level interactions unfolding between neural impulses and nonionizing EMFs. At the molar level, there is an explicit unwanted proximity with radiant infrastructures there for everyone to see. At a molecular level, there is the imperceptible, almost extrasensory intimacy with radiant energies emitted by cell antennas and nuclear reactors. Affect becomes a useful heuristic to comprehend the range of sensations that such entanglements generate. Furthermore, affect becomes a key constituent of the environmental publics that have emerged with the controversies around radiant infrastructures.

Publics exist not only as conversations but also as experiences. Oskar Negt and Alexander Kluge ([1972] 1993) emphasized the need to study everyday experiences as part of investigating public spheres. They offered, from within the Frankfurt School, a rejoinder to Jürgen Habermas's conceptualization of a conversation-oriented, rational-critical public sphere. They argue that "public sphere" refers as much to institutions, establishments, and activities as it does to the "social horizon of experience," which is "something that has to do with everyone and which only realizes itself in the heads of human beings, a dimension of their consciousness" (17–18).[12] While Negt and Kluge associate experience with the mind and consciousness, I have been using the term "affect" to connote both emotions and non-cognitive sensations.

Zizi Papacharissi's (2015) important work on "affective publics" explores what "mediated feelings of connectedness" do for digital politics and networked publics. She examines how the circulation of affect, inside and outside of social media platforms like Twitter, leads to political mobilization. Like Papacharissi, I am interested in affective publics, but my project about environmental publics examines affect in wider media publics, where phenomenological encounters between human bodies and radiant infrastructures (and radiant energies) are important to consider.

Putting emphasis on the embodied aspect of environmental publics means we seriously consider the variety of human bodies and their different interactions with radiant infrastructures, and that we do not believe in standard templates of one nuclear body or one electromagnetic body. The discourse of standardizing templates suggests that a "standard body" can uniformly account for all effects of wireless signals and radioactive rays, which this chapter has demonstrated is simply a myth.

Despite criticism, the cell phone industry worldwide continues to conduct tests on the heating effect of mobile phones based on a standard brain size of a six-foot-two adult white male. Radio waves can penetrate the human body by a few centimeters, leading the water in the body to absorb RF energy, which causes heating. The signal strength of cell antenna and mobile phone radiation determines the amount of heating that takes place. The specific absorption rate (SAR) of energy is a measure of the absorption of radio waves (Drake 2006). In the case of mobile phones, especially because they are held close to ears, the SAR can affect the brain. Every mobile phone manufactured is tested for SAR, but the brain standard used for such simulated tests is that of a six-foot-two adult male. Several counterexperts like epidemiologist and

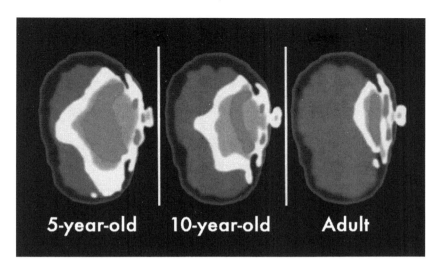

FIGURE 4.14 Difference in heating effect of mobile phone radiation based on age (Snapshot from *Mobilize*, 2014)

founding director of the Center for Environmental Oncology Devra Davis in the documentary *Mobilize* (Kevin Kunze, 2014) explain that this standard testing procedure doesn't take into account that a child's brain absorbs far more radiation than an adult man's brain (figure 4.14). Other experts like Joel Moskowitz (director of the Center for Family and Community Health, UC Berkeley) and Debbie Raphael (director of the Department of Toxic Substances) explain that these SAR tests had been established sixteen years ago (twenty-one years as of 2019) and since then, much has changed with regard to the kind of smartphones manufactured and what we know about cell phone radiation. They express disappointment that despite these changes, there has been no reexamination of the standard procedures for testing.[13]

While tracing the flow of sensations across bodies and matter, it is important not to lose sight of the sociopolitical dimensions of identities, especially the intersection of class and gender. Almost all the subjects in the *Living It Up* episode who were framed inside the house were women, including Karmel Nair. Bodies become gendered as a connection gets made between women and domesticity. One of the producers of *Living It Up* referred to the women interviewed for the episode as the "dames" who had been featured in earlier newspaper articles. The use of the term "dames" suggests that these women were from the upper echelons of society, and that their class backgrounds mattered in their stories getting print space and airtime.

Once a person is exposed to radiation, the not so naturally occurring radioactive isotopes of cesium and strontium become part of the body, decaying slowly and remaining in the skeleton even after the person dies (Brown 2017). Furthermore, brain and heart activities are wavelike phenomena. With electromagnetic processes occurring inside the human body, there is no way to say that nonionizing electromagnetic radiation is only a characteristic of artificial or artifactual technologies such as radios, televisions, and cell phones. Here, again, there is no easy interior-exterior dichotomy, and energetic environments can be found both inside and outside of human bodies. Whether it is a radiation detector or a biomedical visualization, technologies are not just helping us see or sense a radiated environment, but also are making us realize that we, along with our sensors/detectors, coconstitute that environment.

This chapter, which has explored questions of bodily exposure to radiation, and the earlier chapter on regulation of emissions are both an attempt to take the material specificities of radiant infrastructures into account while theorizing environmental publics. The next chapter continues to trace the ways people advocate for emission controls and resist the proximity of cell towers and nuclear reactors, but this time the case studies will center on political subjectivities. While the material specificities of infrastructures and the phenomenological conditioning of irradiated bodies still matter for the arguments presented in the next chapter, the focus shifts now to thinking of the radiant infrastructure as itself a political terrain onto which claims of citizenship are continuously being made and unmade. What kind of environmental claims, political expressions, and everyday experiences congeal around radiant infrastructures as the state and its subjects perform for one another the rules (and rituals) of citizenship?[14] The next chapter posits that the political pulse of antinuke activism and the anti–cell tower campaign in India cannot be explained simply by probing the material characteristics of infrastructures; rather, one needs to examine the organizing networks and actors that are already in place due to particular postcolonial historical and environmental contexts.

O5

Styling Advocacy
Activism and Citizenship

I was at an antinuke energy conference in Ahmedabad in the summer of 2012. On the sidelines of this symposium, over cups of tea, an activist opposing nuclear energy mentioned that the anti–cell tower campaign was a celebrity campaign, and he was sad that no celebrities were coming together to stop nuclear plants. He said he cannot comprehend why film celebrities feel that nonionizing cell antenna radiations are carcinogenic while ionizing nuclear radiations are fine. Speaking from experience, he said that when he and some friends were making a documentary about the Tarapur atomic power station, the only Bollywood actor they found to support their film was Tom Walter, who agreed to do the narration for the film. According to the activist, this was so even though Tarapur is not very far from Mumbai, and celebrities cannot possibly be ignorant of the work practices going on there, but since they were not directly affected, at least not now, they were not concerned. Embracing a similar view, and perhaps making a slight jibe at Bollywood, the Brazilian environmental journalist Norbert Suchanek, while he was crossing through India with his Travelling International Uranium Film Festival, expressed the following wish: "I would love to have Bollywood stars acting in a film related to radioactive contamination or a romance centered around a chemical engineer facing the risks of a nuclear disaster."[1]

However, among the activists opposing nuclear energy, there was a lack of consensus on whether celebrities should become the face of the antinuclear campaign in India. In a casual conversation during a lunch break at a conference on nuclear energy, somebody suggested inducting the Bollywood actor Aamir Khan and using his iconic status to draw the attention of Indian masses toward the ill effects of nuclear energy. A senior activist from the group responded that the antinuclear movement would risk losing its gravity and depth if there was a highly visible celebrity presence. The campaign might become more about Aamir Khan and less about antinuclear concerns. This reasoning was provided despite the fact that Khan has been involved with social movements such as the anti-dam movement Narmada Bachao Andolan (Save the Narmada Movement) and produced the show *Satyamev Jayate* (*Truth Alone Triumphs*, STAR India Network, 2012–), which deals with social issues and environmental concerns such as the toxic effects of pesticides and waste management. When I was in Jaipur in November 2012, I came across newspaper articles in which residents of the city asked Khan to take up the cell tower radiation issue for an episode of *Satyamev Jayate*.

This chapter explores the style and substance of advocacy movements related to antinuke and anti–cell antenna campaigns as a way to extend theorizations of the different environmentalisms and social movements operating in India. We now have a chapter that juxtaposes different radiant infrastructures and the publics formed around them. This juxtaposition and this conversation are important because they help explore the differences and contradictions—both internal and external—encountered by the various social movements and environmental campaigns that are resisting infrastructural development in contemporary India.

In this book, I have developed the concept of "environmental publics," showing how groups gathered around cell antennas and atomic power plants can be understood as issue-based publics. Such publics are spurred to action when radiant infrastructure becomes disruptive, creating problems and issues for affected stakeholders. However, the disruptive quality of radiant infrastructures cannot be the only reason that such publics are conjured. Some organizing networks and actors have to be already in place. Thus, the way in which the publics gather together cannot be ascertained only by focusing on the characteristics of the infrastructure. The alliances that antinuke movements and anti–cell tower campaigns are able to forge with media groups and with other environmental campaigns working on allied issues and concerns are critical to the ways in which such issue-based publics emerge. Such alliances are also shaped by the long history of social and ecological movements in India. Studying such alliances and their histories helps us grasp the distinctive "Indian/South Asian" character of the environmental publics discussed so far.

There is much writing on Indian environmentalisms, but scholars of ecological movements in India often tend to focus on the relationships between state, judiciary, and social movements, relegating media to only a supplementary role (see Baviskar 2011; Gadgil and Guha 1995). I want to foreground the role of media in sustaining such social movements and, in doing so, to also explain how different environmentalisms are mobilized through different mediations.

Affinities and Alliances

In the year 2012, as part of spreading awareness about health effects of cell tower radiation, Prakash Munshi would give weekend PowerPoint presentations to Mumbai residents' associations, including the Napean Sea Road Citizens Forum. Consulting my field notes, I will sketch out how these presentations and discussions unfolded.

In such a presentation, there are slides dedicated to the Men against Rape and Discrimination campaign by Bollywood director and actor Farhan Akhtar. This campaign is related to woman's safety and contains a poem by Akhtar's father, Javed Akhtar, an eminent Bollywood lyricist and screenwriter. During his presentations, Prakash Munshi makes it known that Farhan Akhtar is a friend and has been a big supporter of the campaign against cell antennas; that is why in his own presentations, Munshi believes in spreading the good causes that Akhtar has been working on. Through this citation, Munshi both touches emotional chords and makes his Bollywood connection well known.

Comprehending the associations and affinities of both the antinuke and anti–cell tower campaigns with Bollywood is one essential piece of understanding these campaigns. If we are to fathom the different styles and rhetorics these movements choose for representing themselves and their goals, however, there is another essential piece to this puzzle: the ways in which these movements invoke convergences with and divergences from industrial disasters of the past.

In some of the meetings in Mumbai that I have described, Munshi not only name-dropped Bollywood superstars but also reminded audiences of the Bhopal gas disaster. Munshi addressed his audiences and explained that cell towers were ubiquitous and that multinational corporations (read: cellular operators) were trying to deliberately sabotage any research on harmful emissions from the antennas. Citing the example of what Union Carbide did in Bhopal, Munshi contended that multinational corporations are always running after wealth and cannot be trusted to be concerned about the health of the citizens of India. Munshi thereby suggested that whether it is a chemical company like Union Carbide or a cellular operator such as Vodafone, all of them could be made to fit into the category of the greedy multinational corporation. At the same time, many of the upper-middle-class urban residents that Munshi was addressing were themselves working for multinational corporations.

The links between the advocacy of survivors battling the aftermath of the Bhopal disaster and the antinuclear movement in India, in particular, the agitation against a nuclear reactor in Koodankulam, are more organic than the links Munshi attempts to draw between the Bhopal protests and anti–cell tower movements. Established political parties cite Bhopal in their opposition to the Indo-US nuclear deal and the lack of stringent regulations against foreign nuclear equipment suppliers in the Nuclear Liability Bill discussed in the Indian parliament. Other translocal connections between activist groups have emerged. Two women survivors of Bhopal, Rashida Bee and Champa Devi Shukla, who were at the forefront of the two-decades-long campaign for justice in Bhopal, received the Goldman Environmental Prize in 2004. The prize money went toward building the Chingari Rehabilitation Center in Bhopal, where children of Bhopal are treated. Part of the money was also allocated toward instituting the Chingari Award. The word *chingari*, translated from either Urdu or Hindi, means "flames," which are emblematic of the hard-won battles of the Bhopali women survivors against Dow Chemical and Union Carbide. The Chingari Award is given each year to courageous women and communities in recognition of their fight against the injustice of environmental disasters.

On December 1, 2012, around the twenty-eighth anniversary of the Bhopal disaster, the Chingari Award was given to the women of Idinthakarai and Koodankulam for standing up to both the nuclear establishment and "a nuclear supplier lobby comprising multinational companies who see the entire Indian market shutting its doors to them if the Koodankulam struggle were to succeed."[2] The award's symbolism cannot be overestimated, as it is offered from a disaster survivor to an activist who is boldly struggling to avert a future such disaster. The award citation's explicit reference to foreign suppliers is another reiteration that the lessons learned from Bhopal cannot be forgotten.

I have juxtaposed these stories to argue that the antinuke campaign and the anti–cell tower campaign have fashioned different styles of advocacy. The cell tower campaign not only has better access to the culture industry of Bollywood than the antinuke campaign but also emphatically embraces such connections. The antinuclear movement's position toward Bollywood remains ambivalent; some antinuke activists are opposed to the idea of involving Bollywood, while others who had made overtures to Bollywood celebrities found that the responses to their invitations were lukewarm. While both movements have invoked Bhopal, the antinuclear movement's alignment with the International Coalition for Justice in Bhopal was perceived to be more authentic. Some key campaigners of the antinuke movement, like Nityanand Jayraman, had earlier been part of the movement for justice in Bhopal.

Bollywood and Bhopal represent two "populars" in India, one standing for the national popular cultural industry, and the other representing the groundswell of support for people's movements in India, including other eco-justice movements and new social movements such as the Narmada Bachao Andolan. Both of these antiradiation movements cast themselves against the "infrastructural power" of the Indian state. The anti–cell antenna movement was a movement from within neoliberal India against the excesses of neoliberalism symbolized by the unfettered growth of cellular infrastructure, and the antinuclear movement was part of a long history of subaltern struggles against the state's policy of disproportionately endangering and displacing certain populations in the name of infrastructural development and technological progress. Where these movements differ is in the kinds of media produced by antiradiation activists who organize against these two different radiant infrastructures. Among other things, this book is about the mediation of Indian environmentalisms represented by these two differing strategies.

In its November 2011–January 2012 issue, *Movement of India*, the flagship news magazine of the National Alliance of People's Movements (NAPM), spotlighted the Koodankulam antinuclear struggle. The magazine also covered anti-dam movements in the state of Assam and the plight of unorganized sector workers. By putting Koodankulam on its front cover alongside anti-dam movements and working-class concerns, the magazine proclaimed what it finds worthy of discussion, and what associations it prefers to emphasize. The front cover has a picture of activists jotting down on a piece of cloth what they have learned from the Fukushima nuclear meltdown. The label that runs through the cloth in English and Hindi reads: "Lessons from Japan." Thus, this cover image showcases translocal solidarities with Japanese antinuke activists.

The NAPM is an association of environmental advocates who believe in grassroots activism and in the need for environmental concerns to be interwoven with social justice, global solidarities, and livelihood issues. As an organization, NAPM has faith in collective struggle as a means to empower the subaltern populations of India: it connects antinuclear movements with anti-dam movements because it is convinced that both large dams and nuclear reactors are development projects that displace vulnerable people. There is no mention of anti–cell tower radiation campaigns in NAPM's magazine even though one would have thought there is much that unites nuclear radiation and cell tower radiation.

This omission does not necessarily have to do with the nuclear reactor projects affecting rural areas and the anti–cell tower campaign being an urban phenomenon. The NAPM champions the rights of urban slum dwellers and works for the unionization of urban workers. It remains indifferent to anti–cell tower activism, however, because of the class privilege of those urbanites who consider themselves affected by the cell antennas. The anti–cell tower movement, which is led by upper-middle-class advocates, has little to offer in terms of interweaving environmental concerns with concerns about social inequality.

In the next sections of this chapter, I address the following questions: What political and ecological claims are made in the Indian public spheres by the nation's citizens and populations, and in what ways are these claims being made? How are such claims, concerns, and anxieties being addressed by the state bodies and technical institutions? Which citizen groups get to frame this debate in mediated arenas and make their issues come to matter and for whom?

Differentiated Publics, Different Environmentalisms

In order to make decisions about technical infrastructures such as nuclear reactors and cell towers, the government needs to consult not only scientific experts but also lay experts, those ordinary citizens who have specialized knowledge about an issue because they are affected by its consequences. This is the dictum from a group of science and technology studies scholars belonging to liberal progressive Western societies who advocate for a "technical democracy" based on a level playing field for different kinds of experts (Callon, Lascoumes, and Barthe 2001). These are well-intentioned conjectures, yet they fail to grasp the empirical realities and political expediencies of non-Western contexts such as India, a country that is witnessing an interrogation of the postcolonial project of development from many different constituencies.

India's political and expert class believes that both cell towers and nuclear reactors are essential for the nation's continued development. However, India's politicians and experts treat people who oppose the expansion of cell towers differently than those who want to halt the nation's atomic juggernaut. The Indian government has been more responsive to the concerns of elite urbanites who are alarmed to see cell towers close to their houses than it has been to rural fishermen and farmers who do not want a reactor in their villages. Comparing the environmental debates around these different radiant infrastructures highlights the need to differentiate environmental publics and to empirically examine how each such public (formed around nuclear reactors and cell towers) negotiates the perpetually mutating state-science-society contract.

Political theorist and anthropologist Partha Chatterjee (2004) has contended that only a small group of the Indian citizenry can be considered as belonging to the arena of civil society, meaning those who can confer with the government or state through their membership in formal associations and institutions. A majority of the population in India lives in extremely vulnerable conditions; their very livelihood depends on transgressing laws, and they engage with the government politically through informal associations and paralegal transactions. According to Chatterjee, the government interacts with the majority of the population in India not through formal associations but by making them "targets of policy." These governed populations are part of "political society."[3]

These formulations offer a neat schema, and it would be easy to lump the cell antenna activists in with civil society and then tag the antinuke protesters with political society. In this chapter I will attend to this schema, and sometimes even conform to its categorizations. At other times, however, I shall endeavor to problematize these overly neat distinctions by showing that the Indian antinuclear movement is far more heterogeneous and involves mediations and intersections across civil society members and the so-called governed populations. While discussing the anti–cell tower movement in India, I acknowledge that the government has been more receptive to its demands than to those made by antinuke protesters. That being said, I want to point out certain limitations that still plague the anti–cell tower movement, despite its "civil" society privileges.

It is also crucial to point out that Partha Chatterjee's formulation leaves little room for understanding associational and publicity practices of subaltern populations as part of civil society (Sundar 2010). Furthermore, Chatterjee tends to assume that all middle-class populations enjoy civil society privileges. Such an assumption fails to consider that the Indian middle class is a broad category and that social inequalities exist among middle-class citizens in that country (Fernandes 2011). All such criticisms suggest that one needs to interrogate the civil society–political society categorization postulated by Chatterjee.[4]

Beyond this, several scholars have criticized Chatterjee for failing to account for the constitutive role of media in shaping the relationship between the government and citizens/populations (see Neyazi 2014). Does the media, just like the government, also discriminate between citizens (civil society) and populations (political society)? With a competitive media environment marked by the proliferation of linguistically and thematically diverse media channels, are less privileged middle-class citizens and subaltern populations able to find avenues in vernacular media to express their concerns and make them matter in public discourse? The realm of media is another arena in which to assess the alliances between civil society and political society. Beyond analyzing different movements to make them conform to political categories, I aim to explore how new social movements against radiation in India portray themselves, what affinities and associations they want to build and project, and what this all has to say about radiant infrastructures and the infrastructural power of the state.

The antinuclear movement in India is based on issues like displacement and livelihood, and its origins can be traced back to iconic campaigns against deforestation such as the Chipko—or "tree-hugging"—movement of the 1970s; campaigns against toxic factories built by foreign multinational corporations, such as the one responsible for the Bhopal gas tragedy of 1984; and campaigns against the building of large dams such as Narmada Bachao Andolan from the mid-1980s to the present. The anti–cell antenna movement has a more recent inception and reflects the urge by urban elites to make the government responsive to their need for healthy lives in Indian cities that are increasingly becoming environmentally unsustainable. The antinuke movement can be considered to be part of the long tradition of ecological movements in India and the Global South known as "environmentalism of the poor" (Guha and Martinez-Alier, 1998). In Ramachandra Guha and Juan Martinez-Alier's (1998) influential formulation, such environmental movements, often waged by subaltern classes, have pointed out that ecological sustainability of their livelihoods has been threatened by resource extractivism of the privileged classes and multinational companies (also see Gadgil and Guha 1995). Thus, the environmentalism of the poor shows how the project of ecological justice necessarily includes a component of social justice. Such a history of ecological movements explains why the front cover of NAPM's magazine seamlessly lumps together anti-dam and antinuke movements in India.

Amita Baviskar (2011) detects another strand of environmentalism practiced by elite urban middle-class citizens who want the state, the judiciary, and the regulatory authorities (including municipalities) to immediately attend to their concerns, which have little to do with "lives and livelihoods" but very much to do with "health and hazard" and "beauty and order" (401–402). Baviskar refers to such initiatives and campaigns as instances of "bourgeois environmentalism."

To make sense of how antiradiation activists understand the particularity of their movements, represent their goals, build alliances, and, finally, perceive the threat of radiant infrastructures, I want to nuance these previously mentioned historical trajectories and categories of social movements with some anecdotes plucked from my fieldwork. Through these incidents, I investigate and compare the different strategies of persuasion and publicity chosen by, and available to, antiradiation advocates in the nuclear reactor and cell tower debates based on the different political and cultural imaginaries of the affected communities. I argue that processes of mediation in these two environmental debates cannot be analyzed only by sketching the existing or emerging political contracts between state, science, and society at a macro level. As a media studies researcher, I also remain alert to the cultural protocols of evaluating citizenship, technology, newsworthiness, livelihoods, and lifestyles that operate on the ground among ordinary citizens.

Those supporting the greater regulation of cell towers eschew the activist badge and declare that they are concerned citizens who dutifully pay their taxes to the government and therefore expect the government to pay heed to their demands. Advocates against the proliferation of nuclear reactors are happy to espouse the activist label and want to foreground the state's failure to honor the livelihood rights of subaltern populations. Up until this point, the strategies and tactics of styling each campaign's advocacy seem to operate nicely within the categories of civil society and political society established by the state-science-society contract. However, when anti–cell antenna activists attempt to lean on Bollywood celebrities and when antinuke activists establish solidarity links with survivors of the Bhopal gas tragedy, culture and mediation spread through the state-science-society contract, reminding us that they were in fact always holding this contract together. In the process of documenting the interactions occurring within publics sparked by radiant infrastructures, I want to explore in this chapter the work being done by culture and media in upholding and challenging the categories of civil and political society in India. If the ease and difficulty of crafting alliances with Bollywood and Bhopal indicate the differences between the movements, investigating the way the state views these movements and responds to their demands offers another route to exploring radiant infrastructures. Such an undertaking involves examining the different knowledge practices and techniques of governmentality entailed in state action.

The State and the Public

In December 2012, I sat in the office of the Center for Nuclear Disarmament and Peace (CNDP) conversing with filmmaker Prem Piram about his documentary *3 Miles to Gorakhpur* (2012). In that film, the farmers of Gorakhpur village in Haryana are depicted putting up a spirited fight against the land grab methods of the government. However, Kumar Sundaram, a CNDP member, noted that although during shooting of the film there was indeed significant resistance to land acquisition, the scenario had changed lately. Sundaram, who had recently visited Gorakhpur, informed us that suddenly, one day, the banks in that region started issuing notices to farmers about not paying their arrears on the loans they had taken. These tactics had led many farmers to resign themselves to selling their lands even though they were initially opposed to the idea of nuclear reactors. As Partha Chatterjee (2004) would note, the government/nuclear establishment's "mode of reasoning" or way of negotiating with these farmer groups "is not deliberative openness but rather an instrumental notion of costs and benefits" (34).[5]

The Indian government has deployed coercive tactics to isolate local communities agitating against the construction of nuclear reactors in their area by cutting them off from the influence of outside activists. Section 144 of the Indian Penal Code—which prohibits outsiders from entering places close to a construction site, and forbids locals from organizing protests of more than five members—has been imposed within a seven-kilometer radius in Koodankulam, and also in parts of Jaitapur where the French transnational nuclear supplier Areva is building a plant. This use of Section 144, a law with a colonial legacy, shows the proclivity of the state to create a zone of exception in the name of nuclear.

Across earlier chapters, I have reiterated the class and regional access privileges that the campaign for stricter regulation of cell towers has enjoyed over campaigns by rural communities affected by nuclear reactors. However, this privilege does not automatically translate into access to media, and ascribing the privilege of power automatically to certain identities conveys a certain refusal to comprehend the complexity of media and cultural practices

FIGURE 5.1 Banners (Courtesy Prakash Munshi)

FIGURE 5.2 Banners facing Sahyadri Guest House (Courtesy Prakash Munshi)

involved in the making of news and entertainment. Identity itself is always in the making.

Despite their privileges, actress Juhi Chawla and her neighbor and friend Prakash Munshi could not get the government or the municipality to pay heed to their letters requesting the removal of a cluster of cell tower antennas from the terrace of the Sahyadri Guest House, located on the other side of the road facing their apartment. What finally worked for them was the privilege of their home's location: many state government dignitaries stay in the Sahyadri Guest House, and ministers tend to hold press conferences there. Munshi organized the residents of the apartments to put up banners, which were addressed to the Sahyadri Guest House and listed the ailments caused by cell tower radiation. The concluding banner asked the question: "Who will be responsible for parting of our loved and dear ones?" The banners were signed, "From your Friendly Neighbors" (figures 5.1 and 5.2). Reporters who had come to cover the government-organized press conference literally walked into these banners. The next day, cell tower radiation was news. Since then, Chawla and Munshi have been invited to present their case in front of the interministerial committee that has been taking steps to recommend a new set of regulatory frameworks for cell towers in India. Such open and inclusive invitations for citizens to participate in policy making regarding cell towers are difficult to find in the case of debates about nuclear reactors in India.

Public hearings and the Environmental Impact Assessment (EIA) report are the two civilian avenues available to local communities for engaging with the nuclear state. Often, one of the reasons for conducting a public hearing is to win the consensus of the local community and ascertain whether its members are satisfied with the EIA report. Before getting final clearance to build a large-scale development project, the executioner/developer needs to ensure that the project gets environmental clearance. Nuclear power plants also fall under this law, and yet activists and local community members have often alleged flouting of rules by the nuclear establishment. Surendra Gadekar, a prominent Gandhian, nuclear activist, and physicist, while delivering a lecture at the Convention on Nuclear Energy (figure 5.3), said that in his experience of public hearings related to nuclear matters the local administrative officials conducting them seem to act as *pitthus* (stooges) of the nuclear establishment. For example, despite strong criticism of the EIA reports in these meetings and even as local people raise strong objections to the proposed plant, district collectors would summarize the public hearing succinctly in the following manner: "General opinion favored the project." Gadekar argued that the collector's job is to record honestly what was said, but that is not the practice.

In the same convention, a local of Mithi Virdi, a village in the Bhavnagar district of Gujarat, where a 6,000-MW United States–designed nuclear reactor was going to be set up, complained about both the way the public hearing was conducted and the process by which the EIA report was prepared. He explained that the locals had successfully resisted attempts by officials to do a study of the environment in their village, and so they were surprised that during the public hearing the administrators had presented an EIA report. The villagers suggested that the EIA report had been prepared by studying the soils from villages around the main village where the plant was actually being constructed. The EIA report was printed in English and not Gujarati, thus preventing many villagers from comprehending the potential environmental impact of the project. Another speaker noted that the public hearings are often held about ten kilometers away from the most affected village in order to make the venue difficult to reach, particularly for those villagers who have the most to lose if the plant is built. The village chosen often is one in which people are poorly organized against the plant. These strategies suggest that even as public hearings are civilian avenues, they slant toward unconventional

FIGURE 5.3 Convention on Nuclear Energy in Ahmedabad (Photo by author)

political strategies, which deliberately create spaces where *fair* civil deliberations just cannot happen.

If there was a lack of will on the part of the state to reach out to citizens about public consultations in the case of nuclear reactors as opposed to cell towers, the media could also be blamed for being selective about which issues to highlight on a national scale. The fact that the debate on nuclear reactors never made it to national talk shows on English-language channels leaves open the question of whether such shows remain restricted to entertaining a narrow segment of privileged citizens.[6] The public hearings did get covered by one kind of media, however: the politically committed documentary film.

Documentary filmmaker R. P. Amudhan begins *Radiation Stories 3: Koodankulam* (2011), his film about the Koodankulam nuclear power plant, with archival shots of the nuclear bombs "Little Boy" and "Fat Man" being dropped, and the mushroom-like atomic clouds they formed over the cities of Hiroshima and Nagasaki. Following this opening, the first scene from the Southern Tamil Nadu region is the public hearing about the power project held in Tirunelveli in June 2007. The first six or seven shots of the hearing are striking for the way in which Amudhan, using a handheld camera, focuses exclusively on groups of policemen regulating the flow of people attending the meeting (figures 5.4–5.8). He begins on a narrow road leading to the venue.

FIGURES 5.4 THROUGH 5.6 Snapshots of a public hearing from
Radiation Stories 3: Koodankulam (Courtesy R. P. Amudhan)

Firstly you had promised to give us
the environment impact assessment report in Tamil.

FIGURES 5.7 AND 5.8 Snapshots of a public hearing from
Radiation Stories 3: Koodankulam (Courtesy R. P. Amudhan)

The diegetic voice on a loudspeaker emanates, it seems, from someplace closer
to the venue. It is a commanding voice that instructs the people who have
come to the meeting to behave in an orderly way.

As the filmmaker keeps walking, he pans his camera right to show yet another group of policemen. Continuing to move, he pans left again: more police officers. In the next shot, a police truck is visible straight ahead. The truck
that had seemed far away on the road in earlier shots is now much closer to
the camera. All the while, the diegetic voice on the loudspeaker continues:
"You can follow and obey the procedure . . . meet the District Magistrate and
convey your grievances. But do not behave contradicting the police. There are
symptoms of such behavior. I don't think it is a good idea." The filmmaker
continues to walk with his handheld camera, and the film shows more images
of policemen lined up outside a large, makeshift tent, keeping a close watch

over the structure intended to provide shade to the people who come to attend the public hearing in the summer season. The speaker on the microphone introduces himself as the most senior police officer at the hearing and continues to provide more instructions until, finally, the moving filmmaker frames him holding a microphone. More shots follow of policemen now asking men and women to move in separate lines, and the policeman's voice is replaced by music playing on the sound track.

Documentarian Amudhan explained to me the impulse behind showing the public hearing in this way: "The number of police. The way they surrounded the people. The kind of sticks they carry. I wanted to bring that . . . really we live in a scary place. You have to shut up your mouth and be quiet. That despite the fact, that there is so much police, people could actually speak" (interview excerpt, Chennai, July 12, 2012). In the nuclear energy convention I attended, many other villagers from Mithi Virdi close to a reactor site in the state of Gujarat also alleged that the public hearing was conducted in a very high-handed manner, with more policemen than civilians. I heard this same allegation from locals in Koodankulam and Jaitapur.

A public hearing, which should be a *public* event, often is not publicized enough out of fear that "unruly" elements will gather together to oppose the construction of the plant. Amudhan's documentary brings a mediated publicness to the public hearing. Such a mediated publicness is concerned with representing events as evidence not only in the hearing itself but also around it. Amudhan is careful to document the muscular disciplining presence/role of the deployed policemen around the meeting. Even before the hearing starts, the speech of the police officer suggests that he (like the nuclear state) anticipates mob behavior, as if the people gathered need to be disciplined (and preached to) before they, the "subaltern citizens" of political society, can enter the civil corridors of the space of a public hearing. In my reading, Amudhan's documentary emphasizes that the state cannot openheartedly accept that local communities living around the proposed nuclear plant have enough civic sense to be capable of civil behavior, at least, not right away.

Indeed, as Amudhan mentioned in our interview and shows in his documentary, people spoke at the public hearing: they were angry, they gave vent to their indignation, and they brought out the facts of the Indian government's negligence, but at the same time they argued coherently (see figure 5.8). Even at the collectorate of the Kanyakumari district, the report could not be found. The people's leaders and representatives asserted that the EIA report was not present in the government offices. When the district collector of Tirunelveli mentioned that they had made the report available to NGOs, the people's representatives explained that the report circulated through NGOs was available only in English and not Tamil. When the collector interjected to suggest that the report was available on the collectorate's website, an elderly man from the crowd went to the microphone and asked: "How could the government assume that everybody had TV and internet?" He observed that the report should have been printed and made available to each household.

Amudhan echoes Gadekar when he claims that public hearings are a "lie" and a "cheat" because finally the government does what it wants. His angst as a filmmaker who works closely with social movements in India and has documented these public hearings extensively deserves expansive citation: "Public hearing should be like *Arre Yaar!* (Hey mate!), I have a problem with your project. You listen to me. Yeah. So, *Bolo . . . Kya Bolna hain. Bolo* [Tell, what you have to tell. Tell]. You have told, that's all. We have heard you. Even if you say, I am going to die tomorrow. Yeah, we heard. Go die, but we won't shut the project. It's kind of cheat . . . they are doing it. Some kind of a hypocrisy" (R. P. Amudhan, interview excerpt, Chennai, July 12, 2013). The government in these situations is certainly made to lose face, something that Dipesh Chakrabarty (2007) has described as the postcolonial state ceding to rituals of humiliation practiced by crowds.[7] However, the effect of such rituals/moments of humiliation in the final decision making is limited.

NGOs, RTI, and the Repressive Indian Government

The Indian government's biopolitical measures against population groups considered to be part of political society have been repressive. More recently, its actions against civil society groups that support the struggles of such people's movements against extractive development projects like nuclear reactors, uranium mines, and coal mines have also been intimidating. On June 3, 2014, the Indian Investigative Bureau (IB) submitted a confidential report to the recently elected prime minister, Narendra Modi, arguing that some "select NGOs" were making concerted efforts to "'take down' Indian development projects." These "select NGOs," which included People's Movement against Nuclear Energy and Greenpeace, were then pronounced as engaging in "antinuclear activism" and "anti-coal activism" (among others) that had brought down India's GDP growth by "2–3%."

When I conversed with environmental activists who were named in the report along with their organizations, they speculated that since the report contained such provocative statements about NGOs sabotaging India's growth, and—though it was marked "SECRET"—the report was leaked to the media, the government wanted to create a threat perception about the

NGOs and denigrate them in front of Indian audiences through media trials. The "select NGOs" were those working in the area of human rights, labor issues, and environmental activism, and thus were civil society groups that were actively engaged with subaltern populations doing environmentalism of the poor. The government's anxiety over such environmental NGOs needs to be historically situated in order to comprehend the changing Indian civic landscape. While other sociologists and legal scholars have meticulously sketched this history by paying attention to "judicialized politics" (see Bornstein and Sharma 2016), I shall focus on both trials in/by courts and trials in/by media.

Soon after Indian independence, voluntary associations in the Gandhian mold continued grassroots work. When the Indian Constitution was set up, they used judicial mechanisms to protect Indian citizens' constitutionally granted fundamental rights and check any excesses committed by autocratic governments (De 2014). One significant step in this direction was public interest litigation (PIL), introduced in the late 1970s, which has been used by civil society groups to question government actions and recommend policy interventions: PIL was used by activists fighting for victims of the Bhopal gas disaster and the Narmada Bachao Andolan advocacy groups (Fortun 2001). Since the late 1980s, with the neoliberal restructuring of the Indian economy, NGOs have, on the one hand, been courted by governments in order to widen the ambit of welfare measures and bring in policy reforms to ensure democracy, and, on the other hand, been sharply criticized for overstepping their limits and interfering with the country's politics and development (Bornstein and Sharma 2016).

One of the great success stories of civil society in the neoliberal period in India has been the Right to Information (RTI) Act of 2005, which empowered citizens and made government more transparent. The RTI has been successfully deployed by NGOs and activists to find out more information about development projects and thereby unearth any corruption involved in these projects. While the Indian nuclear establishment is protected under the Atomic Energy Act of 1962 from releasing much information about nuclear matters, PMANE and other antinuclear activists were able to get some details through RTI claims about defective parts being sold by the Russian company ZiO-Podolsk for the Koodankulam reactor (Levy 2015). Many media institutions have also been involved in filing RTI claims and reporting on the government-corporate connivance in urban building projects among other cases, and RTI has become an avenue for ordinary citizens and civil society groups to make government accountable.

Having been at the receiving end of accountability claims for too long, the government may have leaked the IB report as a way to demand accountability from NGOs in return. The IB report stated that several NGOs were foreign funded and were serving the vested interests of foreigners who did not want to see India develop. Soon after the release of the IB report, the foreign funds of Greenpeace and several other NGOs were frozen because they were alleged to have violated the Foreign Contribution Regulation Act (FCRA). The government wanted to send out the signal to the public that NGOs such as Greenpeace were misreporting the contributions they were receiving from their foreign donors. Greenpeace did challenge the government's decision in courts and won the case. However, it remains to be seen whether it will be able to win the perception battle.

This aspersion that NGOs allow foreigners to interfere in Indian policy making and politics had existed before the Modi government. In the book's introduction, I discussed how Prime Minister Manmohan Singh had made similar insinuations about Scandinavian and American funding for antinuclear activities in India. In the IB report, PMANE leader S. P. Udayakumar was alleged to have received funds from a center at Ohio State University. The report further buttressed this foreign angle by mentioning that Udayakumar was supposedly in touch with Rainer Hermann, a German national who had sent him a scanned map of India with nuclear reactor sites prominently marked. I was surprised to see this particular piece of information presented in the leaked report as the result of investigation, because the Rainer Hermann controversy had been widely reported in Indian media channels, and since then, Hermann, who was visiting India, had been deported. I could not fathom what was so secretive about this controversy to have found its place in an investigative report. Hermann was a tourist who had often visited Southern India, and the map he had allegedly sent to Udayakumar could have been found on the internet with a little bit of Google searching. So, what exactly was being classified as a "secret" was unclear.

In December 2014, I was conversing with Anil Chaudhary, convener of Popular Education and Action Center (PEACE) at the organization's Katwaria Sarai office in South Delhi. The IB report had stated that four NGOs were operating from this office space. Chaudhary explained that soon after the IB report was released, many journalists descended on the office space. Chaudhary told them that there is nothing wrong with like-minded organizations sharing office space to cut costs. When I asked Chaudhary to elaborate on his interactions with the journalists, he said that some of them had come with the expectation that they were going on a mission to uncover a lot of insidious details, but they were surprised at the openness exhibited by Chaudhary. I myself had found Chaudhary's office environment to be open and relaxed in my interviews with CNDP activists. Nobody even asked me for identification. The office space was in a bustling area of South Delhi, and many young students studying for civil services examinations lived in the neighborhood. I was therefore surprised at how the sharing of office space was represented as "privileged" information by its inclusion in an IB report. Chaudhary told me that he had complied with FCRA guidelines, and the duty slip and taxi receipts for cars hired to take activists from Delhi to the Fatehabad district in Haryana to protest the construction of nuclear reactors were all filed. Thus, PEACE was not keeping anything hidden from the government. Chaudhary described the leak of the IB report as an effort to create "media euphoria."

Activists and NGOs reacted swiftly to the IB report, declaring that their financial dealings were transparent and they did not have anything to hide. They criticized the government for subjecting them, as civil society groups, to surveillance from an investigative agency that is actually meant for terrorists, spies, and threats to national security (*First Post India*, June 13, 2014). Prominent civil society leaders wrote a letter to the Home Ministry in April 2015, criticizing the government for refreezing Greenpeace's accounts even after the courts ruled in favor of that organization. The letter was widely disseminated through media outlets and contained arguments made by NGOs that the government cannot paint a section of the civil society as "anti-national" just because it holds dissenting or contrary views to those espoused by the government.[8]

Furthermore, PILs and RTIs are not just filed by activists espousing environmentalism of the poor. Anti-poor middle-class elites in urban centers have used the judicial activism of PILs and RTIs to remove slums and "beautify" cities. In a remarkably prescient essay, the geographer D. Asher Ghertner (2011) writes that the early 2000s witnessed a "drastic increase" in PILs against slums by "resident welfare associations." These were property owner associations that gave "neighborhood security" and "local environmental issues" as reasons for evicting slums. In the following section, I examine online blogs maintained by resident associations that targeted slum settlements for removal in their neighborhoods. In these blogs, resident associations also argue that cell antennas are polluters and a public nuisance that should be evicted. The people staying in the slums are an important vote bank, and so it is not easy for governments to remove slums just like that.

While the slums resemble a visible ecological threat, the cell antennas radiate the invisible danger of carcinogenic signals. Many in government see them as part of India's development story, part of the "smart cities" initiative of the ruling administration. Ironically, in this framework the slums become polluters while the orderly and sleek-looking real estate projects and malls are "green" projects, even though several urban planning documents suggest such urban development projects are damaging the water table and flood plain of cities like Delhi and Mumbai (Ghertner 2011). Cell antennas might be aesthetic eyesores for some, but others consider them a part of Indian modernity that guarantees they can use their sleek mobile phones. Thus, they remain ambivalent structures in the urban planning scripts, at once comparable to slums as "polluters," and yet part of urban development projects in the "green" category inhabited by shopping malls and multiplexes.

Ruptures: Civil Society–Political Society

An allegation repeatedly leveled against the anti–cell tower campaign was that it was elitist. Only upper-middle-class urbanites were concerned with such potential health hazards. Several metropolitan activists affiliated with people's ecological movements, trade unions, and social movements dealing with social justice for rural and urban poor told me they were not interested in the cell tower radiation issue. When I asked them to provide me reasons for their indifference, they challenged me to point out media stories where urban slum dwellers had complained about cell antennas.

Elite urbanites certainly had the cultural capital to have stories about their struggles against malpractices of telecom companies be included in the pages of prominent newspapers. The Mumbai edition of *Times of India* (TOI) carried a story titled "No Civic Nod for 3 Cell Towers atop Building: RTI." The article mentioned that Harish Pandey of the New Link Road Residents' Forum had filed an RTI query, which revealed that the mobile operator had installed cell towers atop Victor Shelter without permission of the civic body (figure 5.9). Nilesh society residents at Kandarpada in Dahisar were especially affected by these three unauthorized towers on the rooftop of the Victor Shelter apartments. The apartment residents complained of headaches, lack of concentration, memory loss, and joint pain. These unregulated cell antennas had to be removed.

The same day, the TOI report was posted on the New Link Road blog. This blog is a forum for environmentally conscious Mumbai residents living around the New Link Road area to share their stories about how they are holding the municipality, neighbors, and the government accountable so that people in their neighborhood can enjoy a clean and sanitary life.

The blog post that included the TOI report also contained a bit more backstory: Dr. Mathew, both the president of New Link Road Forum and a physician by profession, had conducted a survey of the neighborhood along

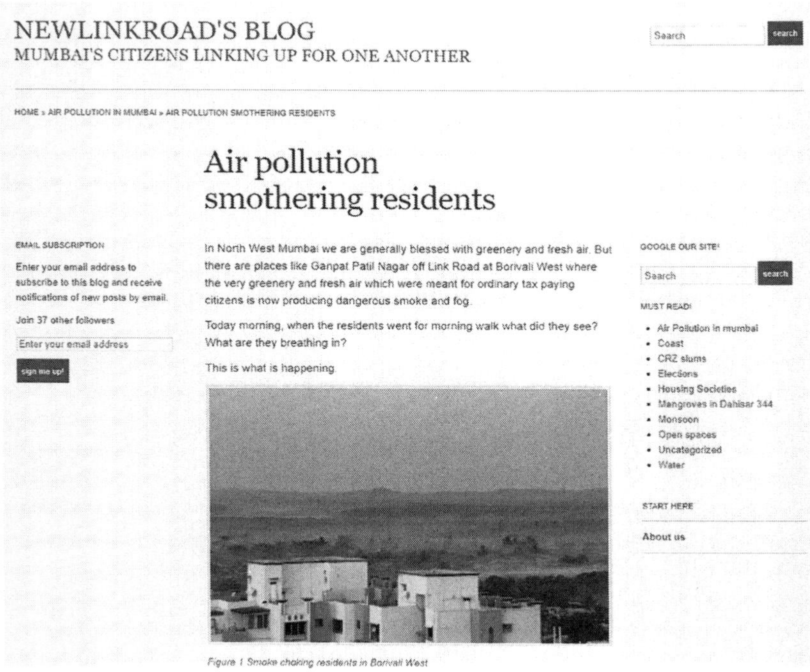

NEWLINKROAD'S BLOG
MUMBAI'S CITIZENS LINKING UP FOR ONE ANOTHER

Search search

HOME » AIR POLLUTION IN MUMBAI » AIR POLLUTION SMOTHERING RESIDENTS

Air pollution smothering residents

In North West Mumbai we are generally blessed with greenery and fresh air. But there are places like Ganpat Patil Nagar off Link Road at Borivali West where the very greenery and fresh air which were meant for ordinary tax paying citizens is now producing dangerous smoke and fog.

Today morning, when the residents went for morning walk what did they see? What are they breathing in?

This is what is happening.

Figure 1 Smoke choking residents in Borivali West

EMAIL SUBSCRIPTION

Enter your email address to subscribe to this blog and receive notifications of new posts by email.

Join 37 other followers

Enter your email address

sign me up!

GOOGLE OUR SITE!

Search search

MUST READ!

- Air Pollution in mumbai
- Coast
- CRZ slums
- Elections
- Housing Societies
- Mangroves in Dahisar 344
- Monsoon
- Open spaces
- Uncategorized
- Water

START HERE

About us

FIGURE 5.9 New Link Road Forum blog photo of proximate cell towers (Courtesy Harish Pandey)

with Harish Pandey and had discovered sites where mobile towers were less than thirty feet from the adjoining buildings. The results from the survey had prompted the RTI query, and then the TOI report had followed. The TOI report included a picture of the antennas. The same picture in the blog had been labeled with a yellow line that joined the rooftops of two apartments. On the line was inserted capitalized text that read: "TOO CLOSE."

The blog contains entries about several such investigations conducted by concerned citizens. While the cell antenna is one kind of obdurate hazard, eyesore, and encroachment, there are others that this citizens' forum remains vigilant about. On October 19, 2014, a blog post mentioned that when the New Link Road Residents Forum found a woman spreading a mat on the footpath and selling vegetables, it immediately asked her to leave. The vegetable vendor initially objected, but she finally had to clear out. In the comments on this blog post, the forum congratulated itself (its active residents) for being ever vigilant.

Continuing this trend, as in the cell tower blog entry and the hawker blog post, the forum congratulated its active residents for posting multiple pictures showing smoke emerging from the Ganpat Patil Nagar slum. The images carry captions that suggest smoke from slums is causing respiratory illnesses. The blogger writes, "We hope and pray that these slums will be removed from here and greenery and fresh air become the norm." In this post from July 12, 2014, the urban elite author mentions that he belongs to the group of "ordinary tax paying citizens" and bemoans the fact that even though he stays amid the greenery of North West Mumbai, the slums produce noxious smoke that renders his morning walks unpleasant. Just like cell towers, the illegal slums are considered carcinogenic. One blog post suggests that the "cancerous growth of illegal slums" is eating away Mumbai's precious mangrove cover.

I write about these other stories of environmental advocacy, carried out by the same urban elites who campaign for stricter regulation of cell towers, to show how this kind of bourgeois environmentalism is very different from antinuke activism. Amita Baviskar (2011) explains that for bourgeois environmentalists, "environmentalism is a mode of expressing and addressing their anxieties about themselves in relation to their habitat, that is their physical surroundings" (401). These urban elites are impatient with bureaucrats and government ministers for not doing enough to remove cell towers, hawkers, and illegal slums. Such privileged citizens pay significant taxes to the government, which makes them believe that the government should address their concerns about the condition of their locality.

As recounted in several other chapters, one central problem with cell towers is their proximity and their obdurate fixity/immobility, which makes them a problem for the locality. The concerns of bourgeois environmentalism are almost always about an individual's immediate surroundings; there is no hint of any activism that would try to build a mass movement. Previously, I have mentioned the techno-struggle of vigilant citizens who keep monitoring the cell antenna signal levels. Similar environmental surveillance activities can be seen in the way the New Link Road residents surveilled hawkers on their footpaths, captured pictures of smoke coming from slums, or snapped images of power cables being laid out. Just like paying taxes, keeping vigil is key to being ideal citizens for these elites.

There is a rupture here between civil society and political society. The upper-middle-class urbanites who belong to civil society ask local administrators to evict cell towers in the name of public interest. They are the same urbanites who also ask authorities to evict illegal slums where populations belonging to "political society" reside, citing environmental concerns. Such environmental concerns might seem genuine, but they do little to address social inequities. In fact, as in the latter case, they perpetuate such inequities. Thus, there is a fundamental disconnect between concerned citizens and governed populations. The urban elites might say that the urban poor and slum dwellers are equally vulnerable to the harmful effects of cell tower radiation. That being said, if the urban elites continue to treat both cell towers and urban slums as carcinogenic encroachments, how can there be intersections across these two groups? My online research and off-line fieldwork in Jaipur and Mumbai suggest that bourgeois environmentalism is very much alive in these cities. I often heard residents belonging to apartment associations in upscale neighborhoods overtly discussing how street hawkers were a nuisance.

Intersections: Civil Society–Political Society

Not all middle classes are the same, and neither are all anti–cell tower advocates indifferent to the concerns of urban poor. Shipra Mathur and Prakash Munshi mentioned their concerns that slums in Jaipur and Mumbai were affected by cell tower radiation and they wanted to do whatever they could to evict unregulated towers from poor tenements. Mathur and Munshi added that cell tower regulation was an even more pressing concern for the urban poor than for the urban middle class because poor residents could not afford to pay their medical bills if they were affected by cancer. Keeping these conversations in mind, it is important to clarify that there were indeed well-meaning elite urbanites who cared for the health of all. The tendency to equate slums or street encroachments with cell towers did not pervade every elite urban activist protesting cell towers.

The middle class in India needs to be internally differentiated. While one group of middle-class citizens are only interested in ensuring that their individual bourgeois desires are addressed by the state, another group of middle-class activists have engaged in contentious politics and social movements supporting social justice and equality. A number of city-based activists have always been part of the antinuke movement. These activists have maintained connections with rural communities affected by nuclear projects and uranium mining. Metropolitan activists worked together with local communities opposing nuclear plants in their region. Such alliances and networks also took the form of conventions attended by affected local communities, antinuclear activists, journalists, and academics.

I was present at one such convention in Ahmedabad on July 2013, where the people's charter against nuclear energy was going to be drafted based on consultations with the gathered actors. Some of the major public intellectuals associated with the antinuke struggle in India such as Achin Vanaik, Praful Bidwai, and Surendra Gadekar were present at the meeting. Xavieramma, one of the key figures in the PMANE movement from the Idinthakarai village, shared the stage with other activists, each of whom reported about antinuclear campaigns they had been part of in different regions of India, such as Chutka, Jaitapur, Rawatbhata, and Gorakhpur. Xavieramma courted arrest on September 9, 2012, while drowning in the sea as part of the protests. The police arrested her and four other women and kept driving them in a police van for two days in various towns of Tamil Nadu before finally incarcerating them in Madurai, charging them with sedition and waging war against the nation. They are now out on conditional bail and are required to visit the Madurai police station once each week.

Xavieramma, aided by a translator, animatedly told this story. She sang songs and raised slogans in Tamil; many others in the convention center joined her in chorus. Mostly English-, Hindi-, and Gujarati-speaking, not knowing Tamil, the crowd followed her rhythm and intonations. Xavieramma has told her story, and her presence is sought by many venues, including documentary film festivals and book launches related to nuclear issues. Along with Udaykumar, the leader of the PMANE movement, she is the face of the antinuclear campaign. The organizers of this convention expressed hope that her and her community's stories of perseverance will help to rally activists and locals opposing nuclear power plants in other regions of the country who have also come to the gathering. The organizers extolled her courage many times.

Gyanendra Pandey's (2010) use of the term "subaltern citizens" helps to mobilize discussions of subalternity away from dichotomies of authentic/inauthentic, visible/invisible, and voice/voiceless and toward contingent stagings of subaltern voices in situated contexts. The term invites explorations of the "citizenly," the political potential in subaltern subject positions (7). Was Xavieramma the subaltern or the subaltern citizen, in this gathering that can be construed as being peopled by civil society members? Her speech was celebrated. This was, in many ways, a safe space for expression. There was genuine admiration for her struggle and her fortitude.

As Gayatri Spivak (1999) famously observed in *A Critique of Postcolonial Reason*, "All speaking, even seemingly the most immediate, entails a distant decipherment by another, which is, at best, an interception" (309). Is Xavieramma's speech deciphered/intercepted in the right way in contexts such as that described here? Her views in this activist space are certainly not dismissed as "unscientific," which has been the case when her audiences have been officials of the nuclear establishment. Are her agency and her speech appropriated within the power structures of the activist convention? In certain ways, they have been. Her presence lent credibility to the convention and her speech energized the fellow activists working in various regions, but her participation in preparing the people's charter against nuclear energy seemed limited. The debates about what to include or exclude in the charter preoccupied long-term antinuke activists and academic-activists. The charter, once debated and passed in the convention, would then be circulated among the general public and political parties. Political parties would be asked to agree or indicate their stand on the demands made in the charter. Xavieramma was not a central player in this civilian procedure of political negotiation. To put it in Partha Chatterjee's (2010) terms, Xavieramma has voice and has rights, but she still cannot be thought to belong to the properly constituted civil society, and so she is a subaltern citizen: "subalterns who are nonetheless citizens, but not quite proper citizens" (202).

However, we should also ask a different question: Do subalterns necessarily need to conduct themselves in a way that makes them ideal citizens? Xavieramma's speech displayed, for lack of better terms, "agency" and "political consciousness." She was aware of the context in which her speech emerged. The convention was held at the Gujarat Vidyapeeth with many university students in the audience, and Xavieramma was quick to point out that movements based on fishermen-student alliances had always succeeded in India. She mentioned her interest in antinuclear movements in different parts of the country and expressed her desire to help out in any way. It also needs to be noted that before the Fukushima disaster, Xavieramma did not heed the advice of Udaykumar and other antinuke activists who had been asking villagers at Idinthakarai to protest against nuclear reactors. Nonetheless, after seeing the television coverage of the Fukushima disaster, Xavieramma and her friends in the village called a meeting and asked Udaykumar, who was then living in Nagercoil, along with other activists, to come and lead the movement against the construction of the power plant. Here, the so-called subaltern citizens engaged with civil society of their own volition and on their own terms, when they deemed it necessary.

While it is important to contest unequal power relations, it is also crucial to question the efficacy of boxing communities within political categories such as "political society" and "subaltern." It is one thing to theorize how the state and the mainstream media view the fishing communities in Koodankulam; it is another thing to begin to comprehend how such communities make sense of their own lives and struggles. The mainstream media does exhibit a proclivity to sensationalize the affective and performative aspects of Koodankulam protesters, especially their protest tactics of Jal Satyagraha and the digging of mass graves. Such proclivities do make India's middle class pay attention to antinuke struggles, but they also lead to reifying Koodankulam protesters as subalterns. Chemmencheri (2015) contends that mainstream media portrayals of such Gandhian values and tactics make the subalterns heard, but in doing so, they also serve to reinforce their subalternity.

Less attention has been paid to how a relay fast of 1,754 days has been sustained by villagers around Koodankulam through rotating responsibilities among fifteen villages and through Theripu, an innovative tax system that requires every participating fisherman to part with one-tenth of his earnings from the daily catch. The involvement of the church in the locality suggests its key mediating role between citizens and the state. Theripu, the church, and the relay fast gesture to the rich civic associations that exist among rural communities in India. Writing about similar civic engagements of rural fishworkers in South India, Aparna Sundar (2010) argues against Chatterjee's tendency to suggest that civil society does not exist among subaltern rural populations.[9]

My point is that there indeed are concrete practices of managing populations that the Indian government exercises over Koodankulam fishworkers, and so there is something gained by studying state-population negotiations within the rubric of political society as suggested by Partha Chatterjee. However, what the antinuke struggle and its mediations suggest is that there is a room created for intersections between civil society and political society. Furthermore, the formulations of political society cannot account for all associational activities practiced by Koodankulam fishworkers, and hence one needs to move beyond the dichotomies proposed by Chatterjee.

Intimate Mobilizations

People living in the surroundings of cell towers in Mumbai and Jaipur or living close to the Koodankulam or Jaitapur nuclear plant share an unwanted intimacy with these infrastructures. In several chapters of this book, I have elaborated on how these unwanted intimacies create affect worlds of premonitions and prehensions, which then lead to political mobilizations against such infrastructures. As I have explained in this chapter, media representation shapes the styling of advocacy for anti–cell tower and antinuke activism, though the style is different in these two cases. On one side, Bollywood celebrities and lifestyle shows represent anti–cell tower activism, while on the other, radical magazines and politically committed documentary films are venues for publicizing antinuke organizing. The different characters of these mobilizations result from the different structuring conditions of media access and the rural-urban/civil society–political society divides between the two cases.

I have further argued that the antinuke movement espouses livelihood concerns in the tradition of the environmentalism of the poor and provides spaces for civil society and political society members to gather together, interact, and forge meaningful alliances. The anti–cell tower movement, as an instance of bourgeois environmentalism, has been unable to forge solidarities across urban elites and urban poor because in the eyes of particular privileged urbanites, both cell towers and slum dwellers are encroachments to be evicted so that elites can enjoy an ordered and sanitized environment. Indeed, for certain middle-class urbanites, the proximity of cell towers and slum dwellers are both unwanted intimacies. This tendency of equating towers with slums, I have also clarified, cannot be said to have been espoused by all urbanites: indeed, many anti–cell tower activists I met such as Prakash Munshi and Shipra Mathur felt that they should organize against such towers across all classes because the radiation norms would have an effect on everybody.

Furthermore, media channels and practices cannot be neatly slotted into the poles of the civil society–political society and environmentalism of the poor/bourgeois environmentalism divides. Such is the plurality of media forms, genres, and outlets that one should endeavor to examine how mediation both enacts and refashions these divides. Vernacular-language TV channels operating at a local level have been covering the cell tower radiation issue in many towns and cities of India. While a mainstream English-language TV channel like CNN-IBN frames mostly individual stories or individual citizen journalists like Prakash Munshi or Juhi Chawla, the local TV9 Marathi covered residents of an entire apartment society gathering together and expressing their angst about cell antennas erected close to their house. TV9 assembled a whole collective of apartment society residents to provide a team interview while covering the 4G cell tower problems in Mulund, Mumbai.[10]

It might be possible that some members of the middle class who would never have been able to influence state authorities to act are able to do so today because of their easy access to local vernacular media that creates pressure on the city's municipality to be accountable. A significant amount of administrative work in municipalities is conducted in local languages, and hence a local reporter has a better chance of establishing connections with local government authorities. This is especially relevant for the cell tower radiation issue because as I have discussed previously, such an issue is both a national public health concern and a hyperlocal issue, with disputes emerging over siting of particular cell towers.

Throughout this book, I have tracked the interaction of actors involved in debating radiant infrastructures. This chapter, which compares the different publics that different radiant infrastructures gather around them, has shown how mapping the genealogies and networks of different actors imbricated in any environmental controversy is incomplete without an analysis of the structures and contingencies that mark class, caste, regional, and environmental advocacy coalitions of Indian democracy. Such coalitions are key to how unequal power relations are both contested and lived out within environmental publics in India.

I have shared many stories in this book about environmental debates that continue to unfold. While studying vibrant public cultures and complex infrastructures, one should appreciate chaos and hoopla, acknowledge the value of incertitude and uncertainty, but that does not mean there is no room left for analysis. If humans have intentions, infrastructures have tendencies. Stories about infrastructures that people told me illuminated something about those technologies, and at the same time, I was left with a feeling that there was another backstory about an organization's (un)declared intentions and motivations, an infrastructure's (un)anticipated tendencies, potentials, and dispositions. According to Keller Easterling (2016), "disposition" describes "an unfolding relationship between potentials," and paying attention to "disposition" helps us uncover "covert" and "accidental" forms of power "hiding in the folds of infrastructure space" (73).

The lack of clarity about certain technologies made radiant infrastructures exhibit varying tendencies. If aluminum foil could indeed reflect back cell antenna radiation, then the whole cell antenna assemblage would undergo a change; now, not only were the apartments facing cell antenna beams under threat, but the apartments whose rooftops housed the beams were similarly affected. People whose apartments were facing the antenna beams could now have aluminum shades in their houses, which would reflect the beams back to the apartments hosting the antennas. All this being said, it is still to be scientifically established whether aluminum foil can actually reflect electromagnetic rays. Currently, it is simply not possible to ascertain the impact of aluminum foil, and that means we will just have to wait for answers. The relationship between aluminum foil and electromagnetic radiation is still unfolding; it is part of "undone science" (Frickel et al., 2010; D. Hess 2016) that dissident scientists/counterexperts and concerned citizens are teaming up together to comprehend.

In a country like India, the public health effects of emerging technologies such as cell towers become difficult to gauge because of the state of environmental reporting. Often, there is little reporting on science, health, and environment issues. Several journalists who cover the environmental beat expressed concerns that newspapers devote little space to health columns compared with the number of pages dedicated to discussion of business and politics. A journalist who writes on health issues in a leading English newspaper told me that she had meticulously researched the health effects of cell tower radiation in Mumbai and published a piece on it. A few weeks later, another reporter from the same paper wrote an article in the business section that put the cellular operators in a favorable light and dismissed concerns about the health effects of nonionizing radiation. This was not so much a case of a newspaper's general bias toward a particular issue, but rather the different tilts of particular sections of a newspaper toward the issue. Cultures of uncertainty get shaped by institutional cultures of value: matters of health are not valued as much as those relating to politics or money.

Cultures of uncertainty are also influenced by cultures of trust. I have written extensively in several chapters about the local newspaper *Rajasthan Patrika*'s close relationship with its readers. The newspaper made itself accessible to its readers, whereas the government seemed aloof and indifferent to their problems. Such cultures of trust cultivated between newspapers and readers shape cultures of uncertainty during an environmental controversy. I gained this understanding when I asked Shipra Mathur, one of the editors of *Patrika*, about the general culture of risk in the city. She noted that in times of crisis, the people trusted *Patrika* more than the municipality:

> One thing is . . . the faith of people . . . [in] the system has gone down. It is going down constantly. This is the condition . . . some small incident happens . . . there was an incident in IOC [Indian Oil Corporation] . . . fire erupted there . . . phone calls started coming to our office . . . phone calls should come to our office or go to the government. This kind of faith in readers . . . like . . . any big crisis happens, any big crime occurs . . . the phone starts to ring in Patrika. (interview excerpt, Jaipur, December 19, 2012)

I have quoted Mathur's praise of *Patrika* not because I necessarily agree with her, but her way of expressing the position of the newspaper in the configuration of the relations between the government and citizens demands attention. Mathur views *Patrika* as not only a provider of objective reporting but also a supplier of public services and security. In fact, *Patrika* seems to be taking on the role of governance, which has been diminished in the wake of an emaciated state that is perceived to be corrupt and inefficient. The Indian government has in many cases abdicated its responsibilities toward its own citizens. Within such a context, it is not surprising that Jaipur's denizens believed *Patrika* when the newspaper portrayed cell towers as hazardous infrastructures. The locals did not trust the Jaipur municipality's reassurances that it was regulating the cellular operators and their activities, but they trusted *Patrika*.

I have presented several examples throughout the book of occasions on which the media amplified particular uncertainties about radiant infrastructures. That being said, at times, the media's quiescence on some issues could lead to rumors about infrastructures spreading virally as well. Around mid-October 2012, while I was traveling in several cities of Tamil Nadu, the topic of conversation would often shift to state-sponsored shutoffs of electricity. Some information technology professional friends of mine in the state of Tamil Nadu would complain that the weather there was quite hot; although they were fine in the office with the air-conditioner perpetually on, spending time at home for them was becoming unbearable. The power shutdowns were becoming so rampant that another friend in Tirunelveli got a generator at his house so that his children could study during the evenings. This was also around the time that the agitation in Koodankulam was gaining ground, and many blamed the delay in construction of the Koodankulam nuclear plant (and the power shutdowns) on the protesters. The state's chief minister M. S. Jayalalithaa had initially opposed the construction of the plant but later agreed with the Central Government and Nuclear Power Corporation of India Limited plans, declaring publicly that the plant would help to mitigate cuts in the power supply.

Small-scale industries such as those of power loom workers were hit badly, and in interviews, members of fishing communities in Idinthakarai explained that the government should find alternative sources of energy to solve the state's electricity woes (Subramanian 2012). The power failures were getting worse with every passing day, and conspiracy theories were making the rounds that the government was deliberately cutting power to make the Koodankulam agitators look bad. No news report I came across explicitly suggested that the government was intentionally indulging in electricity distribution irregularities, and the people I talked to who alleged that this was indeed the case never mentioned a news source; they seemed to just know it. Rumor as a form of popular discourse plays a role in dampening the technopolitical pressure exerted by the nuclear establishment: while the government may not have had any hand in the increasing power cuts, it sought to gain public support for the Koodankulam nuclear reactor project from the power failures. To understand why the present configuration of environmental publics is the way that it is, analyzing official news would prove insufficient; examining rumors is just as important. Rumors and cultures of uncertainty need to be studied together.

The cultures of uncertainty that I have discussed are often encountered by regulators of the cell tower and nuclear energy industries. The regulator's predicament involves balancing entwined sustainability concerns: sustaining calls/data traffic and energy needs and at the same time sustaining citizens' health.

National Infrastructures and Regulatory Conundrums

Nuclear reactors and cell towers are national infrastructures because they touch the lives of many people in the country. The Indian public becomes a population statistic to be flaunted as future potential, with many promises being made in the name of 1.25 billion Indians. The scale is planetary as India houses every sixth person in the entire world. Out of 1.25 billion Indians, 400 million do not have electricity, and, according to the Indian government, nuclear reactors are the answer to this problem. In Micha Patault and Sarah Irion's documentary *Are-Vah!* (2014), the French nuclear company Areva's former chairperson, while describing the company's partnership with the NPCIL in building reactors at Jaitapur, hailed India an "energy giant." There is a focus on the scale of reactors, the scale of electricity generated, and the scale of India's energy demand. Areva's reactor in Jaitapur is going to be the largest on planet Earth.

Patault and Irion's documentary is full of vignettes that show the living Indian population in public spaces (such as overcrowded train stations and subways) as well as shots of what forms electricity takes: the illuminated high-rise apartment buildings in Mumbai's nightscape, lighting in street parades as part of religious festivals, and the flickering tubelight in a poor fisherman's room in rural India (figures C.1 and C.2). By stitching together these vignettes, Patault and Irion recognize the energy needs and desires of India's teeming millions, but they further argue that the demographic dividend that seems to benefit nuclear commerce could also potentially backfire by magnifying nuclear risks. The sites chosen for construction of reactors in Jaitapur are going to affect the livelihoods of ten thousand fishermen and mango farmers. Amid population pressure and a resource crunch, it is difficult to find land for building nuclear parks that is not already being used for other purposes.

Patault and Irion document hundreds of tangled electrical cables precariously hanging over streets, incidences of sparks in those web of wires, and malfunctioning electricity meters to highlight the energy losses that India's power

FIGURES C.I AND C.2 Mumbai's electrified nightscape and Delhi subway (Screen grabs from *Are-Vah!*, 2014)

infrastructure suffers from (figures C.3 and C.4). Some of these moving images are stilled, other shots are presented in the form of still photographs, and several of them are also rendered through long takes with slow vertical pans: all such aesthetic decisions ask audiences to contemplate the ruined state of infrastructure, its messiness, and the all-pervasive transmission losses, theft, and leakages of electricity. The experts who are interviewed in the documentary note that every year, 30 to 35 percent of electricity produced is lost while it is being distributed. The Indian government's answer to the energy problem is not to spend money to develop better energy distribution infrastructure

FIGURES C.3 AND C.4 *Top:* Tangled electrical cables; *bottom:* compromised electric meters in Old Delhi (*Are-Vah!*, 2014)

in order to connect the yet unconnected 600,000 villages and 400 million households, but to invest in European pressurized reactors imported from Areva/France. The technological wisdom and the economic basis of such governmental actions are called into question in *Are-Vah!*

The regulation of electricity distribution infrastructure has been a problem for a long time. While the rampant corruption that sustains such power leakages and thefts does need to be condemned, it is also an empirical reality that a significant section of low-income households in India simply cannot afford electricity by legal means. They depend on informal workarounds

FIGURE C.5 Cell antennas atop Hotel Supreme (Photo by author)

devised by *katiyabaaz(s)* who can switch or extend electricity connections for a small amount of money.[1] It is tricky to navigate the terrain of regulatory frameworks for many different infrastructures, not just energy distribution but also the telecom network.[2]

Regulations set by the Indian Department of Telecommunication and municipal corporations were openly being flouted by tower companies and commercial establishments that offered their rooftops to cellular operators to set up towers. Gaurav Bhatia lives in Clover Apartments in the Cuffe Parade area in Mumbai. He fears for the health of his preteen son and daughter because of twenty-nine cell antennas that are located on the rooftop of Hotel Supreme, a commercial lodge next to his residential apartment. A photograph that I took from Bhatia's balcony of the Hotel Supreme terrace gives some sense of just how brazenly the laws regarding cell antenna siting have been disregarded (figure C.5). Hotel Supreme is only three floors tall, but the apartments that surround it have more than twenty floors. The antennas are angled upward, which makes residents of the posh apartments very worried about their safety. It remains debatable whether the weight of twenty-nine antennas can be sustained by the Hotel Supreme structure itself. Due to these reasons, the Brihanmumbai Municipal Corporation of Mumbai cannot possibly allow the structures to remain.

Bhatia and residents of other neighboring apartments had moved a petition to the Mumbai High Court, and after the ruling, there were delays in the implementation, but finally a number of antennas were removed in March 2017. After the eviction drive that took place that same month, only seven antennas remained, but in May 2017 more constructions went up, and more towers were added, bringing the number of antennas to twenty-two. With the entry of Jio, a new cellular operator, and the promise of 4G connections, regulating cell antenna siting became even more difficult. Bhatia spotted Jio workers installing 4G LTE antennas one morning when he was reading a newspaper while drinking tea. Bhatia showed me the video he had recorded on his cell phone.

The Hotel Supreme owner continues to violate municipality regulations because the hotel does not run well, and to make ends meet, he depends on the rent that he receives from the cellular operators/tower companies for use of the rooftop space. The unbridled violation of rules suggests the desperation of cellular operators to expand their infrastructural footprint in an industry that is witnessing cutthroat competition to win more customers and deliver better service. When asked for explanations, they also, like the nuclear establishment, emphasize the pressure to deliver cheap broadband and calling services (substituted here for electricity from the former) to the large population of India at the lowest possible rates in the world.

Even telecom regulators decided to normalize cell towers. J. S. Deepak, the secretary of the Department of Telecommunications, noted at an "awareness session" on October 28, 2016, that "if we want good quality communication 24/7, mobile towers will have to present just like overhead tanks."[3] Through this infrastructural analogy, the DoT secretary was arguing that just as every terrace had an overhead tank for water supply, terraces should have a cell antenna for information connection. The mobile phone had become a great equalizer, allowing many poor people to enter the Indian economy with new vibrancy. As such, stopping the growth of telecom infrastructure in the name of environmental ramifications, Deepak warned, was going to perpetuate the digital divide. The telecom regulator, just like the power regulator, explains that too much regulation will create infrastructural inequities, and hence distributional injustices. While such arguments can surely be challenged, what is not accounted for here is what kind of infrastructural violence will be unleashed from such regulatory paralysis if the environmental impact of nuclear reactors and cell towers is factored in. The regulators consign the apocalyptic time of the environment to the distant future, while present-day expediencies of digital divides and energy shortages are given top priority.

The regulators, like politicians and other governmental bodies, do not merely have practical considerations of infrastructures; they also build an infrastructural imagination based on aspirations of technological modernity that encompasses the whole nation, by discussing India's digital divide (as in the case of cell towers) and energy needs (as in the case of nuclear reactors). But beyond the nation, there are conversations happening between state and nonstate players about what to do about the environmental impact of radiant infrastructures. The DoT secretary likes to bring telecom experts from the United States and the United Kingdom for promotional campaigns and "awareness sessions" in which these experts argue that there is nothing wrong with cell towers. The anti–cell tower campaigners in India are in touch with like-minded people in Canada and the United States who believe cell antenna signals are potentially carcinogenic. I have discussed the use of microwave ovens to demonstrate radiation in Mumbai. This is not something particular to India, but has also been used in Canada and elsewhere by antiradiation activists like Magda Havas. Prakash Munshi, whose demonstrations I attended in Mumbai, knows about the work of Havas and has been in touch with critics of cell tower radiation in many parts of the world, including Devra Davis in the United States and Lyn McLean in Australia. The lateral local-local collaborations between antinuke activists in India and Japan are even more organic, and these translocal connections are important to think about as a way to conceptualize radiant infrastructures beyond the nation.

Translocal Connections: Techno-struggle and Indigenous Cosmopolitics

For many years, the eminent nuclear physicist and Gandhian antinuclear activist Surendra Gadekar edited *Anumukti*, one of the only antinuclear journals of its kind in India. In 2004, he wrote a piece in *Anumukti* about the high radiation levels plaguing the region of Jadugoda (where uranium mining was carried out). These findings were ignored by the Indian nuclear establishment but were seriously considered by Hiroaki Koide, a nuclear engineer at the Research Reactor Institute at Kyoto University. Koide flew to India with thermoluminescent dosimeters to study background gamma radiation in Jadugoda (Levy 2015). He stealthily took soil and water samples with the help of local residents and carried them back to Japan, where he tested them for radon, uranium, and other nuclides in state-of-the-art laboratories not available to antinuclear activists and dissident nuclear scientists in India. As they struggle to understand the effects of nuclear technologies, antinuke activists in India find new allies in other countries. The publication of measurement results in *Anumukti* served the purpose of mediating the infrastructure of the uranium mine; this mediation produced a techno-struggle to comprehend radioactivity in Jadugoda through new translocal connections and collaborations between activist-scientists or, still better, dissenting scientists in India and Japan.[4]

The participation of ordinary citizens in radiation detection in post-Fukushima Japan is unprecedented, whether it is crowd-funded radiation-mapping exercises or opening up radiation screening centers to test food grains and vegetables produced in areas close to Fukushima. Yet, they still needed counterexperts/dissident scientists like Koide to indicate which dosimeters could be relied on and how to interpret the results. Translocality is helpful in understanding the connections between antiradiation activisms unfolding in different places across the globe.[5]

Anthropologist Kath Weston (2017) argues that citizen science in post-Fukushima Japan was about "techno-struggle," about struggling with one technology like the Geiger counter to combat the radioactivity of another technology, the nuclear reactor. This scientific citizenship was about food safety, measuring radioactive contamination accurately, and determining appropriate threshold levels. The antinuke activism was less interested in agitating against the Japanese government and more interested in finding ways to protect oneself and one's family from imperceptible radioactive contamination.[6]

In both Japan and India, popular epidemiology requires investigations and detections. However, there are limitations to this "techno-struggle": the phenomenological translations afforded by dosimeters and radiation detectors tend to work on neoliberal ("care for the self") and technologically deterministic assumptions. The movement championing greater regulation of cell towers in India also failed to contest science beyond the technical vocabulary of standards, thresholds, and signal intensities. There was much here in terms of embodied experiences and affective reverberations, but little in terms of alternative imaginaries.

I want to think of popular translations/popular detections of radiation in the register of imaginaries. The Indian nuclear establishment's uranium mining practices in Jadugoda have led to increasing incidences of cancer in the area, which is mostly inhabited by indigenous populations who had no previous history of cancer in their families.

Ghanshyam Birulee, a local *Adivasi* (twin translations: indigenous person/original inhabitant) from Jadugoda, has helped Surendra Gadekar and Hiroaki Koide to carry out radiation measurements in the villages neighboring the uranium mine.

FIGURE C.6
Surendra Gadekar
measuring radiation
around a school
wall in Jadugoda
(Snapshot from
Jung Aur Aman)

Anand Patwardhan's film *Jung Aur Aman* (*War and Peace*, 2002) includes scenes based in Jadugoda in which antinuclear activists and dissident nuclear physicists can be seen wielding dosimeters and conducting readings in different parts of the village. Uranium rock had been used as ballast for road leveling and house building, and to construct a local school and clinic. Through their Geiger counters, the activists (such as Surendra Gadekar) demonstrate in Patwardhan's documentary that the radiation levels, in the school wall and the streets on which open trucks carry nuclear waste, are four to five times more than the average background radiation (figure C.6). In places close to the mines and in residential areas near the tailing ponds, radiation levels have far exceeded the safety limits prescribed by the international community.

Beyond this techno-struggle, Birulee has other perspectives on the nuclear issue. When interviewed in Shriprakash's documentary *Buddha Weeps in Jadugoda* (1999), Birulee likens uranium mining to interfering with snakes. He says if you go inside the burrow of the snake and interfere with its life, the snake will come out and bite you. Taking uranium out of the ground is like provoking a snake, for it has left the *Adivasi* community poisoned (figures C.7 and C.8). Elsewhere, Birulee has recounted an urban legend about a haunted castor oil tree where people were told not to go. Pregnant women would suffer miscarriages or have children with congenital deformities if they ventured close to the tree. Only people who dug holes went to the tree, and soon the bore turned into a mine (Levy 2015). These are powerful fables that mark how indigenous populations are attempting to understand radioactivity through a process of translation; these are impactful metaphorical translations of uranium mines critical to forming shared understandings about "the nuclear."

FIGURES C.7 AND
c.8 Ghanshyam
Birulee in *Buddha
Weeps in Jadugoda*
(Snapshot)

Like a snake...if you leave the
snake alone...it will not harm you

So we want the uranium to be left
where it was buried under the earth

Such stories get dismissed as part animism, part superstition, and part
ignorance, but what if they are about alternative imaginaries, about pluri-
verses, about "indigenous cosmopolitics" (de la Cadena 2010) where the "cosmos refers to the unknown constituted by these multiple, divergent worlds"
(Stengers 2005, 995) and it brings earth beings as political actors to public
debate on environmental controversies. Translating radiation, or interpreting
radiant infrastructures, is not only a technological exercise but also a sociocultural endeavor in which tactics of coping (and perhaps "wisdom") might
(even) lie in speculations, premonitions, and myths.

It is important to interpret Birulee's testimony and Shriprakash's documentary as not just situated critiques that celebrate "place" and an "ethics

FIGURE C.9 Koide in Jadugoda (Screen grab from *Nabikei*, 2017)

of proximity" (Bauman 1993). Birulee believes in tactically assisting in the scientific endeavors of Koide as he procures soil samples from Jadugoda in order to prove that the radiation levels close to the mine are indeed dangerous (figure C.9). Such a belief in science and scientific method does not stop Birulee from believing in ancient legends that compare the uranium mine to a snake. Shriprakash stresses the attachment indigenous people of Jadugoda have to their lands and forests by depicting their rituals and ceremonies involving animal sacrifice and song-and-dance routines. However, by invoking the rhetoric of place as a contingent strategy of protest against exogenous development projects (setting up of uranium mines), *Buddha Weeps in Jadugoda* does not seek to essentialize place. Shriprakash shows Jadugoda to be shaped by and shaping national and global networks of social relations and understandings. At one point in the film, Shriprakash takes his slides to a meeting of the Atomic Energy Regulatory Authority in Delhi with the hopes that the power structures that impinge on the porous boundaries of Jadugoda (as a place) will end the exploitation of tribals. Shriprakash has screened his documentary in numerous film festivals, including the 2000 Earth-Vision International Film Festival in Tokyo, where it won the Grand Prize. Over the years, through documentaries like *Nabikei* (2018), Shriprakash has made translocal connections between the conditions of the Santhals in Jadugoda with indigenous communities inhabiting the irradiated sites of erstwhile tailing dams (of uranium mines) in the Navajo Nation

FIGURE C.10 Churchrock tailings spill site, New Mexico, United States, 1979
(Screen grab from *Nabikei,* 2017)

(New Mexico/southwestern United States) (figure C.10). Such translocal connections suggest that eco-documentaries like *Buddha Weeps in Jadugoda* that privilege place-based struggles are not necessarily antithetical to "eco-cosmopolitanism." Instead, they possess an understanding that environmental injustices must be fought by bridging the local and global with an awareness of the scale of capitalistic and ecological forces that impinge on a particular locality (Heise 2008).

I have been using the term "translocal" to explain collaborations between Koide, Birulee, and Gadekar because, unlike "transnational," such local-local connections do not privilege either "national" or "global" frameworks, and sometimes they even bypass such frameworks. Translocality stresses both situatedness and connectedness of places across spaces and scales (Brickell and Datta 2011).[7] While these translocal connections are key to antinuke activism, post-Fukushima documentaries in Japan also emphasize "home" and the radioactive landscape as crucial to nuclear imaginaries.

Abandoned Homes/Haunted Landscapes

While filming *Nuclear Hallucinations*, documentarian Fathima Nizaruddin found Koodankulam locals telling her about the fictional Tamil film *Citizen* (2001, Saravana Subaiya) in which a village disappears from the map of India. In places like Koodankulam, where locals anticipate a Fukushima-like disaster, the speculative fiction of *Citizen* has a certain affective charge.

Fresh from the sea

FIGURE C.11 Kenji eating fish and talking about home (Screen grab from *Furusato*; courtesy Thorsten Trimpop)

Depopulated ghost towns also exist in Japan in the "red zone" surrounding the Fukushima nuclear plant that were evacuated because of fears of radioactive contamination after the 2011 Tohoku earthquake and tsunami led to a nuclear meltdown.[8] Filmmakers Mark Olexa and Francesca Scalisi entered this zone in 2016 and documented a resident still living there, a farmer named Naoto Matsumura, in their film *Half-Life in Fukushima*. The documentarians wear hazmat suits and protective gear while shooting Matsumura, who wanders around the city and its haunted landscapes clad in plain clothes, without a mask, picking mushrooms and playing golf.[9]

Perhaps Koodankulam's residents fear Matsumura's solitary existence; they fear not so much evaporating as being abandoned. Matsumura might be an extreme case, but there are others, like residents of Minamisoma, located at such a distance from the reactor that the border between the officially uninhabitable and the inhabitable runs through the center of the city. Some of the residents were evacuated from the region and lived in school dormitories before returning. They want to return to normal life, but what does such a desire for normalcy look like? Thorsten Trimpop, in his documentary *Furusato* (2016), records one such resident, Kenji, eating fish caught fresh from the ocean very close to the reactor. Kenji does not run a Geiger counter over the fish. He simply eats it with soy sauce on the boat and pronounces it delicious (figure C.11).

FIGURE C.12 Bags of contaminated soil close to ocean on the right
(Screen grab from *Furusato*)

Kenji then talks about home: "I think home is a place you go back, you feel relaxed, you feel that you belong there, you are safe, you are happy.... I think that is where home is." But, and here is the irony: the safety, happiness, and relaxation of home (Minamisoma) that Kenji wishes for cannot be guaranteed because there is uncertainty about the levels and health effects of imperceptible radiation. Normalcy will return if there is no reason to use a Geiger counter in Minamisoma. Can one stop using it now?[10] Trimpop has often wondered whether this pretense of normalcy reflects an unwillingness to leave home and become nuclear refugees.[11] This would explain the title of the documentary *Furusato*, which literally means "home" in Japanese.

Beyond "home," the word Furusato has a more poetic meaning: "the first and last landscapes one sees." This probably is the reason for the observational style of documenting that Trimpop espouses in order to communicate the deeper relation between Minamisoma residents and their (now) wounded landscape.[12] It is a landscape where the topsoil has been scraped away from parks and children's playgrounds. In an aerial shot with lateral and vertical pans, Trimpop shows thousands of bags of contaminated topsoil that have been collected and piled in temporary storage plots close to the ocean for the indeterminable future (figure C.12).

Ontological Renderings of Expert-Layperson Divides within Environmental Publics

One of the key sites of contention that emerge when analyzing the environmental publics of radiation-related controversies is the expert-layperson divide. The friction between scientists who voice extreme consent and activists who proclaim intense opposition to radiant infrastructures is even starker in the case of debates about nuclear energy. In this book, I have explained how media (with examples ranging from talk show debates to documentary films) negotiates and complicates the expert-layperson divide when controversies unfold about the health effects of radiation.

So far, most of the case studies of mediations of nuclear reactors I have discussed present the clash of knowledge systems in epistemic terms. Patault and Irion, the makers of *Are-Vah!*, explicitly relate the fishermens' knowledge systems to their ontological lived realities. Like Amudhan, Shriprakash, and Nizaruddin (whose documentary works have been discussed in various chapters of this book), Patault and Irion associate themselves with the antinuke social movement in India and interrogate the state-corporate nexus that is degrading environmental habitats. Thus, they seem as politically committed as the rest of the filmmakers, but what makes their documentaries incisive environmental/ ecological documentaries (or ecodocs) is their ability to image the nonhuman as central to their affective political address to viewers (Smaill 2016).[13]

The village Sakhri-Nate is part of the Jaitapur region where the French corporation Areva is setting up a nuclear plant. The plant is estimated to discharge 52,000 million liters of hot water into the Arabian Sea through hoses. The fishermen are concerned that this thermal discharge will affect the marine ecosystem on which they rely to catch fish that is exported to many European countries (Hardikar 2013). In 2010, addressing numerous press briefings and academic talks in various cities of Maharashtra, the Atomic Energy Commission chairman, Anil Kakodkar, reassured reporters and students that "the site had been selected after carrying out thermal ecology studies" and "the nuclear plant at Jaitapur would not be a threat to agriculture or marine ecology."[14]

Patault and Irion stage the clash of knowledge systems between Majeed Latigowarkar, the fisherman in Sakhri-Nate village, and Kakodkar. At one point in the documentary, Latigowarkar exclaims, "Anil Kakodkar said that the hot water won't cause any problems. If he really wants to know, let him

FIGURE C.13 Fish under water (Screen grab from *Are-Vah!*, 2014)

come here. Here, we don't work behind a desk like Anil Kakodkar." As if to actualize Latigowarkar's comparison of his lived and embodied knowledge with Kakodkar's bookish knowledge, Patualt and Irion follow Latigowarkar on his fishing expedition. The documentarians are on a fishing boat with Latigowarkar in the middle of the creek.

As Irion recounts to me in an interview, during this trip to the creek with Latigowarkar, Patault at one point sees a dead fish and then decides to put the GoPro camera on his chest and dives down to capture it (figure C.13). In this unsettling scene with muffled yet evocative sound, Patualt and Irion ask audiences to encounter the fish in its own milieu, something that the fishermen of Sakhri Nate do every day. It is their lived ontologies that provide the fishermen with the confidence to discern even the minutest differences in water temperatures and the health of the fish.

In framing this sensual assemblage of sea, fishermen, boats, and fish, the documentarians are not practicing the kind of sonic ethnography that Lucien Castaing-Taylor and Véréna Paravel have repeatedly executed in their much-discussed films like *Leviathan* (2012). Castaing-Taylor and Paravel's approach to a postcinematic and new materialist documentary is so complete, so absolute, that they find little use for narrative or argumentation. In their portrayal of nonhumans (fish), Patault and Irion connect material politics with an explicit environmental politics around livelihood and socio-ecological justice.

Patault and Irion's filmmaking techniques diversify the strategies that antinuke documentaries can espouse, and their documentary offers a counterpoint to some of the *diktats* propounded by the "expert" Anil Kakodkar. This counterpoint is made not just through commentaries and testimonies by counterexperts, affected communities, and activists but also through the documentary's portrayal of nonhuman assemblages.

The ability of media to interrogate the expert-layperson divides within environmental publics of cell towers and nuclear reactors has been a key concern for me throughout this book. Another concern has been the ways in which intermedial approaches can help ordinary people understand the complexities of radiant infrastructures and the issues at stake in environmental controversies.

Infrastructural Complexities and (In)Visibilities

Certain parts and configurations of infrastructures may not be visible because of the sheer scale of their operations. At times, it is simply not possible for people to gain a comprehensive understanding of infrastructures, partly because of technical details, and partly due to the impossibility of physically observing all the working parts of a vast infrastructure. Mediation of infrastructures during environmental controversies could be a way of understanding the relational complications that characterize an infrastructure's workings across local-global scales. Lisa Parks (2015, 359) asks media scholars and media audiences to cultivate an "infrastructural disposition" when watching media representations of infrastructures. She notes that "it would be impossible to present a photorealist view of an entire postal infrastructure within a single view," but if analysts/viewers are able to activate an infrastructural disposition, then they can approach "what is framed as a starting point for imagining and inferring other infrastructural parts or resources" (359). One can say the same for an infrastructure like the nuclear reactor: if analysts and viewers are presented with exterior domes, they can be curious about nuclear technologies and ask questions about coolant chambers, and if they are presented with the whole nuclear reactor, they can ask further questions about the mines from where the uranium is brought for the reactor. The reactor can be in Koodankulam, South India, but with infrastructural intelligibility, audiences can imaginatively travel to the Jadugoda uranium mines in Jharkhand and ask questions about the translocal circulation of energy resources.

To further extend Parks's point, during environmental controversies, different media (an ad by the nuclear establishment or an antinuclear documentary) might present different aspects of an infrastructure like the nuclear reactor, and so stitching together the different observations of the nuclear energy infrastructure through an intermedial approach might be another way to cultivate an infrastructural disposition. This is something I have done throughout this book as an analyst/media scholar. Can such an endeavor be undertaken by an affected community member? I believe it can be done, with due caveats placed for constraints of time and access. My larger point is that people do engage with various media that focus on or choose to highlight different facets of and gaps in infrastructures, and juxtaposing/comparing these different mediated representations of infrastructures might not necessarily be something that only an analyst does. Rather, ordinary people who are curious about the issue of nuclear or cell tower radiation are indeed adopting such intermedial approaches to understand reactors and towers. Infrastructural disposition and intermedial approach can indeed be seen as both analytical tools and empirical conditions. That being said, in suggesting this, I do not want to dismiss or conflate the analyst's privilege and the specific empirical practices.

Radiant infrastructures, like other infrastructures, symbolize national innovation and achievement through their successful technological development. The same radiant infrastructures, however, unlike other infrastructures, specifically emit radiations, whether ionizing or nonionizing. And that makes the governance of radiant infrastructures an act of controlling their material emissions and knowledge about such emissions. Media, whether in the form of science journalists getting access to interior parts of nuclear reactors or in the form of Web 2.0 e-portals mapping out cell towers and their signal strengths (through radiation detectors), becomes an active part of governing radiant infrastructures. These new transparencies afforded by radiometers and electroencephalograms help affected communities to apprehend the uncanny radiations that eluded their sensory faculties. That being said, such transparencies do not always lead to certainties. Radiation detectors operating on different threshold levels can cause anxiety about whether or not somebody is in a safe zone.

Therefore, with radiant infrastructures and radiant energies, there are limits to visibilities and transparencies, and while some visibilities afford greater certainties, particular indeterminacies about the workings of infrastructures and uncertainties about the environmental impact of radiations remain.

Speculative Fiction

Students at the Coimbatore Institute of Technology created an animated film about a vigilante going by the name "Stranger Electrifier" who magically completes all the remaining work left to make the Koodankulam nuclear reactor fully operational. Other than this work of speculative fiction, the majority of

FIGURE C.14 Pakshi Rajan in human form among birds near a cell tower
(Screen grab from *2.0*)

media texts I have discussed in this book have been news stories and documentaries (though, as I have stressed, documentaries like *Nuclear Hallucinations*
do not serve merely instrumental/activist functions, but demonstrate an urge
to speculate about a dystopic future of nuclear ruination). Nonetheless, this
book has focused on what is typically described as "nonfiction." Nuclear issues
have been taken up by fictional films made in both Bollywood and regional film
industries, and yet such films have dealt exclusively with atom bombs and other
nuclear weapons (Kaur 2013b). Bookending the Bombay film industry's engagement with nuclear weapons are two films: the Homi Wadia–directed *Atom
Bomb* (1947) and *Parmanu: The Story of Pokhran* (2017). The original posters
for *Atom Bomb* depict a scientist leaning over a laboratory experiment, his linea-
ments suggesting he has cracked the "atomic secret" (Kaur 2013b). *Parmanu*,
which stars John Abraham and Diana Penty, retells the story of the prepara-
tions made for the 1998 nuclear tests at Pokhran, India. Despite these two
films and those made in the long intervening years, India still awaits a Bollywood film about the issue of nuclear energy that focuses on nuclear reactors.[15]

Relative to nuclear reactors, cell towers are a new infrastructure. Yet, in late
2018, just as I was completing this book, the Tamil film industry and Bollywood
collaboratively released a film that engages with the issue of mobile tower radiation. This recent Bollywood/Tamil film, titled *2.0*, depicts an ornithologist,
Pakshi Rajan (which is Sanskrit/Tamil for "king of birds"), who is pained by the
detrimental impact of cell tower radiation on bird life (figure C.14). Pakshi

FIGURE C.15 Posthuman Pakshi Rajan, part human, part bird, part cell phones (Screen grab from *2.0*)

Rajan takes on a posthuman figuration, that is, a "humanimal machine" (part human–part bird–part machine) form to kill key figures in the cell phone industry (corporates and corrupt regulators who are amassing wealth from the growth of cell towers).[16] This is his way to exact revenge for what cell towers have done to the birds, who have been his research interest and dearest companions all through life. Pakshi Rajan (played by Bollywood actor Akshay Kumar) in his human form resembles Salim Ali, India's famous ornithologist. When Pakshi Rajan transitions to the posthuman humanimal machine form, his/its body undergoes rapid transformation as he/it gathers wings akin to those of birds, and both the bird's wings and body plumage are constituted of cell phones (figure C.15). These cell phones have been snatched away from their human users by Pakshi Rajan, who believes the needless and irresponsible chitchat on mobile phones that humans indulge in is the reason that cell towers emit harmful wireless signals. Each time Pakshi Rajan transforms into the posthuman monster figure (combining the human, bird, and cell phone forms), we see a swarm of cell phones flying in formation like a flock of birds, gathering together to exact revenge on humans, with ominous music playing on the sound track.

The film *2.0* is a sequel to *Enthiran*, a Tamil/Hindi film about a genius scientist Vasikaran (played by Rajnikanth), who creates an andro-humanoid robot named Chitti. Chitti is at once very efficient and devoted to Vasikaran, and at the same time has a Frankenstein-like potential to wreak havoc. An updated version of Chitti, addressed as Chitti 2.0, in the new film *2.0* by Vasikaran, does finally annihilate the posthuman humanimal machine figuration of Pakshi Rajan with some stupendous and sumptuous action scenes and questionable application of electromagnetic wave theory. That being said, what fascinates me is the embodiment of Pakshi Rajan.

Pakshi Rajan as a "posthuman monster" figure does trouble (and dissolve) the ontological categories of flesh/metal and human/nonhuman about which Rosi Braidotti (2011) and Abhishek Lakkad (2018) have written. But there is more here, as Pakshi Rajan also recalls mythological figures like Jatayu/Garuda from ancient Hindu epics, some of whom were indeed hybrids of humans and birds. Garuda is a bird creature from Hindu mythology that has a mix of human and eagle features. In *2.0*, Garuda's human-bird combination is further technologized for Pakshi Rajan, who has the added component of cell phones in the body. This suggests a tendency in *2.0* (and in some other recent Indian science fiction films) to layer myth over cutting-edge technologies. More specifically, *2.0* suggests that to make sense of high-tech peril like the cell phone or the cell antenna radiation, scientific explanations will not be enough, and that such anxieties about uncanny (spectral) and ethereal radiations will have to be poured into a wider sea of mythical time and affects. Technoscience provides some answers in *2.0*, but when technoscience lacks rational answers for the imaginative leaps made in the film's narrative and action sequences, audiences are asked to supplement such a lack with references to a mythic past where posthuman hybrids existed. Past anteriors and future imperfects are invoked in the way this "speculative fiction masala" depicts Pakshi Rajan asking audiences to think not in linear time but in cyclical time (A. Basu 2011; Kaur 2013b).[17]

What stands out is how much *2.0* focuses on birds, depicting them as the primary victims of cell towers. The film mentions in passing that humans have been affected too, but through selection and salience it chooses to emphasize the effect of such radiation on birds. Perhaps, imperfectly so, the film gestures to the sensitivity of birds to such radiation.[18] This opinion that birds are extrasensitive, and hence better than humans at perceiving nonionizing electromagnetic fields is also found in the jeweler Kasliwal's story that I recounted earlier, wherein peacocks become a heuristic by which radiation can be most reliably measured. The film *2.0* does take liberty with the science and technology of EMFs, but in its imaginative meanderings and sensationalist depictions, the film is able to translate and channel some of the anxieties and uncertainties about contemporary technological gadgets like cell phones used by billions of Indians. The posthuman figuration of Pakshi Rajan allows for the possibility of interspecies mediations across humans and birds when it comes to electromagnetic signals.

One scene in *2.0* has Pakshi Rajan (in his human form) vehemently oppose the construction of a cell tower, and listening to his opposition, a telecom engineer exclaims that this is not a nuclear reactor site. This reaction from the engineer suggests that Pakshi Rajan's frustration with a cell tower site is inexplicable. So, in a way, protesting nuclear reactors is considered normal, but protesting construction of a cell tower is seen as ridiculous. This is perhaps another comparative story to be kept in mind as we think of contemporary Indian reception to these two infrastructures.

Infrastructural Change

Infrastructures keep changing, planned and tinkered with by a range of human and nonhuman actors. There is no way to correctly speculate whether infrastructural change will be progressive or rational or better. During the Cold War era, the race for atomic bombs and the health effects of nuclear testing sullied the reputations of the United States and the Soviet Union. Both nations responded by launching "atoms for peace" programs whose stated goals were to generate "electricity too cheap to meter." The two superpowers entered into a new race to outproduce each other in the number of nuclear power plants installed in their respective countries and by their allies (Brown 2017, G39). One would have thought that after the partial fallout in the Three Mile Island reactor, and then the Chernobyl and Fukushima atomic disasters, nuclear technologies would lose public support. Indeed, there have been periodic lulls in the construction of nuclear reactors, and yet support for atomic energy (as a clean and green energy form that could supplement solar, wind, and geothermal energy resources) comes from unexpected quarters. Lisa Lynch (2012, 327) writes that "some of the hastiest defenders of nuclear power in the wake of Fukushima were environmentalists." Post-Fukushima, Gaia theorist James Lovelock, global warming alarmist George Monbiot, and *Whole Earth Catalog* author Stewart Brand reassured the public in media interviews that their enthusiasm for nuclear energy had not diminished (Lynch 2012, 328).

Tech titans and venture capitalists in Silicon Valley are funding nuclear startups that are building next generation nuclear reactor designs that work with innovative fuels and alternative coolants. Nuclear engineers Leslie Dewan and Mark Massie were funded by a Bill Gates–backed nuclear start-up named TerraPower to build their "waste-annihilating molten salt reactor," which aims to use existing nuclear waste to produce electricity (Koch 2015). If their reactor design works, nuclear wastes will have new radiant afterlives, and the planet might just be saved. Dewan is an avowed environmentalist who believes her reactor designs are the answer to carbon-free electricity. Nuclear energy divides environmentalists. Some, like Matthew McKinzie, affiliated with the environmental group Natural Resources Defense Council, believe that Dewan's nuclear reactors look good on paper but are far too complex to be actually realized. That being said, such next-generation nuclear reactor stories are often featured in media outlets like *National Geographic* magazine, which lends credibility to the narrative that new technologies will solve problems instigated by old technologies.

Sometimes an old technology, ignored for a century, is found to be of great value. This certainly is the case with mobile communications adopting new frequency bands to cater to a data saturated planet. The story of these new frequency bands takes us back to the colonial history of India. At a Calcutta town hall in 1895, the scientist J. C. Bose used a spark-gap transmitter to send a 60-GHz signal through three walls and the body of the region's lieutenant governor to a funnel-shaped horn antenna and detector 23 meters away (Rappaport, Roh, and Cheun 2014). This was a demonstration and so it had to be proved that the signal had indeed followed that trajectory. The signal, when it reached the antenna, triggered a simple contraption that rang a bell, fired a gun, and exploded a small mine. These millimeter waves were not considered a resource by wireless engineers for whom the ideal frequency range has for a long time been 300 MHz to 3 GHz (Shepherd 2012). However, the 4G LTE networks are facing a saturation crisis with the demand for more and more data-intensive broadband traffic. The millimeter wave band spans from 30 to 300 GHz, and this is where 5G (fifth generation) wireless networks are being prepared. Since the millimeter band had long been ignored by the telecom industry, the initial RF circuit and antenna equipment was unsophisticated and costly, and it took twenty years for wireless science to come up with better designs for antenna so that 5G wireless technology can be commerically rolled out (Rappaport, Roh, and Cheun 2014).

Millimeter waves do not exactly link the cell tower and mobile phone but are better deployed to transfer larger amounts of data over short distances between machines. That, however, means that "smart" 5G antennas will have to be installed closer to homes on perhaps every second electric pole of our residential streets. This has made antiradiation activists in the Bay Area protest against California's SB 649 bill that reduces the local government's planning authority over wireless facilities on publicly owned streets and properties. Some professors of medicine are unsure about the effects of millimeter waves on the human body and do not want small antennas to come on public streets.[19] As the telecom industry transitions from 4G to 5G wireless technologies, it makes relevant again a 120-year-old millimeter wave technology that had remained previously ignored. In doing so, wireless enterpreneurs face new hurdles from public health professionals who emphasize the need for caution and ask for more tests that probe the health effects of millimeter waves. New radiant technologies are resisted for the darkness they might spread. New uncertainties emerge alongside new potentials.

In my documentation of the biomedical crises refracted by processes of mediation, authoritative expert knowledge backed by coercive power is resisted through formal and informal environmentalisms, explicit and implicit environmental politics. I have attempted to expand both the forms of media and the kind of environmental politics that can be taken into account while studying environmental controversies. Controversies are conjunctive moments, and that allows a science studies/media studies researcher to examine both radiation science and indigeneous cosmopolitics, both local newspapers and lifestyle shows, which on first glance might seem disjunctive forms/practices but then end up being connected to the same environmental issue.

The analysis of radiant infrastructures often has to engage with both light and shadows. Nuclear reactors are associated with illuminating lives by bringing electricity, and yet they are also a cause of cancer and thus need to be analyzed from the shadows. What happens if and when we consider radiant infrastructures as dysfunctional entities from the point of view of the affected populations rather than their beneficiaries? Radiant infrastructures then do not remain just economically and socially productive forces but rather provoke critical and palliative forms of care. The invisibility and imperceptibility of radioactive isotopes and cell antenna signals further extend questions of shadows in relation to light/radiance, of what can and cannot be seen in, and through, the radioactive light and electromagentic signals.[20]

The infrastructural violence of radiant infrastructures has to do with uncontrolled emissions. Such radiological violence confounds perceptibility and amplifies uncertainty: the slow but accretive quality of the heating effects of nonionizing EMFs do not lend themselves well to spectacle, nor do the (un)diagnosed mutations in the irradiated human body's cells due to radioactive cesium isotopes make for good reality TV. And yet, across genres there have been mediations that render the nuclear bodies as situated and reflective subjects. However disturbing the scars on their bodies, the survivors of nuclear disasters in the documentaries of Amudhan and Shriprakash offer sensuous and expressive testimonies. Even though the recent HBO TV miniseries *Chernobyl* (2019) manipulates the facts of the 1986 nuclear fallout and mischaracterizes the behavior of Soviet scientists, it has been able to stir worldwide interest in a decades-old disaster (Gessen 2019). The miniseries has audiences addictively watching a tragedy that has often been considered unwatchable, and instigated some to google search esoteric scientific details about the disaster (Saraiya 2019). The TV critic Emily Nussbaum (2019) champions the narrative power of this distressing thriller, which has firefighters dying in agony and courageous whistleblowers challenging the nuclear establishment.[21] One poignant scene at the end of the first episode conveys the invisibility of radioactivity. Ordinary citizens living close to the reactor do not yet know about the imperceptible danger; they go about their lives chatting in parks, children romping about as they return from school, oblivious to the radioactive air they are breathing in the absence of atmopsheric cues. As ominous music plays, and the audience knows something is amiss, the camera pans and tracks to show these vignettes (and perhaps manifests the dread of the audience), searching for some visible sign of an impending disaster in this uneasy calm until it finally finds a bird dropping dead to the ground.

The 5G revolution envisions connecting millions of devices instantaneously, thereby making the Internet of Things more efficient. Such a revolution is not merely about upgrading cell towers and mobile phones but also about shifting protocols and practices related to privacy and security. These upgrades and shifts continue to be entangled in controversies related to anxieties about public health and local control of public space, which to some extent are similar to problems I have discussed in this book regarding siting of cell antennas. Some objections to cell antennas, and now to 5G, might indeed be considered unscientific or opportunistic obstructionism, and yet a more historical approach suggests "deep legacies of environmental and infrastructural injustice" (Mattern 2019). National and international pressure can possibly prevent nuclear and telecom lobbyists from manufacturing doubts about correlations between radiation and ill health. Such doubts help to normalize the slow violence faced by affected community members living in proximity to radiant infrastructures. Projects to interrogate regimes of imperceptibility will require careful listening, seeing, smelling, sensing, and witnessing. Uncertainties will not end merely by a radiation sensor or a radiation map. The mediation of radiation and electromagnetic interference through detectors and electroencephalograms, carried further through intermedial relays with documentary films and lifestyle shows, will (have to) be conveyed to translocal audiences across the world. Such translocal witnessing has to translate into attention to slow violence, curiosity about infrastructures, and understanding the stakes of participating in reconfiguring technologies of perceiving radiation. This book is written with just so much expectation.

NOTES

Introduction

1   Air pollution was still a serious environmental concern as of 2015; see Sehgal and Bennett (2016). Beyond vehicular pollution, Dewali firecrackers are one reason for the poor air quality. Another reason is crop burning in states surrounding Delhi. Despite a temporary ban on firecrackers in November 2017, air pollution in Delhi has again reached "public health emergency" levels. See "Delhi Air Pollution a 'Public Health Emergency,'" *The Wire*, November 7, 2017, https://thewire.in/195106/delhi-air-pollution-public-health-emergency-says-ima-kejriwal-suggests-shutting-schools-days/. The *hawa badlo* (change the air) campaign was launched. Its website is http://changetheair.org. While some particulate matter (PM 2.5) can make air look hazy, not all air pollution is visible, especially that caused by nitrogen dioxide.

2   A *TV9 Maharashtra* show on cell towers, broadcast on November 3, 2011, labeled the danger as *khamosh khatra*: see "Mobile Tower and Children: Silent Killers—Prof Gisish Kumar and Juhi Chawla—TV9," YouTube, posted October 28, 2013, by NesaRadiationSolns, https://www.youtube.com/watch?v=XEM5xsOoka4.

3   Gabrielle Hecht, in her book *The Radiance of France* (2009b), discusses how national identity in post–World War II France became associated with grand technological projects of nuclear power. In India, postcolonial national identity became increasingly entwined with mastering the science of the atom.

4   Throughout this book, I have used *Koodankulam* and *Kudankulam* interchangeably as both spellings have been used in many places while discussing the nuclear reactor.

5   If the Indian nation has its own kind of modernity, then science, duly inflected by cultural processes, had a role to play in it. The "multiple modernities" thesis postulates that "each nation or region produces its own distinctive modernity in its encounter with the allegedly culture-neutral forms and processes," including science, technology, and industrialization, as part of societal modernization (Gaonkar 2002, 4).

6   The Non-Proliferation Treaty is an international treaty whose member nations vow not to expand nuclear weapons and to cooperate with other members for peaceful nuclear energy production.

7   See the Indus Towers web page: http://www.industowers.com/who_we_are.php.

8   (Nuclear) energy and information transmission (cell antenna signals) might be considered separately nowadays, but in the late nineteenth century, as Ghislain Thibault (2014) notes, "information and energy" were "part of the same ecology and their separation was artificial" (96). Even as the electromagnetic spectrum came to be understood as the medium of information transmission, the electromagnetic radiation in that spectrum is part of energy phenomena.

9   The atom bomb joined photography, X-ray, and cinema as new technologies of light, and this light (and radiance) was associated with totalitarianism and alterity, "with knowledge and its destruction, and with the visible and the invisible" (DeLoughrey 2009: 478; Lippit 2005). This paradox of light, both in its physicality (particle and wave nature) and metaphorical usage (illuminating and blinding) can be extended to think of how radiance (and radiation) is a double-edged sword. More on this follows in the book.

10 Refer to research by Elisabeth Cardis and the Interphone Study Group (2010) on brain tumor risk in relation to mobile phone use. While this book focuses on cell towers, apprehensions about mobile phones causing cancer, since they maintain communication with cell towers through EMFs, surface in the public sphere. The possible harmful effects of mobile phones erupted into the American public sphere when on January 21, 1993, David Reynard told CNN's Larry King that his wife Susan Reynard died of brain cancer caused (or accelerated) by cell phone use (Kurtz 1996). Anxieties about health effects of contemporary media technologies is not recent and did not start with cell phones. Susan Murray (2018) writes about the discourses of possible danger from proximity of television screens to human bodies in the 1950s and '60s. Around 1967, it was found during routine testing that specific large-scale-screen models of GE color TV sets were emitting X-ray radiations beyond desirable threshold levels. From there, a swift response to this revelation lead to better regulatory protocols and vigilant checking. As television historian Lynn Spiegel (1992) has noted, in the mid-1930s, owing to confusion about broadcast technology, there were public fears about the contaminating effects of the electric space of television spreading into the real physical environment. Complaints about harmful effects of mobile phones and cell towers are not restricted to cancer but include nausea, memory loss, headache, and muscular pain. I discuss particular cases of electro-sensitives who claim to be hypersensitive to the electromagnetic fields emitted by cell towers and wi-fi routers in chapter 4.

11 Kate Brown (2013), in her insightful book *Plutopia*, explains how medical radiologists in the Manhattan Project had preferred plutonium over radium, since the former emitted fewer gamma rays than the latter. And yet, the radioactive isotopes emitted by plutonium were able to insert themselves into biological processes inside the human body, including blood and bone marrow, with terrible consequences.

12 The information is from the NPCIL/Vigyan Prasar poster, published in leading English dailies in India.

13 This is a statement that Raminder Kaur (2013a) finds Robert J. Oppenheimer invoking from *Bhagavad Gita* to describe the sublime feature of the July 1945 atomic tests. In the late 1950s, the US Atomic Energy Commission undertook

a secret program called "Operation Sunshine" to measure radioactive isotope strontium-90 levels in humans, plants, and animals from militarized nuclear radiation (see DeLoughrey 2009). This blurring of boundaries between background radiation from sun and anthropogenic radiation from nuclear weapons and nuclear reactors is problematic.

14 Refer to the fact sheet on TRAI's Tarang Sanchar site: https://tarangsanchar.gov .in/emfportal.

15 Medical oncologist Siddhartha Mukherjee (2011) reassures us that, at the low power levels of cell towers and mobile phones, it has been epidemiologically difficult to establish that radio-frequency energy at nonthermal intensities causes cancer. That being said, scientific studies have not overruled the possibility that chronic exposure to cell antenna signals can stimulate chemical reactions that might aggravate or accelerate tumors or physiological (e.g., brain glucose) activity.

16 Discussing Bose's writings, Ashis Nandy (1972) notes that "Mahashakti" as "ultimate power" is "represented by the dominant mother-deities of Bengal" (40). On electro-sensitivity, that is, sensitivity of human bodies to electromagnetic fields at particular frequencies, read Lisa Mitchell and Alberto Cambrosio's (1997) early article on the invisible topography of EMFs.

17 Noortje Marres (2005, 2010) and Jane Bennett (2005) have stressed that, for Dewey, a public is not just another collective of individuals or a social community: "Dewey makes it clear that a public does not preexist its particular problem but emerges in response to it" (Bennett 2005, 100). In Marres's (2010) formulation, Dewey was interested in how social actors who went about their everyday lives had to break from their habitual ways and attempt to forge a public when they found themselves affected by the consequences of an issue or a problem that was beyond their control.

18 The term "environmental public" in other literature on this topic, like Robert Cox's (2010) *Environmental Communication and the Public Sphere*, is often used as part of "environmental public sphere(s)," "environmental public interest litigation," or "environmental public health." While I do include such uses of "environmental publics" because I am dealing with environmental controversies, I also use the term to stress the environmental or ecological aspects of infrastructures (in general, and radiant infrastructures in particular) and media networks/ systems that cover such infrastructures.

19 In a special issue of the *LIMN* magazine in July 2016, Collier, Mizes, and von Schnitzler (2016) invoke the term "infrastructural publics" in a Deweyian sense to study social collectives that gather around infrastructural connections and flows and define technical standards. However, in addition to studying publics "called into being" by infrastructures, they are interested in publicness of infrastructures, that is, how the government (the public sector) has traditionally planned and constructed infrastructures for preconstituted publics. This interplay between public infrastructures and infrastructural publics is fascinating and something that I study in this book as well. That being said, my central preoccupation remains ecological/relational aspects of infrastructures and environmental impacts of radiant infrastructures.

20 In her recent book *Rethinking Media Coverage: Vertical Mediation and the War on Terror*, Lisa Parks (2018) offers a capacious definition of media coverage so that "coverage" does not become reduced to merely news stories but also includes satellite mapping and digital monitoring practices. In my own case studies, media technologies of biomedical imaging and radiation sensing technologies account for media's role not only in propaganda and publicity but also in mapping and monitoring. Intermediality helps to connect these different mediatic operations of publicity, monitoring, and mapping. I am also not suggesting via intermediality that mediations are ubiquitous or total. Intermediality points to (unstable) configurations of interlinked media systems (and issue-based publics), which are almost always shifting, contingent, and partial.

21 For Jill Bennett (2007), intermediality in contemporary art practice operates "between media" and cannot be subsumed within descriptors like "mixed media" and "appropriation" (434). In crossing media boundaries, there is more than just a play of language and sign system. That is, there are intersections of practices and technologies in intermediality.

22 For Herkman (2012), the term "intermediality—more than concepts such as "re-mediation" and "convergence"—helps explain the sociohistorical contexts within which media changes happen. While there are media technologies that are converging—for example, the smartphone of today can be seen as a convergence or even remediation of radio, television, and telephone—it is also the case that cultural forms and statuses of different media have not simply evaporated. For example, electronic television programs still maintain a hold on Indian masses even as social media is beginning to make a dent in the credibility of television channels. Furthermore, politically committed documentary films continue to be the medium for social justice and environmental justice campaigns in India, even though ad filmmakers are also getting interested in taking up such topics.

23 See Bagla and Stone's (2012) interview with Manmohan Singh.

24 In August 2012, then Indian prime minister Manmohan Singh had equated national development (including "energy security") with national security: "If we do not increase the pace of the country's economic growth, take steps to encourage new investment in the economy, improve the management of government finances and work for the livelihood security of the common man and energy security of the country, then it most certainly affects our national security." Refer to ET Bureau (2012).

25 The bill in its present form makes foreign nuclear suppliers liable, but only for any catastrophe that occurs within five years of the plant's installation. After that period, compensation for damage due to nuclear leaks or a nuclear disaster will be the responsibility of the sole nuclear operator in India, NPCIL.

26 It is important here to mention the cultural dimension of phenomenological encounters. Emotions or sensations felt by humans are not universal; they are specific, situated, and culturally inflected.

27 Nuclear physicist Surendra Gadekar first wrote about this in the April/May 1993 issue of India's only antinuclear journal at the time, *AnuMukti*. In the face of the Indian nuclear establishment's apathy, local communities and antiradiation activ-

ists have created their own epidemiological studies, such as the one published in *AnuMukti*. This study found many different pathways for radioactive pollutants to affect human bodies living around the plant. For example, radionuclides emitted by the plant could settle over the soil and find their way into the local produce eaten by the people there. Another vulnerable group identified were the casual workers at the plant (Gadekar 1993).

28 The project of ecological justice necessarily has a component of social justice in the "environmentalism of the poor." Amita Baviskar (2011) points to another kind of environmentalism, called "bourgeois environmentalism," which is practiced by Indian urban middle-class citizens. Such urban elites want governmental authorities to immediately address their concerns about "beauty and order" in the city even at the cost of poor people's "lives and livelihoods" (401–402). There is little hint of any activism that would try to build a mass movement. I shall discuss these different environmentalisms in greater detail in chapter 5.

29 A liberal public sphere consisting of bourgeois voluntary associations did appear in colonial India in the late nineteenth century, but these liberal public spheres were soon challenged by the crowd of the streets. The nationalist freedom fighter B. G. Tilak promoted Ganesh festivals as a way to conjoin varied, vibrant public cultures. Barton Scott and Brannon Ingram (2015) argue that, with the arrival of cinema and other mass media in early twentieth century, the crowd increasingly became the face of the public in India, displacing civic associations.

30 Chatterjee (2004) has contended that a majority of the population in India does not have access to formal means of engaging with the government. He is categorical that these population groups have a "political relationship" with the state based on informal associations that do not conform to the "constitutional depiction of the relation between the state and members of civil society" (38). He asks scholars to study the distribution of governmental benefits and the relationship between the state and population groups under the rubric of "political society" or the "politics of the governed."

31 Aparna Sundar (2010), writing about the civic engagements of rural fishworkers in South India, argues against Partha Chatterjee's tendency to suggest that civil society does not exist among subaltern rural populations. Ajay Gudavarthy (2012) has edited a collection of essays that celebrate and criticize Chatterjee's formulation of "political society."

32 It is certainly important to recognize that there is a reality out there and that facts have a currency in professional journalism (Zelizer 2006). So, objectivity as a journalistic value is still held in high esteem. That being said, several Indian journalists said "subjectivity" in journalism could mean many things, such as writing reports influenced by corporate and political funding or writing based on feelings and not facts. However, "objectivity" should not necessarily imply "neutrality." Shoma Chaudhury, a premier Indian journalist who writes for *Tehelka* magazine, said that to improve the quality of journalism, journalists should ascertain facts, speak to everyone involved, and then be ready to put their "moral weight behind that version of story." She was not happy with just "he said, she said" reporting. See Timmons (2012).

33 Circulation of issues across porous boundaries of various media publics suggests that there are more ways in which one can categorize and compare media publics rather than just the linguistic split public that Rajagopal delineates. In the nuclear energy issue, documentary publics indulge in remarkably different modes of media practice compared with mainstream television news publics. When I speak of "splits" here, I am trying to pay attention to the boundary crossings of media and the need to study the reconfiguration and transformation of those boundaries themselves.

34 National TV channels can also become hyperlocal if they have ordinary citizens act as journalists and report issues from their locality. CNN-IBN's *Citizen Journalist* is one such program. With the passing of the Right to Information Act and the rise of anticorruption movements (like the one led by Anna Hazare), Indian citizens have been asking for greater governmental accountability.

35 In India, Twitter is dominated by upper-middle-class youth and is not representative of the wider Indian population. Furthermore, the issues supported through hashtags on Twitter become hierarchically trending based on ambivalent algorithms (Gillespie 2012). Nevertheless, Twitter is a place where politicians, journalists, and common people *seem to interact*. Journalists promote their shows on Twitter, and politicians publicize their policy-making schemes and believe Twitter to be an integral part of reaching out to the public. Common people can invoke or tag famous politicians and journalists. Influential journalists and politicians in India rarely follow back or respond to the invocations (and provocations) of ordinary citizens, but when they do, one gets to witness both performances of power and celebrations of digital democracy (Pal 2015).

36 Post-1985, with the advent of neoliberalization in India, media has been opened to private channels, a move that seemed finally to create the possibility of an independent press free from state interference and censorship. While there has been a greater diversity of programs and channels in the Indian mediascape since then, many commentators feel the scope for criticism has been crowded out by "commercial concerns that govern media organizations" (Chaudhuri 2010, 61). There has been growth of reality shows like *Bigg Boss* (Sony TV, 2006; Colors TV, 2007–) that have *aam janata*, or laypeople, as the main protagonists. Television shows have become more interactive, and audiences participate in these shows through Facebook, Twitter, and mobile messaging services. Yet Maitrayee Chaudhuri (2010) argues that, while the transformed Indian publics as represented in the media seem more ordinary, visible, interactive, and diverse, "they do not add up to a more critical public sphere" (62). These scholarly ponderings have led me to comparatively assess the outcomes of show formats that claim to afford audiences greater participation and interaction.

37 Here, Harvey, Jensen, and Morita (2016) are working through a key debate about the infra-ness of infrastructures. Bowker and Star (1999) have noted that the mundane standards and routines that make an infrastructure function are hardly attended to by users of their facilities. Only at the moment of the breakdown/splintering of infrastructures or through research by infrastructure scholars does one get an analysis of the hidden workings of infrastructures. More recently, Brian Larkin (2013) has noted that invisibility might not be the defining characteristic of infrastructures, because some infrastructures are indeed very noticeable and are

championed and publicized by the government. Harvey, Jensen, and Morita (2016) contend that it is one thing to glorify mediated images of satellites and another to understand the actual operations of satellites. I agree with them but disagree with their suggestion that media tends to emphasize only the former and not the latter.

38 Some of the debates and issues related to radiant infrastructures persist, making my archive of media objects, media events, and media genres related to these issues ever-expanding. At times, the issues are out of circulation for a while and then come back again. The catalysts and triggers that bring them back into the news vary: the announcement of a new policy measure with respect to cell towers, the opening of a film festival on uranium, a report of a cell tower antenna turned in the direction of a celebrity's balcony, steam spillage from a nuclear reactor, a viral tweet about a mishap in a nuclear power plant, or corruption charges related to buying nuclear equipment. The issues have continued to grab media attention because the objects' technical specificities lend them ontological indeterminacies, and their ability to attach discourses and institutions to them gives them long mediated biographies. Radiant infrastructures become part of the tales being told about their acquired *associates* (organizations and ideologies) as well.

39 I have avoided essentializing the differences between the two infrastructures and their respective environmental publics. I have refused to dismiss the agitation of wealthy urbanites against cell towers as just another case of NIMBYism ("not in my backyard"–ism). To not be able to sympathize with their heightened sensitivity toward EMFs would be a refusal to acknowledge a fellow human being's pain and sensorial knowledge. That being said, to fail to call out the state and the media on their hypocrisy and double standards when dealing with two different populations (wealthy urbanites and rural fishermen) would be irresponsible. Likewise, I cannot just treat the affected fishing community fighting against nuclear reactors in Koodankulam as collateral damage. They are people with remarkable vitality and agency, as demonstrated by their resilient protests.

40 Sheila Jasanoff's *Designs on Nature* (2007), as a comparative study, examines one technology (biotechnology) in three developed countries: the United Kingdom, the United States, and Germany. In contrast, my attempt in this book is to look at two different infrastructures within the same nation. My comparative project could have explained how cultural differences in India and the United States influence antinuclear activism, or I could have enumerated the similarities and differences between Indian and British ways of apprehending nonionizing EMFs from cell towers. Instead, I have chosen to compare controversies related to two infrastructures to suggest that radiation, India, and media are not a monolith. I have tried to stress differences internal to India, radiation, and media.

1. Debating Cell Towers

1 After new laws prescribing stricter regulation of cell tower signals were passed in late 2012, public anxiety about cell towers subsided for a bit only to rise up again in early 2015 with the call drops issue (Roy 2014).

2 The number keeps increasing; for a more up-to-date figure, consult the Indus Towers website: http://www.industowers.com/who_we_are.php (accessed July 12, 2015).

3   Mobile phones in their communication with cell antennas also emit signals, and there were concerns raised about risks from cell phones in India as well. However, people felt they could regulate their use of mobile phones, while exposure to base station signals was beyond their control. Jack Stilgoe (2005), discussing mobile phone risks in the late-1990s United Kingdom, mentions similar public fear. Schulz, Hartung, Diviani, and Keller (2012) take this a bit further by suggesting that while experts present cell phones as more risky than cell towers, the wider society considers radiation emissions from cell towers to be more dangerous than cell phone radiation. These health communication scholars suggest that this divergence in views between experts and laypersons can be explained by how media coverage impacts perception. Their paper's contentions about expert-layperson differences and newspaper coverage seem specific to Switzerland, and hence difficult to generalize. In this book, I have tried to think of cell towers as infrastructures (not in isolation but) in relation to cell phones.

4   "Is Radiation from Mobile Towers Dangerous?," broadcast on CNN-IBN's *Living It Up*, October 6, 2012. See "Living It Up_Is Radiation from Mobile Phone Towers Dangerous," YouTube, posted March 25, 2013, by NESARADIATIONS, http://www.youtube.com/watch?v=S3C10yC50bg.

5   Deora's Twitter feed can be viewed at https://twitter.com/milinddeora/status /247561524892270592.

6   Around the time that NDTV dedicated an episode of *We the People* to the cell tower radiation issue, another leading television channel, CNN-IBN, also reported on this issue in its lifestyle show *Living It Up*. This is discussed further in chapter 3.

7   Wayne Munson (1993) provides a lovely articulation of how "talkshow" combines the two communicative paradigms of "talk" and "show": "The 'talkshow' fuses and seems to reconcile two different, even contradictory, rhetorics. It links conversation, the interpersonal, and the premodern oral tradition, with the mass-mediated spectacle form of modernity. It becomes, among other things, a recuperative practice reconciling technology and commodification with community, mass culture with the individual and the local, production with consumption" (6).

8   Talk shows are not merely deliberative forums but are also experiential platforms. The affective charge of televisual testimonies and heated arguments should not be reduced to stage-managed spectacle. Talk shows connect intimate private feelings and public sentiments, and disrupt the individual-collective dichotomy (see Berlant 2008). Talk shows on Indian television channels have been compared to think tanks (Mehta 2013) and to commercial infotainment (achieved by mixing news and reality show qualities) (Thussu 2014). I believe *We the People* can be considered to have both of these characteristics, but these generalizations do not do justice to what happens in a specific episode or the particular characteristics of media practices that govern the production of *We the People*. The preoccupation with texts and their meanings eschews discussion about the spatiotemporal experiences of their production and reception contexts, and I hope my methodology has been a corrective.

9   While *We the People* does not display real-time tweets in the form of scrolling text (moving across the television screen) during the show, the Twitter activity

surrounding the show can be tracked by collecting the tweets associated with the talk show's Twitter handle @WeThePeopleNDTV and Dutt's own Twitter handle (@bdutt) on June 28, 2015, the day of the screening. *We the People* collection of tweets from June 28, 2015, https://twitter.com/search?vertical=default&q=%40WeThePeopleNDTV%20since%3A2015–06–28%20until%3A2015–06–29&src=typd.

10 "Call Drop Compensation Rules Stay, TRAI to Hear Out Telecom Operators," *Indian Express*, December 25, 2015, http://indianexpress.com/article/technology/tech-news-technology/call-drop-compensation-rules-stay-trai-to-hear-out-telecom-operators/.

11 "No Compensation for Call Drops, TRAI Regulation Unreasonable, Arbitrary: Supreme Court," *Indian Express*, May 12, 2016, http://indianexpress.com/article/technology/tech-news-technology/trai-regulations-on-call-drops-arbitrary-unreasonable-says-sc/.

12 See "VK Residents Protest DDA Nod to Cell Towers," *Times of India*, August 26, 2015, http://timesofindia.indiatimes.com/city/delhi/VK-residents-protest-DDA-nod-to-new-cell-towers/articleshow/48674339.cms.

13 There are many ways of hiding or making inconspicuous cell antenna structures. For a consideration of such practices, see Lisa Parks's (2010) essay on antenna trees.

14 Unlike antinuke campaigns, the anti–cell tower movement is not focused on street protests. There were a few street protests by antiradiation activists. In New Delhi, the DoT facilitated negotiations between regulators, cellular operators, concerned citizens, and parliamentary boards.

15 The work of scholars on toxic e-waste and the enormous amount of energy required to maintain the data storage centers of social media companies like Facebook and of search engine giants like Google has challenged assumptions about "clean" and "green" ICTs (see Grossman 2007; Hogan 2015b).

16 Scandals related to the allocation of the 2G spectrum for cellular traffic transmission that began in 2008 revealed that some government officials and Indian politicians were colluding with cell phone companies (Jeffrey and Doron 2013).

2. Contested Nuclear Imaginaries

1 Following the 2008 Indo-US nuclear deal, Indian markets have been opened to investment from foreign nuclear energy corporations like Areva (France) and Toshiba-Westinghouse (Japan–United States). What were once touted as indigenously developed nuclear energy technologies developed by Indian scientists now have begun to be seen as dependence on foreigners for nuclear fuel and reactor designs. Earlier, the Indian nuclear corporation could afford to remain insulated, but now with opening itself up to foreign suppliers and investors, it has also exposed its activities to public criticism from Indian citizens.

2 Such mediations carry embodied meanings and material effects: they sound the alarm for communities living close to plants or allay their apprehensions regarding proximate reactors, they bolster or break the confidence of some people who believe nuclear energy is the solution to India's power problems, they prompt the state to be politically responsive toward affected populations, or they continue

to make the government and middle class treat certain populations as expend-
able. Thus, mediating nuclear reactors is soaked in affective intensities, and such
intensities have material consequences.

3 The NPCIL stages plays for the general public in sites where new nuclear plants
are being built, inevitably featuring a character who opposes nuclear energy and
who often happens to speak "Butler English," connoting his scientific illiteracy.

4 In Nagercoil and Idinthakarai in January 2018, I spoke to several antinuke
activists from Tamil Nadu who mentioned that journalists in India lack both
funds and training to fact-check and verify aspersions cast by the government
on PMANE activists. The journalists just repeat the words of the government.
Furthermore, living in New Delhi, some mainstream media journalists simply do
not know what is happening in Tamil Nadu or the lived realities of the people of
the state.

5 The *Chai Kadai* blog became a site of networked convergence where news and
reports from various media formats were aggregated. The blog's operators and
moderators are from Chennai, which is the capital of the state of Tamil Nadu,
the same province where Koodankulam is located. The Chennai Solidarity
Group for Koodankulam Struggle had taken up the cause of the Koondakulam
protesters, and the *Chai Kadai* blog became the site to mediate the activities in
Koodankulam to the world and the responses of the world regarding Koondakulam. A glance through the blog reveals a remarkable heterogeneity: a scanned
letter by the eminent writer and activist Mahashewta Devi to the Congress Party
president Sonia Gandhi (urging the latter to visit Koodankulam and to ensure that
people there are treated with compassion) can be found alongside poems written
by Koodankulam activists. The stress in these blogs is on details that cannot be
accommodated in mainstream media: a number of long reports such as site evalu-
ations for proposed nuclear power plants, reports of juries of the High Court, and
sections (laws) under which people around Koodankulam have been charged.

6 This alternative mediation arrangement had its own gatekeeping tactics. The
following is what Jayaraman had to say on that topic: "We have set up a response
team . . . that will do nothing but get information, verify, because there is a lot of
bad information coming. Not intentionally, but people panicking, saying they
are going to attack us now. I cannot keep putting that out because what it does is,
it is making my thing valueless. Crying hoax. What we stopped was predictions,
but happenings we would report. After cross-verifying. One people. Two people"
(Nityanand Jayaraman, interview excerpt, Chennai, November 20, 2012).

7 See Jyothy Karat's photo-essay on Koodankulam, accessed June 20, 2015, https://
www.scrollkit.com/s/c5sV4bz.

8 See the News-X channel news segment titled "Kudankulam Protest: Activists Find Welcome Ally in Facebook," YouTube, posted September 22, 2012, by
NewsX, https://www.youtube.com/watch?v=y5n_AHfK8mo.

9 Some antinuclear activists are aware of the existence of Twitter trends and Facebook's news feed algorithms and have received offers to buy services from social
media and crowdsourcing companies in order to increase the visibility of their
blogs and campaigns.

10 The fasting/protesting responsibilities have been divided between fifteen villages; these villages send designated people each day to fast, and the responsibilities rotate. The money for the protests comes from an innovative tax system called Theripu, in which, once a week, fishermen have to part with one-tenth of the revenue they earn from their day's catch. If fishing is stopped, sometimes as a mark of protest, women make *bidis* (tobacco rolled in leaves) while fasting to sustain themselves economically. Sometimes, food supplies and money come from neighboring fishing hamlets. These organizing methods, based on the ideas and practices of commons, solidarity, and cooperation, ensure a long life for the protest.

11 Some of these disruptions can be seen as affective responses to technological disruptions (leakage of steam, aka "hot run"), the discursive spillage of fear (news of the Fukushima disaster), and the visceral intensity of police brutalities (lathi charges). That being said, each such "spontaneous" protest cannot be all that spontaneous; it needs some organization. Not only do the long intervals between disruptions require organizing, but disruptions too have their collective dynamics, which cannot merely be reduced to self-organizing (autopoeisis).

12 Narmada Bachao Andolan is the famous anti-dam movement in India, seeking to resist the largest river valley hydro-irrigation project of the country across the Narmada River.

13 As a child, Stephen was raised among narratives extolling the wonders of nuclear power and the safety of atomic power plants. Raminder Kaur (2017) discusses similar nuclear subjectivities and imaginaries being cultivated among people living in Anushakti Nagar, the atomic township of the Bhabha Atomic Research Center in Mumbai, where the virtues of nuclear power as the technology of producing electricity with the lowest greenhouse gas emissions were often touted. To continue with Stephen's story, it was during his stint as a photojournalist in Bangalore that he heard about an accident in Kaiga (Kaiga is in the state of Karnataka and Bangalore is the capital of that state). That was when Stephen decided to question the efficacy of nuclear power and comprehend the risks of producing atomic electricity.

14 I interviewed Stephen at Dr. Udayakumar's Nagercoil residence on January 1, 2018. I have paraphrased some of his answers.

15 It would be simply inadequate to reduce PMANE's struggles to antinuclear imaginaries of future (nuclear) calamities. Disaster scripts have been one kind of nuclear imaginary brought forth in popular protest culture, but they are limiting because they remain contained within the nuclear domain and do not engage with the rich material worlds of the protesters. The antinuclearism of PMANE may sound stubborn; protesters' suspicion of the government might seem to be bordering on psychosis, but their right/claim/voice/insistence to script their own future cannot be denied.

16 Jayaraman's piece, entitled "No More Empty Promises: Koodankulam Wants Concrete Safety Measures," can be found at the *Tehelka* magazine site: http://archive.tehelka.com/story_main53.asp?filename=Ne220912No.asp.

17 These fireworks are often used in the festival of Diwali, and 70 percent of India's total fireworks production takes place in Sivakasi.

18 The French nuclear supplier Areva's project MW Olkiluoto in Finland is behind schedule, and spending on the plant has been 50 percent more than the initial budget. Many countries, such as Egypt, Turkey, and South Africa, would like to open nuclear plants, but there is no funding.

19 The prime minister at the time, Manmohan Singh, was hailed as "Singh Is King" by a section of the Indian press for his dogged pursuit of the deal against some stiff opposition from various political parties and civic organizations. See Katyal (2015).

20 See "No Nuke Deals in India Unless Liability Issue Is Resolved," *Hindu*, July 11, 2014, http://www.thehindu.com/news/national/no-nuke-deals-in-india-unless -liability-issue-is-resolved/article6200641.ece.

21 The second film, completed in 2012, deals with cancer cases in the vicinity of the Kalapakkam reactor, which is also located in the state of Tamil Nadu. The third film, released in 2012, shows the enthusiasm and courage of fishing communities that protest against the nuclear reactor in Koodankulam. Considered together, the three documentaries help us comprehend the infrastructure of nuclear reactors, not in isolation but in relation to uranium and monazite mining.

22 Anand Patwardhan is not only one of the founders of the independent political documentary film movement in India but also one of the first Indian filmmakers to take up the nuclear issue as a documentary subject. Patwardhan's *Jung Aur Aman* (War and peace), an epic documentary made in the wake of nuclear tests conducted by India and Pakistan in May 1998, contains footage taken over three years (beginning in 1998) across India, Pakistan, Japan, and the United States. Patwardhan's documentary critiques the ideologies and practices behind the growth of nuclear weapons in India and relates such activities to more than fifty years of history, geopolitical transformations, politico-economic, and sociopsychological issues, as well as environmental and ethical concerns (Hess 2005, 155). Patwardhan has most certainly been an influence on Amudhan, and when queried about transnational inspirations, Amudhan somewhat predictably cites Latin American directors like Fernando Solanas and Patricio Guzmán. Patwardhan has often noted the influence of revolutionary Latin American cinema (including Solanas and Guzmán) on the alternative documentaries he has made since the late seventies (Patwardhan 1984; Hanlon 2014). I further queried Amudhan if he has watched Patricio Guzman's *Nostalgia for Light* (2010), where the legendary documentarian is in his lyrical essayistic avatar. Amudhan replied that he identifies more with the (earlier) Guzman of *Battle of Chile*, which appeared in three parts in 1975, 1976, and 1979.

23 They depict nuclear workers, villagers, and children living close to uranium mines and nuclear reactors whose bodies carry the scars of persistent exposure to radioactivity. Despite this corporeal evidence, there is scant official dosimetry research on irradiated populations, and the health authorities and nuclear physicists belonging to the nuclear establishment are found in the documentaries to be denying any correlation between cancer and nuclearization activities. I shall discuss this aspect in later chapters.

24 Hanlon (2014) writes about the "talking groups" interview strategy in the following manner: "The overlapping voices, captured in lengthy takes, create a revela-

tory pro-filmic rough cut of the film determined by the subjects that precedes and limits the filmmaker's later ordering of the material. Combined with the lack of voiceover narration, this technique ensures that the film's subjects have some degree of control over the film" (5).

25 Shriprakash's talk is available on YouTube: "Media Workshop—Shri Prakash (part 1)," YouTube, posted June 22, 2011, by kvtay, http://www.youtube.com/watch?v=2CvIgwoqIho&list=PL05CF2BCCB21ADA4D.

26 This particular interview must, however, be interpreted within the broader context of Shriprakash's documentary oeuvre. In all his films, the lived experiences of affected communities gain precedence over expert commentaries. Shriprakash's films demonstrate great sensitivity toward his documentary subjects. He has returned again and again to Jadugoda to work with local activists as people of that region continue to suffer because of UCIL's criminal negligence. He made another documentary, *Jadugoda—The Black Magic*, which was screened for the first time in 2007.

27 EPRs are the latest design in pressurized water reactors where cooling water surrounding the reactor core is kept at high pressure to prevent it from boiling. These reactors, Areva claims, generate more electricity using less fuel. Being a new design, EPRs in Finland and Hinkley Point are taking a very long time to construct. See Marshall (2013).

28 While the nuclear establishment centralizes power in its three institutions— Atomic Energy Regulatory Board, Nuclear Power Corporation of India Limited, Department of Atomic Energy—it carries out mining operations, runs nuclear reactors, and enacts waste disposal in a variety of regions in India, meeting opposition that is both politically and culturally diverse. An activist once told me that there is no one antinuclear movement in India. Some organizations oppose nuclear energy because it is not the best science for electrifying India, and others find it to be infringing on the livelihood rights of displaced farmers and fishermen.

29 It is true that this book contains analysis of more nonfictional texts than fiction media. One of the main reasons is that the controversies I study are fairly recent, and hence not many fiction works have emerged as yet. Another reason is that Bollywood has never produced a definitive work on the nuclear energy issue. That said, Bollywood has significantly engaged with the nuclear weapons issue. More on why that is the case will be discussed in chapter 5.

3. Emissions

1 Ramana (2009) adds that whenever the NPCIL has been asked for information related to nuclear weapons and/or nuclear energy, it invokes the 1962 Atomic Energy Act and the Official Secrets Act to justify its refusal to divulge information that might embarrass the nuclear establishment or provide damning evidence of cover-ups.

2 While one could argue, and some have, that Indian taxpayers basically fund the NPCIL's activities and hence it is answerable to Indian citizens, the relationship or connection between the entities seems indirect.

3 Soon after India's independence, as citizens of a newly postcolonial developing nation, many Indians were in awe of cutting-edge nuclear technologies and
believed that embracing nuclear science would make India a superpower in the
future (Chaudhuri 2012). The public euphoria in India that followed the successful testing of nuclear arsenals in 1998 was termed "nuclear nationalism" by
Bidwai and Vanaik (1999). The tests were touted as having led to a resurgence
of national pride in India's sovereignty, development programs, and scientific
capability.

4 Many infrastructure scholars have noted that human workers are very much a
part of infrastructural processes and should be accounted for in any infrastructural analysis (Parks 2015).

5 As part of the nuclear workforce, casual workers/contract laborers are exploited
not only in India but also in many other parts of the world. In Fukushima's and
Chernobyl's post–nuclear fallout, it was contract laborers who were involved
in cleaning radiation from reactors' drywells and spent-fuel pools. See Tabuchi
(2011) and the remarkable work of anthropologist Adriana Petryna (2013). In
India, such workers are paid low wages and often do not receive health benefits.

6 See the home page for the portal: https://tarangsanchar.gov.in/emfportal.

7 Sinha quoted in "Now a Portal to Check Mobile Tower Radiation," *Times of
India*, May 2, 2017, http://timesofindia.indiatimes.com/business/india-business
/now-a-portal-to-check-radiation-level-of-mobile-towers/articleshow/58528978
.cms.

8 R. S. Sharma is cited here in the Ministry of Communication's own press release
about the launch event: "Department of Telecom (DoT) Launches Tarang
Sanchar, a Web Portal for Information Sharing on Mobile Towers and EMF
Emission Compliance," Press Information Bureau, Government of India, May 2,
2017, http://pib.nic.in/newsite/PrintRelease.aspx?relid=161464.

9 Sharma in "Department of Telecom (DoT) Launches Tarang Sanchar."

10 While espousing a very different political ideology than Modi, former president
Barack Obama too was criticized for mobilizing certain ideas of transparency
to boost his presidential persona, campaigns, and governmental activities. By
exposing some of the Bush-era secrets regarding the "War on Terror," by creating
Gov 2.0 through Web 2.0–enabled sites sharing climate change and other data
gathered by federal agencies, and by issuing intra-agency reviews of classification
procedures, Obama attempted to show a commitment to transparency. That
being said, much of the information made transparent regarding Guantánamo
Bay or water boarding–related torture activities was not actionable. Thus, transparency helped Obama gain moral credit through revelation, but it did not help
victims or survivors seek justice. Claire Birchall (2011) has powerfully made this
argument about the limitations of Obama's transparency initiatives. Thus, Modi
and Obama share transparency as a neoliberal ideal of governance.

11 Such a metadata-generation facility was encoded into crowd-sensed radiation-
map platforms during the period after the Fukushima Daiichi disaster to ascertain safe radiation levels in Japan. For more, see Jean-Christophe Plantin's work
"The Politics of Mapping Platforms" (2015).

12 Details about Airtel's Open Network Initiative can be found at https://www
.airtel.in/opennetwork/.

13 Refer to the CIS analysis of the Open Network Initiative at https://cis-india.org
/telecom/blog/airtel-open-network.

14 Dietmar Offenhuber (2017) makes a similar point, tying together infrastructural
governance and infrastructural representation through a different case study,
that of information about waste infrastructures and their various information
visualizations.

15 See the paper written by former Atomic Energy Regulatory Board chairman A.
Gopalakrishnan, "Resolve Koodankulam Issues" (2013).

4. Exposures

1 See "Chernobyl Sheep Controls Lifted in Wales and Cumbria," BBC, March 22,
2012, http://www.bbc.com/news/uk-wales-17472698.

2 "Unwanted intimacy" is an analytical category that anthropologist Kath Weston
uses to explain the nature of the entanglement of bodies and radiation in post-
Fukushima Japan. Unlike cases where controlled radiation is used to medically
treat cancer, Weston (2017, 80) writes, Japanese citizens did not ask for uncontrolled radiation fallout from Fukushima, and they did not invite radioactive
isotopes to find home in their bodies. Thus, this kind of radioactive embodiment
was an "unwanted intimacy."

3 Uranium mines and nuclear wastelands form, respectively, the front end and
back end of the nuclear energy infrastructure, as the former provides uranium for
the nuclear fuel cycle and the latter deals with the waste generated as a by-product
of energy-making activities in the atomic power plant. In considerations of the
sustainability of civilian nuclear energy, uranium mining activities and nuclear
waste storage and treatment often get little attention in popular discourse as both
pro-nuclear and antinuclear advocates concentrate on nuclear reactors. Writing
about the geopolitics of nuclear technoscience, the historian of science Gabrielle
Hecht (2009a) has noted that uranium mining was not even considered "nuclear"
activity for a long time, even as several public health experts have contended that
"uranium miners . . . as a group, are exposed to higher amounts of internal radiation than are workers in any other segment of the nuclear energy industry" (901).

4 There are three types of ionizing radiation in nuclear production: alpha particles
travel short distances and can be stopped by a thin sheet of paper; beta particles
travel twenty feet and require plastic shielding; and gamma rays travel farther
than one hundred feet and penetrate the human body.

5 In his remarkable book *Atomic Light (Shadow Optics)*, Akira Lippit (2005)
describes psychology, cinema, and X-rays as "phenomenologies of the inside" to
understand the twentieth-century drive (amid the catastrophic atomic bomb-
ings) for hypervisibility, for lighting up the depths of the interior body, and for
making everything transparent.

6 Monazite is a complex mineral from which radioactive thorium is extracted. It is
hoped that thorium will be used in fast breeder nuclear reactors, which will reduce
India's dependence on uranium as the key nuclear ore. India has rich deposits of

thorium but scant quantities of uranium. This explains the attraction for thorium. However, thorium-based reactors in India (and worldwide) have not yet been realized; they remain in research or planning stages. As Itty Abraham (2012) writes, "After 15 years of research and development and 10 years of construction, India's first 'prototype' fast breeder reactor is due to be commissioned in 2012. However, it will not use thorium as fuel. Thorium remains a value *in potentia*" (110).

7   Christine Marran (2017) emphasizes this specificity of the human body's reaction to external pollutants and its documentation in films by Noriaki Tsuchimoto about Minamata mercury poisoning.

8   In an incisive and evocative essay, Brian Taylor (1997) explains how photojournalist Carole Gallagher's documentary images of "downwinder" (nuclear) bodies in *American Ground Zero: The Secret Nuclear War* contest the official epidemiological discourse of the US nuclear state. Gallagher's pictures are of people in Utah who encountered radioactive nuclides as they traversed downwind from the Nevada nuclear testing site. Amudhan's and Gallagher's camerawork strives to convey what it means to experience radioactive embodiment.

9   Some experts are sympathetic to the concerns of electro-sensitives but argue that reasons for their fear of EMFs have less to do with the intensity of radio waves and more to do with their own psychological condition. Psychological medicine scholars James Rubin and Simon Wessely (2015) explain that electro-sensitives definitely respond with symptoms (of breathlessness and irritation) when exposed to EMFs, and these responses are far more heightened than when they are not exposed to such energy fields. However, when the same experiment is performed double-blind with neither the researcher nor the participant knowing in which scenario a particular stimulus (EMF or non-EMF) has been introduced, the responses become random. According to Rubin and Wessely, electro-sensitives cannot quite detect with accuracy whether an EMF source is on or off. These scientists contend that electro-sensitives show a tendency to feel unwell when they think they have been exposed to EMFs, and so they are responding not to EMFs per se but to the fear of exposure to EMFs.

10 Some of the imaging techniques discussed here from X-rays to MRI scanning are themselves radiant technologies as they light up the inside of a human body, thus complicating boundaries between the public and the private, the interior and the exterior, scientific knowledge and popular culture. The luminosity of cinema and X-ray has been written about in compelling ways in canonical studies by Lisa Cartwright (*Screening the Body*, 1995) and Akira Lippit (*Atomic Light (Shadow Optics)*, 2005). Furthermore, the propensity of antinuke documentary filmmakers, radiologists, and lifestyle show hosts (discussed in this chapter) to lay bare the interior of the body to make evidentiary claims about radiation exposure could well be purported to have a voyeuristic or sadistic gaze. However, it will be reductive to view the filmmaker, radiologist, and researcher as mere voyeurs because there is indeed so much more at stake about fighting obstinate nuclear plant operators and the greedy cellular phone industry with "scientific" evidence. Radiologists and documentary filmmakers make themselves vulnerable to exposure while filming or scanning radiated subjects, and thus their own bodies

occupy an unstable position with respect to the gaze. Within a more historical context, Cartwright (1995) discusses this complicated relationship between bodies, images, and the X-ray apparatus.

11 Affect is emotion and visceral intensity, and it is not fundamentally opposed to knowing/knowledge (see Soneryd 2007). Being affectively moved by patient testimonies and cell phone/antenna signals contributes to a sensory knowledge and is part of a phenomenological adjustment to the environment.

12 The stress on the experiential and the everyday, in addition to the often exclusively dominant discursive ethos of defining publics (seen in the work of even Warner and Fraser, not to mention Habermas) that Negt and Kluge emerge with, makes their take on the public sphere truly refreshing. Generative links can also be found between Kluge's work and Lauren Berlant's (2011) formulation of intimate public sphere.

13 Furthermore, SAR at best tests for (only) heating effects, and there are no tests for biological effects.

14 As Aihwa Ong (1996) notes, citizenship is not just an assignation but a "political subjectification" that needs to be iteratively performed by the state and its subjects. Nikhil Anand (2017) has usefully extended such studies of citizenship to matters of infrastructure in postcolonial India through his book *Hydraulic City*.

5. Styling Advocacy

1 See Anupam Chakravarty's interview with Suchanek (Chakravarty 2013). Suchanek's answer pinpoints something that at once is almost an essentialist thing to utter and at the same time seems very apparent: it is highly improbable that a politically committed Indian documentarian will make a film on cell tower radiation and that a mainstream television lifestyle show (like *Living It Up*) will feature fishermen communities affected by the construction of the Koodankulam nuclear reactor. *Living It Up* is an urban lifestyle show, but then, when has a lifestyle show not been urban? Can we think of fisherwomen communities in rural Tamil Nadu as having a lifestyle? Why do these communities seem to be talked about only in relation to their livelihoods? Perhaps vocabularies are not that innocent; they stand in for, are convenient shorthands for, and sometimes hide knowledge practices within them.

2 See "Koodankulam Women Get This Year's Chingari Awards," DiaNuke.org, December 2, 2012, http://www.dianuke.org/koodankulam-women-get-this-years -chingari-awards/.

3 Borrowing from Chatterjee's work, science studies scholars such as Shiju Varughese (2012) have suggested that people's engagement with the state-technoscience (Government of India–NPCIL) duo in India cannot always be conceptualized within the legitimate sphere of civil society. There are "scientific-citizen publics" (civil society) and "quasi publics" (political society): while the scientific-citizen publics are part of technical democracy in the same way that Western liberal democracies envisage public engagements with science to be, the "quasi-publics" of science are treated as populations to be governed and not to dialogue with. There is thus a hierarchy of publics to be found in the deeply

divided social fabric of India. Are the anti–cell tower radiation activists part of the scientific-citizen publics? Do the antinuke activists belong to quasi publics?

4   Indeed, Ajay Gudavarthy (2012) has edited a collection of essays that celebrate and criticize Chatterjee's formulation of "political society."

5   *Matru Ki Bijlee Ka Mandola* (dir. Vishal Bhardwaj), a Bollywood film released in January 2013 and set in the state of Haryana, shows how a politician and local industrialist who are initially unable to acquire land from villagers to build a car factory then instigate the banks to ask for loan repayments from those rural farmers. The film in fact goes further and highlights a whole set of dependencies that the government can exploit to pressure farmers: as it proceeds, the government prevails on wholesale dealers to stop buying grains from obdurate farmers unwilling to sell their land, who have had a good crop but do not know where to sell it. With the government storage facilities also out of the fighting farmers' reach, in *Matru* we see their grain finally being spoiled by rain. I raise these representations of political negotiations between the Indian state and population groups to suggest that nuclear reactors are not the only contexts in which such relationships unfold, and at the same time to emphasize that we need to explore the nuances of these political relationships and not concentrate only on "nuclear" issues while discussing nuclear energy debates in India. In fact, discussing only nuclear issues tends to isolate the plight of local communities that have to struggle against such coercive tactics by the government.

6   *We the People*, NDTV's most prestigious talk show, never took up the nuclear energy issue. Is *We the People* symptomatic of the media's commitment to the principles of liberal democracy, which fails to attend to the problems of the subaltern populations? These questions are critical and need to be asked. However, can the absence of debates about the nuclear issue on *We the People* be less about structural constraints and more about media practices? The antinuke activists may not have approached Barkha Dutt with a request for highlighting their issue, something that Sudhir Kasliwal, the jeweler from Jaipur, had done. Did antinuke activists not have the contacts to reach Barkha Dutt, or did they of their own volition not think *We the People* to be a suitable venue for publicizing the issue? I have already discussed how some of the debates on other news segments and special features of NDTV dealt with the issue of mushrooming nuclear reactors. What was missing from all such shows was an engagement with people who were going to face the consequences of the reactors being built close to their homes. NDTV never covered a public hearing where affected populations gathered to voice their apprehensions about such reactors.

7   Raminder Kaur (2013c) contends that Chakrabarty's description cannot be said to account for everything that happens at a public hearing. Kaur herself attended a hearing related to the construction of the Koodankulam plant on October 6, 2006. Rather than providing a snapshot of particular spectacular events, Kaur's ethnographic account of the hearing stresses the processual nature of activities that occurred: the hearing includes moments where the officials are indeed humiliated by the gathered public, but it also affords a space where antinuclear activists and local communities can network with other concerned antinuclear

campaigners and work toward sustaining their movement against nuclear energy. The public hearing also provides opportunities to government officials to identify key dissenters and mark them for further surveillance and intimidation.

8 All this is not to suggest that the government does not have its own vision of the environment or that the government does not support a certain variant of environmentalism. Consider, for example, the cleaning drives by Prime Minister Narendra Modi for his campaign Swacch Bharat (Clean India!). India does face sanitation problems with household waste being thrown in public and the widespread practice of open defecation. While the Modi government has tried its best to scuttle the environmental activities of Greenpeace, it has contributed substantial funding to clean Indian public spaces. Modi's campaign is mostly targeted toward middle-class urban populations receiving endorsements and support from corporate and entertainment elites on social media and beyond. The buzz around the hashtag #MyCleanIndia is immense, and the participation of Indian middle-class youth in such a project as responsible citizens is laudable. That being said, the program targets elite urban youth and portrays urban poor as lesser citizens who engage in uncivil behavior by not being able to observe proper sanitation habits. The anthropologist Assa Doron (2016) points out that the Swacch Bharat campaign "endorses a narrowly defined view of citizenship that has an understanding of civility and public behavior that is rarely afforded to the 'unruly' urban poor" (3–4). This kind of bourgeois environmentalism has been practiced for a while in urban areas.

9 Aparna Sundar (2010) finds that fishworkers in South India participate both in civic organizations emerging due to the expansion of state and capital and in their own autonomous local associations. This leads Sundar to argue that "civil society is present as a sphere of autonomous and routinized association and publicity—among subaltern groups in rural India" (30).

10 See the TV9 Marathi coverage at https://www.google.com/url?q=https://www.youtube.com/watch?v%3DB8_NMBuiInw&source=gmail&ust=155078082999 4000&usg=AFQjCNElDdJjgvAMzJXJtM1SEK1cxEhoBw.

Conclusion

1 For more on electricity connections in India, see Leo Coleman's (2017) recent book and the documentary *Katiyabaaz* (2013) by Deepti Kakkar and Fahad Mustafa.

2 Indeed, several other infrastructures can be mentioned, especially the infrastructure of water access. Nikhil Anand (2017) has written an important book about water pipes in Mumbai, and the publics, political subjectivities, and regulatory frameworks that enfold such an infrastructure.

3 See J. S. Deepak's October 28, 2016, speech on YouTube: "Shri J S Deepak, Secretary DoT, on the Role of Telecommunication in India (Part 2)," YouTube, posted October 28, 2016, by Cellular Operators Association of India (COAI), https://www.youtube.com/watch?v=A4pZr5KZoac.

4 See Koide (2011). Due to his active involvement in antinuclear movements, Koide earned himself "an honorable form of purgatory as a permanent assistant

professor at Kyoto University." Before March 11, 2011, Koide's antinuke activism was regarded merely as noise. However, it became music after the Fukushima meltdown. Koide was widely interviewed on television, becoming "a new pop star," so to speak.

5   There have been collaborations between concerned Japanese and Belarusian mothers about the fate of their children following nuclear meltdowns. Director Hitomi Kamanaka, while documenting the efforts made by Japanese mothers to protect their children amid official secrecy in her film *Little Voices of Fukushima* (2015), travels to Belarus to learn more about how mothers have cared for their children there since the 1986 Chernobyl nuclear disaster.

6   Aya Hirata Kimura (2016) explains that antinuke activism was more about "concern" than "outrage." There is a gender politics to this popular scientific citizenship movement and to the government's reactions. Many of these "citizen scientists" were women: mothers trying to make sure their children did not consume cesium-137, mothers equipped with Geiger counters attempting to find their way (often unsuccessfully) into government schools to test the playground/ soil for radioactivity, mothers taking their children off the government-provided school lunch, and mothers opening radiation screening centers where food is tested by stricter standards than in the government-initiated program. We see some of these activities in Kamanaka's documentary *Little Voices of Fukushima*. The Japanese government has taken steps to ensure food safety, but the government has also sponsored the risk communication campaign "Eat to Support." In this campaign, these mothers were labeled "Radiation Brain Moms" and were criticized for their tactics of avoiding food from particular regions. Their worries and anxieties were labeled "unscientific," and their recalcitrance toward government-sanctioned food was seen as inflicting enormous economic and social damage on Japan.

7   Brickell and Datta (2011) argue that translocality as a "form of local-local relations" needs to be comprehended in the simultaneous "situatedness and connectedness" of these locales across "spaces, places and scales beyond the national" (3–4).

8   I wonder how Koodankulam locals will react to the documentary footage from ghost towns like Pripyat (close to Chernobyl), particularly the haunting drone footage of Chernobyl taken by British freelance filmmaker Danny Cooke for CBS's *60 Minutes*. Pripyat is not so much out of the map of Ukraine as simply peopleless (or almost so). Various flora and fauna flourish, undergoing strange mutations, but people have mostly abandoned the place.

9   Sometimes, nondiegetic sounds of ambulance vehicles, loudspeakers, and people's voices in consternation are inserted to connote the experience of haunting. At other times, the diegetic/ambient sounds of winds blowing and waves hitting the shore captured by the documentarians as Matsumura walks along the railway station and the beach are enough to convey the specter of radiation that is all around yet invisible.

10 Trimpop recounted this during a question-and-answer session following the screening of excerpts from *Furusato* at Philadelphia during an event (Documenting Nuclear Afterlives) that I co-organized in October 2017.

11 Thorsten Trimpop, *Furusato* Press Kit.

12 Trimpop is not alone in attending to the landscape. In the immediate aftermath of the Fukushima catastrophe, Toshi Fujiwara made a documentary, *No Man's Zone* (2011, "Mujin Chitai"), by entering the forbidden zone, where there still were people who could not leave (due to age or infirmity) or just did not want to leave. While interviewing people who continue living in the "red zone," Fujiwara does not linger on their faces or gestures in medium close-up but rather chooses to show the landscape, often in a controlled manner through long shots from a camera mounted on a tripod. See the work of Rachel DiNitto (2014, 348) and Joel Neville Anderson (2015).

13 I am referring to Belinda Smaill's book *Regarding Life* (2016). Smaill's concerns are with animals, and I am interested in other nonhuman things (and not just life) as well. Furthermore, Smaill uses the word "emotion," while I prefer "affect," while thinking of how nonhumans are used in ecodocs to persuade audiences.

14 See "Jaitapur Nuclear Plant No Threat to the Environment: Kakodkar," *Indian Express*, December 1, 2010, http://indianexpress.com/article/cities/pune/jaitapur-nuclear-power-plant-no-threat-to- environment-kakodkar/.

15 There are several reasons for the lack of fictional films directly engaging with nuclear reactors in India. There have not been any large nuclear reactor disasters in India, and the smaller accidents in the atomic power stations are brushed aside by the Indian nuclear establishment, as I have discussed at several places in this book. In some Bollywood films, there are generic references to nuclear scientists, and most of them seem to work on the bomb, but for some it remains unclear whether they work to produce nuclear energy or nuclear weapons. Some nuclear reactors also produce plutonium, which can be used for making bombs, and hence references to plutonium are both ambivalent and connect nuclear reactors with atomic weapons. Nuclear reactors are considered peaceful structures of technological modernity devoid of much action, and hence inadequate for a happening Bollywood film. For these insights, I am indebted to an email conversation with media anthropologist Raminder Kaur. Kaur agreed that while there are stray references here and there to reactors in films and comic books, she does not remember them being visualized in popular film. Kaur's co-authored book on adventure comics begins with a vignette that mentions Indian superheroes fighting insurgents around a nuclear reactor, and a "mini plutonium bomb" stolen from the Narora atomic power station (Kaur and Eqbal 2018, 1).

16 "Humanimal" is Pramod Nayar's (2014) term for a part-human, part-animal posthuman monster. The machinic aspect of Pakshi Rajan, along with it being part human and part bird, made me term it "posthuman humanimal machine."

17 Indeed, to use Raminder Kaur's (2013b) phrasing, *2.0* is more appositely understood as a speculative fiction than science fiction given its imaginative departures from scientific practices. Furthermore, it might best be called "speculative fiction masala" (Kaur 2013b) as it adds the *masala* elements such as melodramatic dialogues and song-and-dance routines to a routine sci-fi film. This gesture of invoking an ancient Indian civilizational past for posthuman figurations of the present can also be seen as a nod to the present Hindutva nationalism instincts that have

always problematically claimed a hypertechnologized mythic past. Here, the suggestion is that while presently India might not yet be a technological leader, in the past the nation was technologically supreme. Initially, the film *2.0*, by making the present estranged and open to uncertainties of electromagnetic signals, holds out the promise of "affirmative speculation" in its narrative, and yet by the end of the film, cellular phone technology is considered manageable, its uncertainties (embodied by Pakshi Rajan) can be tamed by enhanced updated technologies like Chitti 2.0. Thus, the film *2.0* as speculative fiction no longer makes the future open to radical differences and uncertainties, and thus remains within the ambit of "firmative speculation" (Uncertain Commons 2013).

18 Radio-frequency fields have been found to disrupt the orientation of birds. An article by Roswitha Wiltschko (2014) and her team suggests that radio-frequency fields do affect the avian magnetic compass by interfering with the process of magnetoreception. These scientists are careful to qualify that there are no long-term adverse effects because the birds, after exposure, are able to readjust to the local geomagnetic field after some time.

19 Joel M. Moskowitz, who researches and teaches at the School of Public Health, UC Berkeley, maintains the *Electromagnetic Radiation Safety* blog, where he discussed the 5G networks issue. See Moskowitz (2019).

20 Akira Lippit (2005) discusses optical light and shadow archives in connection to X-rays, another radiant technology.

21 Mike Hale (2019), reviewing *Chernobyl* (2018) for the *New York Times*, finds writer Craig Mazin and director Johan Renck taking too many fictional liberties so as to distract from the tragedy of the nuclear accident. Hale suggests that a documentary miniseries by Alex Gibney or Amy Berg would have offered a more candid portrait. While there is merit to Hale's argument, the narrative and popular appeal of the fictional miniseries is indeed powerful, and the podcasts following the episodes provide crucial fact-checks and admit to some of the manipulations made in service of a compelling narrative. Furthermore, documentary and facts should not be rigidly tied together. Documentary films are as much about desire as they are about evidence, and documentary itself defies genre as it could range from newsreels to docudramas. On a related note, in an email exchange, Raminder Kaur noted that a screening of the BBC docudrama on Chernobyl was received with much interest in Nagercoil in 2006 as audience members there were living about 30 kilometers from the Koodankulam nuclear reactor site. Kaur's forthcoming book discusses this screening in detail.

REFERENCES

Abraham, Itty. 1992. "India's Strategic 'Enclave': Civilian Scientists and Military Technologies." *Armed Forces and Society* 18 (2): 231–252.

Abraham, Itty. 2009. "Nuclear Power and Atomic Publics." In Itty Abraham, ed., *South Asian Cultures of the Bomb: Atomic Publics and the State in India and Pakistan*, 1–19. Bloomington: Indiana University Press.

Abraham, Itty. 2012. "Geopolitics and Biopolitics in India's High Natural Background Radiation Zone." *Science, Technology and Society* 17 (1): 105–122.

Adams, V., M. Murphy, and A. Clarke. 2009. "Anticipation: Technoscience, Life, Affect, Temporality." *Subjectivity* 28:246–265.

Agrawal, Parul. 2013. "Citizen Journalism: In Pursuit of Accountability in India." In James Painter, ed., *India's Media Boom: The Good News and the Bad*, 73–86. Oxford: Reuters Institute for the Study of Journalism.

Allan, Stuart. 2010. *News Culture*. 3rd ed. New York: Open University Press.

Alley, Jason. 2011. "Spaces of Reticence." *Media Fields Journal*, no. 3 (September). http://www.mediafieldsjournal.org/spaces-of-reticence/.

Anand, Nikhil. 2017. *Hydraulic City: Water and the Infrastructures of Citizenship in Mumbai*. Durham, NC: Duke University Press.

Appadurai, Arjun, and Carol A. Breckenridge. 1995. "Public Modernity in India." In Carol A. Breckenridge and Arjun Appadurai, eds., *Consuming Modernity: Public Culture in South Asia*, 1–65. Minneapolis: University of Minnesota Press.

Arya, Divya. 2013. "Why Are Indian Women Being Attacked on Social Media?" *BBC Hindi*, May 8. http://www.bbc.com/news/world-asia-india-22378366.

Ashar, Hemal. 2010. "Towers Sending Tumour Signals." *Mid-Day*, January 3. http://www.mid-day.com/news/2010/jan/030110-mobile-tower-cancer-cases -carmichaelroadposh-areas.htm.

Bagla, Pallava, and Richard Stone. 2012. "India's Scholar–Prime Minister Aims for Inclusive Development." *Science* 335 (6071) (February 24): 907–908. http:// science.sciencemag.org/content/335/6071/907.

Barad, Karen. 2007. *Meeting the Universe Halfway: Quantum Physics and the Entanglement of Matter and Meaning*. Durham, NC: Duke University Press.

Barad, Karen. 2017. "No Small Matter: Mushroom Clouds, Ecologies of Nothingness, and Strange Topologies of Spacetimemattering." In Anna Tsing, Heather Swanson, Elaine Gan, and Nils Bubandt, eds., *Arts of Living on a Damaged Planet*, G103–G120. Minneapolis: University of Minnesota Press.

Barton, J. Scott, and Brannon D. Ingram. 2015. "What Is a Public? Notes from South Asia." *South Asia: Journal of South Asian Studies* 38 (3): 357–370.

Basu, Anustup. 2011. "The Eternal Return and Overcoming 'Cape Fear': Science, Sensation and Hindu Nationalism in Recent Hindi Cinema." *South Asian History and Culture* 2 (4): 557–571.

Basu, Nupur. 2012. "Koodankulam's Nuclear Holy Cow." *Hoot*, December 18. http://www.thehoot.org/story_popup/kudankulam-s-nuclear-holy-cow-6375.

Bauman, Zygmund. 1993. *Postmodern Ethics*. Oxford: Blackwell.

Baviskar, Amita. 2011. "Cows, Cars and Cycle-Rickshaws: Bourgeois Environmentalists and the Battle for Delhi's Streets." In Amita Baviskar and Raka Ray, eds., *Elite and Everyman: The Cultural Politics of the Indian Middle Classes*, 391–418. New Delhi: Routledge.

Beck, Ulrich. 1992. *Risk Society: Towards a New Modernity*. London: Sage.

Bennett, Jane. 2010. *Vibrant Matter: A Political Ecology of Things*. Durham, NC: Duke University Press.

Bennett, Jill. 2007. "Aesthetics of Intermediality." *Art History* 30 (3): 432–450.

Berlant, Lauren. 2008. *The Female Complaint: The Unfinished Business of Sentimentality in American Culture*. Durham, NC: Duke University Press.

Berlant, Lauren. 2011. *Cruel Optimism*. Durham, NC: Duke University Press.

Bhadra, Monamie. 2012. "Disaster Scripting in India's Nuclear Energy Landscape." In *An STS Forum on Fukushima*. http://fukushimaforum.wordpress.com/workshops/sts-forum-on-the-2011-fukushima-east-japan-disaster/manuscripts/session-4a-when-disasters-end-part- i/disaster-scripting-in-indias-nuclear-energy-landscape/.

Bidwai, Praful, and Achin Vanaik. 1999. *South Asia on a Short Fuse: Nuclear Politics and the Future of Nuclear Disarmament*. New Delhi: Oxford University Press.

Birchall, Claire. 2011. "'There's Been Too Much Secrecy in This City': The False Choice between Secrecy and Transparency in US Politics." *Cultural Politics* 7 (1): 133–156.

Born, Erik Christopher. 2016. "Sparks to Signals: Literature, Science, and Wireless Technology, 1800–1930." PhD diss., University of California, Berkeley.

Bornstein, Erica, and Aradhana Sharma. 2016. "'The Righteous and the Rightful': The Technomoral Politics of NGOs, Social Movements, and the State in India." *American Ethnologist* 43 (1): 76–90.

Bowker, Geoffrey, and Susan Leigh Star. 1999. *Sorting Things Out: Classification and Its Consequences*. Cambridge, MA: MIT Press.

Brabham, Daniel. 2013. *Crowdsourcing*. Cambridge, MA: MIT Press.

Bradbury, David. 2013. "David Bradbury on Idinthakarai's Anti-nuclear Front Line." *Independent Australia*, March 16. https://independentaustralia.net/politics/politics-display/david-bradbury-on-idinthakarais-anti-nuclear-front-line,5105.

Braidotti, Rosi. 2011. "Meta(I)morphoses." In *Nomadic Theory: The Portable Rosi Braidotti*, 55–80. New York: Columbia University Press.

Brickell, Katherine, and Ayona Datta. 2011. "Introduction: Translocal Geographies." In Katherine Brickell and Ayona Datta, eds., *Translocal Geographies: Spaces, Places, Connections*, 3–20. Farnham, UK: Ashgate.

Brown, Kate. 2013. *Plutopia: Nuclear Families, Atomic Cities, and the Great Soviet and American Plutonium Disasters*. Oxford: Oxford University Press.

Brown, Kate. 2017. "Marie Curie's Fingerprint: Nuclear Spelunking in the Chernobyl Zone." In Anna Tsing, Heather Swanson, Elaine Gan, and Nils Bubandt, eds., *Arts of Living on a Damaged Planet*, G33–G50. Minneapolis: University of Minnesota Press.

Bruns, Axel, and Jean Burgess. 2011. "The Use of Twitter Hashtags in the Formation of Ad Hoc Publics." In *Proceedings of the 6th European Consortium for Political Research (ECPR) General Conference 2011*, University of Iceland, Reykjavik.

Burgess, Adam. 2004. *Cellular Phones, Public Fears, and a Culture of Precaution*. Cambridge: Cambridge University Press.

Burgess, Anthony. 2010. "Media Risk Campaigning in the UK: From Mobile Phones to 'Baby P.'" *Journal of Risk Research* 13 (1): 59–72.

Butler, Judith. 1990. *Gender Trouble: Feminism and the Subversion of Identity*. New York: Routledge.

Butler, Judith. 1993. *Bodies That Matter: On the Discursive Limits of "Sex."* New York: Routledge.

Button, Gregory. 2010. *Disaster Culture: Knowledge and Uncertainty in the Wake of Human and Environmental Catastrophe*. Walnut Creek, CA: Left Coast Press.

Callon, Michel, Pierre Lascoumes, and Yannick Barthe. 2001. *Acting in an Uncertain World: An Essay on Technical Democracy*. Cambridge, MA: MIT Press.

Canetti, Elias. 1984. *Crowds and Power*. New York: Farrar, Straus and Giroux.

Cardis, Elisabeth, and the Interphone Study Group. 2010. "Brain Tumor Risk in Relation to Mobile Telephone Use: Results of the INTERPHONE International Case-Control Study." *International Journal of Epidemiology* 39:675–694.

Cartwright, Lisa. 1995. *Screening the Body: Tracing Medicine's Visual Culture*. Minneapolis: University of Minnesota Press.

Chakrabarty, Dipesh. 2000. *Provincializing Europe: Postcolonial Thought and Historical Difference*. Princeton, NJ: Princeton University Press.

Chakrabarty, Dipesh. 2007. "'In the Name of Politics': Democracy of the Power of the Multitude in India." *Public Culture* 19 (1): 35–59.

Chakravarty, Anupam. 2013. "Bollywood Stars Could Act in the Romances around Nuclear Contamination." *Down to Earth*, January 4. http://www.downtoearth.org.in/content/bollywood-stars-could-act-romances-around-nuclear-contamination.

Chanan, Michael. 1990. "Rediscovering Documentary: Cultural Context and Intentionality." In Julianne Burton, ed., *The Social Documentary in Latin America*, 31–47. Pittsburgh: University of Pittsburgh Press.

Chatterjee, Partha. 2004. *The Politics of the Governed: Reflections on Popular Politics in Most of the World*. New York: Columbia University Press.

Chatterjee, Partha. 2010. "Democracy and Subaltern Citizens in India." In Gyanendra Pandey, ed., *Subaltern Citizens and Their Histories: Investigations from India and the USA*, 193–207. London: Routledge.

Chaudhuri, Maitrayee. 2010. "Indian Media and Its Transformed Public." *Contributions to Indian Sociology* 44 (1–2): 57–78.

Chaudhuri, Pramit Pal. 2012. "Someone's Got a Secret." *Bulletin of the Atomic Scientists: Nuclear Journalism in the Developing World*, December 19. http://thebulletin.org/nuclear-journalism-developing-world.

Chemmencheri, Sudheesh Ramapurath. 2015. "Subaltern Struggles and the Global Media in Koodankulam and Kashmir." *South Asia: Journal of South Asian Studies* 38 (2): 187–199.

Clarke, Bruce, and Linda Dalrymple Henderson. 2002. "Introduction." In Bruce Clarke and Linda Dalrymple Henderson, eds., *From Energy to Information: Representation in Science and Technology, Art and Literature*, 1–17. Stanford, CA: Stanford University Press.

Coleman, Leo. 2017. *A Moral Technology: Electrification as Political Ritual in India*. Ithaca, NY: Cornell University Press.

Collier, Stephen, James Christopher Mizes, and Antina von Schnitzler. 2016. "Preface: Public Infrastructures/Infrastructural Publics." *LIMN*, no. 7 (July). https://limn.it/articles/preface-public-infrastructures-infrastructural-publics/.

Collins Harry. 1987. "Certainty and the Public Understanding of Science: Science on Television." *Social Studies of Science* 17 (4): 689–713.

Cottle, Simon. 2013. "Environmental Conflict in a Global, Media Age: Beyond Dualism." In L. Lester and B. Hutchins, eds., *Environmental Conflict and the Media*, 19–33. New York: Peter Lang.

Couldry, Nick. 2010. "Theorizing Media as Practice." In Birgit Brauchler and John Postill, eds., *Theorizing Media and Practice*, 35–54. New York: Berghahn Books.

Couldry, Nick, and Anna McCarthy. 2004. "Orientations: Mapping MediaSpace." In Nick Couldry and Anna McCarthy, eds., *MediaSpace: Place, Scale and Culture in a Media Age*, 1–18. New York: Routledge.

Cox, Robert. 2010. *Environmental Communication and the Public Sphere*. Thousand Oaks, CA: Sage.

Cram, Shannon. 2016. "Living in Dose: Nuclear Work and the Politics of Permissible Exposure." *Public Culture* 28 (3): 519–539.

Daigle, Katy. 2011. "Delhi's Air as Dirty as Ever Despite Some Reforms." Associated Press, December 16. http://phys.org/news/2011–12-delhi-air-dirty-reforms.html.

Dayan, D., and E. Katz. 1992. *Media Events: The Live Broadcasting of History*. Cambridge, MA: Harvard University Press.

De, Rohit. 2014. "Rebellion, Dacoity, and Equality: The Emergence of the Constitutional Field in Postcolonial India." *Comparative Studies of South Asia, Africa and the Middle East* 34 (2): 260–278.

Dean, Jodi. 2002. *Publicity's Secret: How Technoculture Capitalizes on Democracy*. Ithaca, NY: Cornell University Press.

de la Cadena, Marisol. 2010. "Indigenous Cosmopolitics in the Andes: Conceptual Reflections beyond Politics." *Cultural Anthropology* 25 (2): 334–370.

Delicath, John W., and Kevin Michael DeLuca. 2003. "Image Events, the Public Sphere, and Argumentative Practice: The Case of Radical Environmental Groups." *Argumentation* 17 (3): 315–333.

DeLoughrey, Elizabeth. 2009. "Radiation Ecologies and the Wars of Light." *Modern Fiction Studies* 55 (3): 468–498.

Dembo, D., W. Morehouse, and L. Wykle. 1990. *Abuse of Power: Social Performance of Multinational Corporations: The Case of Union Carbide*. New York: New Horizons Press.

Dewey, John. (1927) 1991. *The Public and Its Problems*. Athens: Swallow Press, Ohio University Press.

DiNitto, Rachel. 2014. "Narrating the Cultural Trauma of 3/11: The Debris of Post-Fukushima Literature and Film." *Japan Forum* 26 (3): 340–360.

Doron, Assa. 2016. "Unclean, Unseen: Social Media, Civic Action, and Urban Hygiene in India." *South Asia: Journal of South Asian Studies* 39 (4): 715–739. http://dx.doi.org/10.1080/00856401.2016.1218096.

Dourish, Paul, and Genevieve Bell. 2001. "The Infrastructure of Experience and the Experience of Infrastructure." *Environment and Planning B: Planning and Design* 34 (3): 414–430.

Easterling, Keller. 2016. *Extrastatecraft: The Power of Infrastructure Space*. Brooklyn, NY: Verso Books.

Escobar, Arturo. 1999. "After Nature: Steps to an Antiessentialist Political Ecology." *Current Anthropology* 40 (1): 1–30.

ET Bureau. 2012. "Failure to Step Up Growth Could Impact National Security." *Economic Times*, August 16. https://economictimes.indiatimes.com/news /politics-and-nation/failure-to-step-up-growth-could-impact-national-security -manmohan-singh/articleshow/15509238.cms.

Fernandes, Leela. 2011. "Hegemony and Inequality: Theoretical Reflections on India's 'New' Middle Class." In Amita Baviskar and Raka Ray, eds., *Elite and Everyman: The Cultural Politics of the Indian Middle Classes*, 58–82. New Delhi: Routledge.

Fortun, Kim. 2001. *Advocacy after Bhopal: Environmentalism, Disaster, New Global Orders*. Chicago: University of Chicago Press.

Fortun, Kim. 2012. "Biopolitics and the Informating of Environmentalism." In Kaushik Sunder Rajan, ed., *Lively Capital: Biotechnologies, Ethics, and Governance in Global Markets*, 306–326. Durham, NC: Duke University Press.

Fortun, Kim, Lindsay Poirier, Alli Morgan, Brandon Costelloe-Kuehn, and Mike Fortun. 2016. "Pushback: Critical Data Designers and Pollution Politics." *Big Data and Society*, July–December, 1–14.

Foucault, Michel. 1978. "The Incitement to Discourse." In *The History of Sexuality*, trans. Robert Hurley, 17–36. New York: Pantheon Books.

Frickel, Scott, Sahra Gibbon, Jeff Howard, Joana Kempner, Gwen Ottinger, and David Hess. 2010. "Undone Science: Social Movement Challenges to Dominant Scientific Practice." *Science, Technology, and Human Values* 35 (4): 444–473.

Friedman, S. M. 2011. "Three Mile Island, Chernobyl, and Fukushima: An Analysis of Traditional and New Media Coverage of Nuclear Accidents and Radiation." *Bulletin of the Atomic Scientists* 67 (5): 55–65.

Friedman, Susan Stanford. 2013. "Why Not Compare?" In Rita Felski and Susan Stanford Friedman, eds., *Comparison: Theories, Approaches, Uses*, 34–45. Baltimore: John Hopkins University Press.

Fuller, Matthew. 2005. *Media Ecologies: Materialist Energies in Art and Technoculture*. London: MIT Press.

Gabrys, Jennifer. 2010. "Atmospheres of Communication." In Barbara Crow; Michael Longford, and Kim Sawchuk, eds., *The Wireless Spectrum: The Politics, Practices, and Poetics of Mobile Media*, 46–59. Toronto: University of Toronto Press.

Gabrys, Jennifer. 2016. *Program Earth: Environmental Sensing Technology and the Making of a Computational Planet*. Minneapolis: University of Minnesota Press.

Gabrys, Jennifer. 2018. "Environmental Sensing and 'Media' as Practice in the Making." In Jentery Sayers, ed., *The Routledge Companion to Media Studies and Digital Humanities*, 503–510. New York: Routledge.

Gadekar, Surendra. 1993. "A Special Issue on Rawatbhata." *Anumukti: A Journal Devoted to Non-nuclear India* 6 (5): 1–30.

Gadgil, Madhav, and Ramachandra Guha. 1995. *Ecology and Equity: The Use and Abuse of Nature in Contemporary India*. London: Routledge.

Gairola Khanduri, Rita. 2014. *Caricaturing Culture in India: Cartoons and History in the Modern World*. Cambridge: Cambridge University Press.

Gaonkar, Dilip. 2002. "Toward New Imaginaries: An Introduction." *Public Culture* 14 (1): 1–19.

Gessen, Masha. 2019. "What HBO's Chernobyl Got Right and What It Got Terribly Wrong." *New Yorker*, June 4. https://www.newyorker.com/news/our-columnists /what-hbos-chernobyl-got-right-and-what-it-got-terribly-wrong.

Ghertner, D. Asher. 2011. "Green Evictions: Environmental Discourses of a Slum-Free Delhi." In Richard Peet and Michael Watts, eds., *Global Political Ecology*, 145–166. Routledge: London.

Ghosh, Jayati. 2015. "Wake-Up Call on Call Drops—Glare on Tower Campaign, Spectrum." *Telegraph*, July 8. http://www.telegraphindia.com/1150708/jsp /frontpage/story_30340.jsp#.VZ_Z93rZhrJ.

Gillespie, Tarleton. 2012. "Can an Algorithm Be Wrong?" *LIMN*, no. 2 (March). http://limn.it/can-an-algorithm-be-wrong/.

Ginsburg, Faye D., Lila Abu-Lughod, and Brian Larkin, eds. 2002. "Introduction." In *Media Worlds: Anthropology on New Terrain*, 1–36. Berkeley: University of California Press.

Gopalakrishnan, A. 2013. "Resolve Koodankulam Issues." *New Indian Express-Chennai*, April 19. http://epaper.newindianexpress.com/107173/The-New-Indian -Express-Chennai/19042013#page/8/2.

Gordon, Avery. 2008. *Ghostly Matters: Haunting and the Sociological Imagination*. Minneapolis: University of Minnesota Press.

Govil, Nitin. 2015. "On Comparison." *Media Industries* 1 (3): 1–6.

Graham, Stephen. 2010. "When Infrastructures Fail." In Stephen Graham, ed., *Disrupted Cities: When Infrastructures Fail*, 1–27. New York: Routledge.

Grindon, Leger. 2007. "Q&A: Poetics of the Documentary Film Interview." *Velvet Light Trap* 60:4–12.

Grossman, Elizabeth. 2007. *High Tech Trash: Digital Devices, Hidden Toxics, and Human Health*. Washington, DC: Island Press.

Gudavarthy, Ajay, ed. 2012. *Reframing Democracy and Agency: Interrogating Political Society*. London: Anthem Press.

Guha, Ramachandra, and Juan Martinez-Alier. 1998. *Varieties of Environmentalisms: Essays North and South*. Delhi: Oxford University Press.

Hale, Mike. 2019. "Review: 'Chernobyl,' the Disaster Movie." *New York Times*, May 3. https://www.nytimes.com/2019/05/03/arts/television/review-chernobyl-hbo.html.

Hall, Stuart. 1978. "The Social Production of News." In Stuart Hall, ed., *Policing the Crisis: Mugging, the State, Law and Order*, 53–75. London: Macmillan.

Hanlon, Dennis. 2014. "Making Waves: Anand Patwardhan, Latin America, and the Invention of Third Cinema." *Wide Screen* 5 (1): 1–24.

Haraway, Donna. 1988. "Situated Knowledge: The Science Question in Feminism and the Privilege of Partial Perspective." *Feminist Studies* 14 (3): 575–599.

Haraway, Donna. 2003. *The Companion Species Manifesto: Dogs, People, and Significant Otherness*. Chicago: Prickly Paradigm.

Hardikar, Jaideep. 2013. *A Village Awaits Doomsday*. New Delhi: Penguin Books.

Harvey, Penny, Casper Bruun Jensen, and Asturu Morita. 2016. "Introduction: Infrastructural Complications." In Penny Harvey, Casper Bruun Jensen, and Asturu Morita, eds., *Infrastructures and Social Complexity: A Companion*, 1–22. London: Routledge.

Hastie, Amelie. 2009. "TV on the Brain." *Screen* 50 (2): 216–232.

Hay, Colin. 1997. "Political Time and the Temporality of Crisis." In *Contemporary Political Studies* (proceedings of the meeting of the Political Studies Association, Jordantown University, Ulster). www.psa.ac.uk/cps/1997/hay2.pdf.

Hayden, Michael Edison. 2012. "As Tamil Nadu Nuclear Plant Opening Nears, Protests Enter 'Death Throes.'" *New York Times*, May 29. http://india.blogs.nytimes.com/2012/05/29/as-tamil-nadu-nuclear-plant-openingnears-protests-enter-death-throes/?_r=0.

Hecht, Gabrielle. 2009a. "Africa and the Nuclear World: Labor, Occupational Health, and the Transnational Production of Uranium." *Comparative Studies in Society and History* 51 (4): 896–926.

Hecht, Gabrielle. 2009b. *The Radiance of France: Nuclear Power and National Identity after World War II*. Cambridge, MA: MIT Press.

Heise, Ursula. 2008. *Sense of Place and Sense of Planet: The Environmental Imagination of the Global*. Oxford: Oxford University Press.

Helmreich, Stefan. 2007. "An Anthropologist Underwater: Immersive Soundscapes, Submarine Cyborgs, and Transductive Ethnography." *American Ethnologists*, 34 (4): 621–641.

Helmreich, Stefan. 2015. "Potential Energy and the Body Electric Cardiac Waves, Brain Waves, and the Making of Quantities into Qualities." *Current Anthropology* 54 (s7): S139–S148.

Herkman, Juha. 2012. "Introduction: Intermediality as a Theory and Methodology." In Juha Herkman, Taisto Hujanen, and Paavo Oinonen, eds., *Intermediality and Media Change*, 10–27. Tampere, Finland: Tampere University Press.

Hertsgaard, Mark, and Mark Dowie. 2018. "How Big Wireless Made Us Think That Cell Phones Are Safe: A Special Investigation." *Nation*, March 29. https://www

.thenation.com/article/how-big-wireless-made-us-think-that-cell-phones-are-safe
-a-special-investigation/.

Hess, David. 2016. *Undone Science: Social Movements, Mobilized Publics, and Industrial Transitions*. Cambridge, MA: MIT Press.

Hess, David, and Jonathan Coley. 2014. "Wireless Smart Meters and Public Acceptance: The Environment, Limited Choices, and Precautionary Politics." *Public Understanding of Science* 23 (6): 688–702.

Hess, Linda. 2003. "Violence versus Nonviolence: A Call to Engage and Act." *Critical Asian Studies* 35 (1): 153–159.

Hilgartner, S. 2012. "Staging High-Visibility Science: Media Orientation in Genome Research." In S. Rödder, M. Franzen, and P. Weingart, eds., *The Sciences' Media Connection: Public Communication and Its Repercussions*, 189–215. Sociology of Sciences Yearbook. New York: Springer.

Hobart, Mark. 2010. "What Do We Mean by 'Media Practices'?" In Birgit Brauchler and John Postill, eds., *Theorizing Media and Practice*, 55–75. New York: Berghahn Books.

Hogan, Mel. 2015a. "Electromagnetic Soup: EMFs, Bodies, and Surveillance." Paper presented at *Console-ing Passions International Conference*, Dublin, June 18–20.

Hogan, Mel. 2015b. "Facebook Data Storage Centers as the Archive's Underbelly." *Television and New Media* 16 (1): 3–18.

Hom, Anna Garcia, Ramon Moles Plaza, and Rachel Palmén. 2011. "The Framing of Risk and Implications for Policy and Governance: The Case of EMF." *Public Understanding of Science* 20 (3): 319–333.

Huss, Anke, Matthias Egger, Kerstin Hug, Karin Huwiler-Muntener, and Martin Roosli. 2007. "Sources of Funding and Results of Studies of Health Effects of Mobile Phone Use: Systematic Review of Experimental Studies." *Environmental Health Perspectives*, 115 (1): 1–4.

Ihde, Don. 1990. *Technology and the Lifeworld*. Bloomington: Indiana University Press.

Irwin, Alan. 2006. "The Politics of Talk: Coming to Terms with the 'New' Scientific Governance." *Social Studies of Science* 36 (2): 299–320.

Jasanoff, Sheila. 2007. *Designs on Nature: Science and Democracy in Europe and the United States*. Princeton, NJ: Princeton University Press.

Jasanoff, Sheila, and Kim Sang-Hyun. 2009. "Containing the Atom: Sociotechnical Imaginaries and Nuclear Power in the United States and South Korea." *Minerva* 47 (2): 119–146.

Jayaraman, Nityanand. 2012. "This Renaissance Is Just a Fairytale." *Hindu*, June 15. https://www.thehindu.com/opinion/op-ed/this-renaissance-is-just-a-fairy-tale/article3528968.ece.

Jeffrey, Robin, and Assa Doron. 2013. *Cell Phone Nation: How Mobile Phones Have Revolutionized Business, Politics, and Ordinary Life in India*. Gurgaon: Hachette Book Publishing India.

Jensen, Casper Bruun. 2017. "Pipe Dreams: Sewage Infrastructure and Activity Trails in Phnom Penh." *Ethnos: Journal of Anthropology* 82 (4): 627–647.

Jishnu, Latha. 2007. "Running Out of Options." *Business Standard*, December 22. http://www.business-standard.com/article/opinion/latha-jishnu-running-out-of -options-107122201044_1.html.

Jishnu, Latha. 2012. "A Schoolgirl's Nuclear Nightmare." *Down to Earth*, April 5. http://www.downtoearth.org.in/content/schoolgirl-s-nuclear-nightmare.

Jishnu, Latha, Ankur Paliwal, and Arnab Pratim Dutta. 2012. "Koodankulam Melt-down." *Down to Earth*, April 1–15. http://www.downtoearth.org.in/coverage /kudankulam-meltdown—37876#0.

Kara, Selmin, and Alanna Thain. 2015. "Sonic Ethnographies: Leviathan and New Materialisms in Documentary." In Holly Rogers, ed., *Music and Sound in Documentary Film: Real Listening*, 180–193. New York: Routledge.

Katyal, Anita. 2015. "Modi Takes Credit for Nuclear Deal with US, Ignoring Crucial Role Played by Manmohan." *Scroll.in*, January 29. https://scroll.in/article /703049/modi-takes-credit-for-nuclear-deal-with-us-ignoring-crucial-role -played-by-manmohan.

Kaur, Raminder. 2009. "Nuclear Revelations." In William Mazzarella and Raminder Kaur, eds., *Censorship in South Asia: Cultural Regulation from Sedition to Seduction*, 140–171. Bloomington: Indiana University Press.

Kaur, Raminder. 2012. "Atomic Comics: Parabolic Mimesis and the Graphic Fictions of Science." *International Journal of Cultural Studies* 15 (2012): 329–347.

Kaur, Raminder. 2013a. *Atomic Mumbai: Living with the Radiance of a Thousand Suns*. Routledge: New Delhi.

Kaur, Raminder. 2013b. "The Fictions of Science and Cinema in India." In K. M. Gokulsing and W. Dissanayake, eds., *Routledge Handbook of Indian Cinemas*, 282–296. New York: Routledge.

Kaur, Raminder. 2013c. "Sovereignty without Hegemony, Nuclear State, and a 'Secret Public Hearing' in India." *Theory, Culture and Society* 30 (3): 3–28.

Kaur, Raminder. 2017. "A Nuclear Cyberia: Interfacing Science, Culture, and 'E-thnography' of an Indian Township's Social Media." *Media, Culture and Society* 39 (3): 325–340.

Kaur, Raminder, and Saif Eqbal. 2018. *Adventure Comics and Youth Cultures in India*. New York: Routledge.

Kember, Sarah, and Joanna Zylinska. 2012. *Life after New Media: Mediation as a Vital Process*. London: MIT Press.

Kimura, Aya Hirata. 2016. *Radiation Brain Moms and Citizen Scientists: The Gender Politics of Food Contamination after Fukushima*. Durham, NC: Duke University Press.

King, Claire. 2008. "The Man Inside: Trauma, Gender, and the Nation in *The Brave One*." Paper presented at the 94th Annual Convention of National Communication Association's Critical/Cultural Studies Division, November 21, San Diego.

Kirsch, Scott. 2004. "Harold Knapp and the Geography of Normal Controversy: Radioiodine in the Historical Environment." *Osiris* 19:167–81.

Koch, Wendy. 2015. "Could Next-Gen Reactors Spark Revival in Nuclear Power?" *National Geographic*, July 24. http://news.nationalgeographic.com/energy/2015 /07/150724-next-gen-reactors-seek-to-revive-nuclear-power/.

Koide Hiroaki. 2011. "The Truth about Nuclear Power: Japanese Nuclear Engineer Calls for Abolition." *Asia-Pacific Journal* 9 (5), issue 31.

Krishna, Sankaran. 2009. "The Social Life of a Bomb: India and the Ontology of an Over- populated Society." In Itty Abraham, ed., *South Asian Cultures of the Bomb: Atomic Publics and the State in India and Pakistan*, 68–88. Bloomington: Indiana University Press.

Krtilova, Katerina. 2012. "Intermediality in Media Philosophy." In Bernd Herzogenrath, ed., *Travels in Intermedia[lity]: Reblurring the Boundaries*, 37–45. Hanover, NH: Dartmouth College Press.

Kuchinskaya, Olga. 2012. "Twice Invisible: Formal Representations of Radiation Danger." *Social Studies of Science* 43 (1): 78–96.

Kuchinskaya, Olga. 2014. *The Politics of Invisibility: Public Knowledge about Radiation Health Effects after Chernobyl*. Cambridge, MA: MIT Press.

Kurtz, Howard. 1996. *Hot Air: All Talk, All the Time*. New York: Basic Books.

Lakkad, Abhishek. 2018. "Frankenstein's Avatars: Posthuman Monstrosity in Enthiran/Robot." *Rupkatha Journal on Interdisciplinary Studies in Humanities* 10 (2): 236–250.

Langlois, Ganaele, Greg Elmer, Fenwick McKelvey, and Zachary Devereaux. 2009. "Networked Publics: The Double Articulation of Code and Politics on Facebook." *Canadian Journal of Communication* 34:415–434.

Larkin, Brian. 2008. *Signal and Noise: Infrastructure and Urban Culture in Nigeria*. Durham, NC: Duke University Press.

Larkin, Brian. 2013. "The Politics and Poetics of Infrastructures." *Annual Review of Anthropology* 42:327–343.

Latour, Bruno. 2005. *Politics of Nature: How to Bring the Sciences into Democracy*. New Delhi: Orient Longman.

Levy, Adrian. 2015. "India's Nuclear Industry Pours Its Wastes into a River of Death and Disease." The Center for Public Integrity, December 14. https://www.publicintegrity.org/2015/12/14/18844/india-s-nuclear-industry-pours-its-wastes-river-death-and-disease.

Lippit, Akira. 2005. *Atomic Light (Shadow Optics)*. Minneapolis: University of Minnesota Press.

Livingstone, Sonia. 2013. "The Participation Paradigm in Audience Research." *Communication Review* 16 (1–2): 21–30.

Livingstone, Sonia, and Peter Lunt. 1994. *Talk on Television: Audience Participation and Public Debate*. London: Routledge.

Lynch, Lisa. 2012. "'We Don't Wanna Be Radiated': Documentary Film and the Evolving Rhetoric of Nuclear Energy Activism." *American Literature* 84 (2): 327–351.

Mankekar, Purnima. 2012. "Television and Embodiment: A Speculative Essay." *South Asian History and Culture* 3 (4): 603–613.

Marran, Christine L. 2017. *Ecology without Culture: Aesthetics for a Toxic World*. Minneapolis: University of Minnesota Press.

Marres, Noortje. 2005. "Issues Spark a Public into Being: A Key but Often Forgotten Point of the Lippmann-Dewey Debate." In Bruno Latour and Peter Weibel, eds., *Making Things Public*, 208–217. Cambridge: MIT Press.

Marres, Noortje. 2007. "The Issues Deserve More Credit: Pragmatist Contributions to the Study of Public Involvement in Controversy." *Social Studies of Science* 37 (5): 759–780.

Marres, Noortje. 2010. "Frontstaging Nonhumans: Publicity as a Constraint on the Political Activity of Things." In Bruce Braun and Sarah Whatmore, eds., *Political Matter: Technoscience, Democracy, and Public Life*, 177–210. Minneapolis: University of Minnesota Press.

Marshall, Michael. 2013. "How UK's First Nuclear Reactor for 25 Years Will Work." *New Scientist*, October 16. https://www.newscientist.com/article/mg22029392-500-how-uks-first-nuclear-reactor-for-25-years-will-work/.

Masco, Joseph. 2004. "Mutant Ecologies: Radioactive Life in Post–Cold War New Mexico." *Cultural Anthropology* 19 (4): 517–550.

Masco, Joseph. 2006. *The Nuclear Borderlands: The Manhattan Project in Post–Cold War New Mexico*. Princeton, NJ: Princeton University Press.

Masco, Joseph. 2010. "'Sensitive but Unclassified': Secrecy and the Counterterrorist State." *Public Culture* 22 (3): 443–463.

Massumi, Brian. 2002. *Parables for the Virtual: Movement, Affect, Sensation*. Durham, NC: Duke University Press.

Mathai, M. V. 2013. *Nuclear Power, Economic Development Discourse and the Environment: The Case of India*. London: Routledge.

Mattern, Shannon. 2019. "Networked Dream Worlds: Is 5G Solving Real, Pressing Problems or Merely Creating New Ones?" *Real Life Magazine*, July 8. https://reallifemag.com/networked-dream-worlds/.

Maxwell, Richard, and Toby Miller. 2012. *Greening the Media*. New York: Oxford University Press.

Mazzarella, William. 2005. "Public Culture, Still." Special issue, *Biblio: A Review of Books* 10, nos. 9–10 (September–October).

Mazzarella, William. 2006. "Internet X-Ray: E-Governance, Transparency and the Politics of Immediation in India." *Public Culture* 18 (3): 473–505.

Mazzarella, William, and Raminder Kaur. 2009. "Between Sedition and Seduction: Thinking Censorship in South Asia." In Raminder Kaur and William Mazzarella, eds., *Censorship in South Asia: Cultural Regulation from Sedition to Seduction*, 1–28. Bloomington: Indiana University Press.

Mbembe, Achille. 2001. *On the Postcolony*. Berkeley: University of California Press.

McNeill, D. 2012. "Fukushima Lays Bare Japanese Media's Ties to Top." *Japan Times*, January 8. http://www.japantimes.co.jp/life/2012/01/08/general/fukushima-lays-bare-japanese-medias-ties-to-top/#.VQuBBzrZhrI.

Mehta, Nalin. 2008. "India Talking: Politics, Democracy and News Television." In Nalin Mehta, ed., *Television in India: Satellites, Politics, and Cultural Change*, 32–61. New York: Routledge.

Mehta, Nalin. 2013. "Satellites, Politics and India's TV News Revolution: Challenges and Prospects." In Amitendu Palit and Gloria Spittle, eds., *South Asia in the New Decade: Challenges and Prospects*, 137–162. Singapore: World Scientific.

Mercer, David. 2002. "Scientific Method Discourses in the Construction of 'EMF Science': Interests, Resources and Rhetoric in Submissions to a Public Inquiry." *Social Studies of Science* 32 (2): 205–233.

Mitchell, Lisa M., and Alberto Cambrosio. 1997. "The Invisible Topography of Power: Electromagnetic Fields, Bodies, and the Environment." *Social Studies of Science* 27 (2): 221–271.

Moore, Alfred, and Jack Stilgoe. 2009. "Experts and Anecdotes: The Role of 'Anecdotal Evidence' in Public Scientific Controversies." *Science, Technology and Human Values* 34 (5): 654–677.

Moskowitz, Joel M. 2019. "5G Wireless Technology: Millimeter Wave Health Effects." *Electromagnetic Radiation Safety* (blog), July 1 (orig. post. November 14, 2018; updated February 22, 2019). https://www.saferemr.com/2017/08/5g -wireless-technology-millimeter-wave.html.

Mukherjee, Siddhartha. 2011. "Do Cellphones Cause Brain Cancer?" *New York Times*, April 13. http://www.nytimes.com/2011/04/17/magazine/mag -17cellphones-t.html?_r=1.

Munson, Wayne. 1993. *All Talk: The Talkshow and Media Culture*. Philadelphia: Temple University Press.

Murphy, Michelle. 2000. "The 'Elsewhere within Here' and Environmental Illness; or, How to Build Yourself a Body in a Safe Space." *Configurations* 8 (1): 87–120.

Murphy, Michelle. 2004. "Uncertain Exposures and the Privilege of Imperception: Activist Scientists and Race at the U.S. Environmental Protection Agency." *Osiris* 19:266–282.

Murray, Susan. 2018. *Bright Signals: A History of Color Television*. Durham, NC: Duke University Press.

Nambi, K. S. V., and S. D. Soman. 1987. "Environmental Radiation and Cancer in India." *Health Physics* 52 (5): 653–657.

Nandy, Ashis. 1972. "Defiance and Conformity in Science: The Identity of Jagadis Chandra Bose." *Science Studies* 2 (1): 31–85.

Nandy, Ashis. 1998. "The Twilight of Certitudes: Secularism, Hindu Nationalism and Other Masks of Deculturation." *Postcolonial Studies* 1 (3): 283–298.

Natrajan, Vasant. 2013. "Sick of the Cell Phone? No Way." *Hindu Business Line*, September 10. http://www.thehindubusinessline.com/opinion/sick-of-the-cell -phone-no-way/article5113070.ece.

Nayar, Pramod. 2014. *Posthumanism*. Cambridge: Polity Press.

Negt, Oskar, and Alexander Kluge. (1972) 1993. *Public Sphere and Experience: Towards an Analysis of the Bourgeois and Proletarian Public Sphere*. Minneapolis: University of Minnesota Press.

Neville Anderson, Joel. 2015. "Cinema in Reconstruction: Japan's Post-3.11 Documentary." In Alan Wright, ed., *Film on the Faultline*, 215–232. Bristol, UK: Intellect.

Neyazi, Tabarez Ahmed. 2014. "Media, Mediation, and the Vernacular Public Arena in India." *Media International Australia* 152:179–186.

Ninan, Sevanti. 2007. *Headlines from the Hindi Heartland: Reinventing the Hindi Public Sphere*. New Delhi: Sage.

Nixon, Rob. 2011. *Slow Violence and the Environmentalism of the Poor*. Cambridge, MA: Harvard University Press.

Nussbaum, Emily. 2019. "How 'When They See Us' and 'Chernobyl' Make Us Look." *New Yorker*, June 17. https://www.newyorker.com/magazine/2019/06/24/how -when-they-see-us-and-chernobyl-make-us-look.

Offenhuber, Dietmar. 2017. *Waste Is Information: Infrastructure Legibility and Governance*. Cambridge, MA: MIT Press.

Ong, Aihwa. 1996. "Cultural Citizenship as Subject-Making: Immigrants Negotiate Racial and Cultural Boundaries in the United States." *Current Anthropology* 37 (5): 737–762.

Pal, Jojojeet. 2015. "Banalities Turn Viral: Narendra Modi and the Political Tweet." *Television and New Media* 16 (4): 378–387.

Pandey, Gyanendra. 2010. "Introduction: The Subaltern as Subaltern Citizen." In Gyanendra Pandey, ed., *Subaltern Citizens and Their Histories: Investigations from India and the USA*, 1–12. London: Routledge.

Papacharissi, Zizi. 2015. *Affective Publics: Sentiment, Technology, Politics*. New York: Oxford University Press.

Parameswaran, Radhika. 2012. "Watching Barkha Dutt: Turning on the News in Television Studies." *South Asian History and Culture* 3 (4): 626–635.

Parks, Lisa. 2010. "Around the Antenna Tree: The Politics of Infrastructural Visibility." In *Flow: A Critical Forum on TV and Media Culture*. https://www .flowjournal.org/2010/03/flow-favorites-around-the-antenna-tree-the-politics-of -infrastructural-visibilitylisa-parks-uc-santa-barbara/.

Parks, Lisa. 2015. "'Stuff You Can Kick': Toward a Theory of Media Infrastructures." In D. T. Goldberg and P. Svensson, eds., *Between Humanities and the Digital*, 355–373. Cambridge, MA: MIT Press.

Parks, Lisa. 2018. *Rethinking Media Coverage: Vertical Mediation and the War on Terror*. London: Routledge.

Parks, Lisa, and Nicole Starosielski. 2015. "Introduction." In Lisa Parks and Nicole Starosielski, eds., *Signal Traffic: Critical Studies of Media Infrastructures*, 1–27. Champaign: University of Illinois Press.

Patwardhan, Anand. 1984. "The Guerilla Film—Underground and in Exile: A Critique and a Case Study of *Waves of Revolution*." In Tom Waugh, ed., *"Show Us Life": Toward a History and Aesthetics of the Committed Documentary*, 444–464. Metuchen, NJ: Scarecrow Press.

Peters, John Durham. 2015. *Marvelous Clouds: Toward a Philosophy of Elemental Media*. Chicago: University of Chicago Press.

Petryna, Adriana. 2013. *Life Exposed: Biological Citizens after Chernobyl*. Princeton, NJ: Princeton University Press.

Pinney, Christopher. 2004. *Photos of the Gods: The Printed Image and Political Struggle in India*. London: Reaktion Books.

Plantin, Jean-Christophe. 2015. "The Politics of Mapping Platforms: Participatory Radiation Mapping after the Fukushima Daiichi Disaster." *Media, Culture and Society* 37 (6): 904–921.

Prakash, Gyan. 1999. *Another Reason: Science and the Imagination of Modern India*. Princeton, NJ: Princeton University Press.

Punathambekar, Aswin, and Shanti Kumar. 2012. "Television at Large." *South Asian History and Culture* 3 (4): 483–490.

Rajagopal, Arvind. 2001. *Politics after Television: Hindu Nationalism and the Reshaping of the Public in India*. Cambridge: Cambridge University Press.

Rajagopal, Arvind. 2009. "The Public Sphere in India: Structure and Transformation." In Arvind Rajagopal, ed., *The Indian Public Sphere: Readings in Media History*, 1–28. Oxford: Oxford University Press.

Ramana, M. V. 2009. "India's Nuclear Enclave and the Practice of Secrecy." In Itty Abraham, ed., *South Asian Cultures of the Bomb: Atomic Publics and the State in India and Pakistan*, 41–67. Bloomington: Indiana University Press.

Ramana, M. V., and Aswin Kumar. 2013. "'One in Infinity': Failing to Learn from Accidents and Implications for Nuclear Safety in India." *Journal of Risk Research* 17 (1): 23–42. doi:10.1080/13669877.2013.822920.

Rao, Ursula. 2010. *News as Culture: Journalistic Practices and the Remaking of Indian Leadership Traditions*. New York: Berghahn Books.

Rappaport, Theodore, Wonil Roh, and Keungwhoon Cheun. 2014. "Smart Antennas Could Open Up New Spectrum for 5G." *IEEE Spectrum*, August 28. https://spectrum.ieee.org/telecom/wireless/smart-antennas-could-open-up-new-spectrum-for-5g.

Rathee, Kiran. 2016. "Open Network Initiative: Airtel Upgrades 9,000 Sites, Optimizes 30,000 Sites." *Business Standard* (New Delhi), August 25. http://www.business-standard.com/article/companies/open-network-initiative-airtel-upgrades-9-000-sites-optimises-30-000-sites-116082500473_1.html.

Rip, Arie. 2003. "Constructing Expertise: In a Third Wave of Science Studies?" *Social Studies of Science* 33 (3): 419–434.

Roy, Prasanto K. 2014. "Why India's Mobile Network Is Broken." *BBC News*, December 3. http://www.bbc.com/news/world-asia-india-30290029.

Roy, Srirupa. 2007. *Beyond Belief: India and the Politics of Postcolonial Nationalism*. Durham, NC: Duke University Press.

Rubin, James, and Simon Wessely. 2015. "Better Call Saul: Is Electromagnetic Hypersensitivity a Real Health Risk?" *Guardian*, February 15. https://www.theguardian.com/science/shortcuts/2015/feb/15/better-call-saul-electromagnetic-hypersensitivity-real-health-risk.

Saraiya, Sonia. 2019. "The Unique, Addictive Dread of Chernobyl." *Vanity Fair*, June 3. https://www.vanityfair.com/hollywood/2019/06/chernobyl-hbo-catch-22-good-omens-nuclear-power-dread.

Sarkar, Bhaskar, and Janet Walker. 2010. "Introduction: Moving Testimonies." In Bhaskar Sarkar and Janet Walker, eds., *Documentary Testimonies: Global Archives of Suffering*, 1–34. New York: Routledge.

Scannell, Paddy. 1991. *Broadcast Talk*. London: Sage.

Scarry, Elaine. 1985. *The Body in Pain: The Making and Unmaking of the World*. Oxford: Oxford University Press.

Schnitzler, Antina Von. 2016. *Democracy's Infrastructure: Techno-politics and Protest after Apartheid*. Princeton, NJ: Princeton University Press.

Schulz, Peter J., Uwe Hartung, Nicola Diviani, and Simone Keller. 2012. "Dangerous Towers, Harmless Phones? Swiss Newspaper Coverage of the Risk Associated with Non-ionizing Radiation." *Atlantic Journal of Communication* 20 (1): 53–70.

Sehgal, Kunal, and James Bennett. 2016. "New Delhi Takes Private Vehicles Off the Road Every Second Day as Pollution Soars." Australia Broadcasting Corporation, January 1. http://www.abc.net.au/news/2016–01–01/new-dehli-cuts-cars-to -combat-pollution/7059988.

Shah, Nishant. 2007. "Subject to Technology: Internet Pornography, Cyber-terrorism and the Indian State." *Inter-Asia Cultural Studies* 8 (3): 349–366.

Sharma, Nidhi. 2015. "Urban Development Ministry Allows Installation of Cell Phone Towers on Government Buildings." *Economic Times*, September 10. http://economictimes.indiatimes.com/industry/telecom/urban-development -ministry-allows-installation-of-cell-phone-towers-on-government-buildings /articleshow/48900807.cms.

Shepherd, Virginia A. 2012. "At the Roots of Plant Neurobiology: A Brief History of the Biophysical Research of JC Bose." *Science and Culture*, May–June, 196–210.

Simone, AbdouMaliq. 2012. "Infrastructure: Introductory Commentary by AbdouMaliq Simone." In *Curated Collections, Cultural Anthropology Online*, November 26. http://www.culanth.org/curated_collections/11-infrastructure /discussions/12-infrastructure-introductory-commentary-by-abdoumaliq-simone.

Sivakumar, Souwmya. 2012. "In Rawatbhata, Workers Denied Rights to Know Radiation Exposure." *Daily News and Analysis*, August 28. http://www.dianuke.org /in-rawatbhata-workers-denied-right-to-know-radioactive-exposure/.

Slack, Jennifer D. 2012. "Beyond Transmission, Modes, and Media." In Jeremy Packer and Stephen B. Crofts Wiley, eds., *Communication Matters*, 143–158. London: Routledge.

Smaill, Belinda. 2016. *Regarding Life: Animals and the Documentary Moving Image*. Albany, NY: SUNY Press.

Soneryd, Linda. 2007. "Deliberations on the Unknown, the Unsensed, and the Unsayable? Public Protests and the Development of Third-Generation Mobile Phones in Sweden." *Science, Technology and Human Values* 32 (3): 287–314.

Spiegel, Lynn. 1992. "The Suburban Home Companion: Television and the Neighborhood Ideal in Postwar America." *Sexuality and Space: Princeton Papers on Architecture*, 185–218. Princeton, NJ: Princeton University Press.

Spivak, Gayatri Chakravorty. 1999. *A Critique of Postcolonial Reason: Toward a History of the Vanishing Present*. Cambridge, MA: Harvard University Press.

Staiger, Janet, Ann Cvetkovich, and Ann Reynolds. 2010. *Political Emotions: New Agendas in Communication*. New York: Routledge.

Star, Susan L. 1995. "Work and Infrastructure." *Communications of the ACM* 38 (9): 41.

Star, Susan L. 1999. "The Ethnography of Infrastructure." *American Behavioral Scientist* 43:377–391.

Stengers, Isabelle. 2005. "The Cosmopolitical Proposal." In Bruno Latour and Peter Weibel, eds., *Making Things Public: Atmospheres of Democracy*, 994–1004. Cambridge, MA: MIT Press.

Stewart, Katherine. 2007. *Ordinary Affect*. Durham, NC: Duke University Press.

Stilgoe, Jack. 2005. "Controlling Mobile Phone Health Risks in the UK: A Fragile Discourse of Compliance." *Science and Public Policy* 32 (1): 55–64.

Subramanian, Samanth. 2015. "India's War on Greenpeace." *Guardian*, August 11. http://www.theguardian.com/world/2015/aug/11/indias-war-on-greenpeace.

Subramanian, T. S. 2012. "Groping in the Dark." *Frontline* 29 (21). http://www.frontline.in/static/html/fl2921/stories/20121102292112800.htm.

Sundar, Aparna. 2010. "Capitalist Transformation and the Evolution of Civil Society in a South Indian Fishery." PhD diss., University of Toronto.

Sundaram, Ravi. 2015. "Publicity, Transparency, and the Circulation Engine: The Media Sting in India." *Current Anthropology* 56 (S12): S297–S305.

Tabuchi, Hiroko. 2011. "Day Laborers Braved Radiation for a Temp Job." *New York Times*, April 9. http://www.nytimes.com/2011/04/10/world/asia/10workers.html?_r=0.

Taylor, Brian. 1997. "Shooting Downwind: Depicting the Radiated Body in Epidemiology and Documentary Photography." In Michael Huspek and Gary Radford, eds., *Transgressing Discourses: Communication and the Voice of the Other*, 289–328. Albany: SUNY Press.

Taylor, Charles. 2002. "Modern Social Imaginaries." *Public Cultures* 14 (1): 91–124.

Thibault, Ghislain. 2014. "Wireless Pasts and Wired Futures." In Andrew Herman, Jan Hadlow, and Thom Swiss, eds., *Theories of the Mobile Internet: Materialities and Imaginaries*, 87–104. New York: Routledge.

Thussu, Daya Kishan. 2014. "Television News and an Indian Infotainment Sphere." In Biswarup Sen and Abhijit Roy, eds., *Channeling Cultures: Television Studies from India*, 129–141. Oxford: Oxford University Press.

Timmons, Heather. 2012. "A Conversation with: Shoma Chaudhury." *New York Times*, January 16. https://india.blogs.nytimes.com/2012/01/16/a-conversation-with-shoma-chaudhury/.

Tuana, Nancy. 2008. "Viscous Porosity: Witnessing Katrina." In Stacy Alaimo and Susan Hekman, eds., *Material Feminisms*, 188–213. Bloomington: Indiana University Press.

Uncertain Commons. 2013. *Speculate This!* Durham, NC: Duke University Press.

Van Wyck, Peter C. 2004. *Signs of Danger: Waste, Trauma, and Nuclear Threat*. Minneapolis: University of Minnesota Press.

Varshney, Vibha. 2011. "Warning Signal." *Down to Earth*, January 31. http://www.downtoearth.org.in/content/warning-signal.

Varughese, Shiju. 2012. "Where Are the Missing Masses? The Quasi-publics and Non-publics of Technoscience." *Minerva* 50 (2): 239–254.

Visvanathan, Shiv. 2012. "The Meaning of Koodankulam." *Asian Age*, December 24. http://archive.asianage.com/columnists/meaning-koodankulam-958.

Walker, Janet. 2010. "Rights and Return: Perils and Fantasies of Situated Testimony after Katrina." In Bhaskar Sarkar and Janet Walker, eds., *Documentary Testimonies: Global Archives of Suffering*, 47–64. New York: Routledge.

Warner, Michael. 2002. "Publics and Counterpublics." *Public Culture* 14 (1): 49–90.

Waugh, Thomas. 1976. "Beyond Verité: Emile de Antonio and the New Documentary of the 70s." *Jump Cut: A Review of Contemporary Media* 10–11:33–39.

Waugh, Thomas. 1984. "Why Documentary Filmmakers Keep Trying to Change the World or Why People Changing the World Keep Making Documentaries." In Thomas Waugh, ed., *"Show Us Life": Toward a History and Aesthetics of the Committed Documentary*, xi–xxvii. Metuchen, NJ: Scarecrow Press.

Welsh, Ian, and Brian Wynne. 2013. "Science, Scientism and Imaginaries of Publics in the UK: Passive Objects, Incipient Threats." *Science as Culture* 22 (4): 540–566.

Weston, Kath. 2017. *Animate Planet: Making Visceral Sense of Living in a High-Tech Ecologically Damaged World*. Durham, NC: Duke University Press.

Wiltschko, Roswitha. 2014. "Magnetoreception in Birds: The Effect of Radio-frequency Fields." *Interface*, no. 12:1–6.

Winston, Brian. 2000. *Lies, Damned Lies and Documentary*. London: British Film Institute.

Wood, Helen. 2009. *Talking with Television: Women, Talk Shows, and Modern Self-Reflexivity*. Urbana: University of Illinois Press.

Wright, Alan. 2015. "Film Theory as Seismic Research." In Alan Wright, ed., *Film on the Faultline*, 1–20. Bristol, UK: Intellect.

Wynne, Brian, and Kerstin Dressel. 2001. "Cultures of Uncertainty—Transboundary Risks and BSE in Europe." In Joanne Linnerooth-Bayer, Ragnar E. Löfstedt, and Gunnar Sjostedt, eds., *Transboundary Risk Management*, 121–154. London: Earthscan.

Zelizer, Barbie. 2006. "When Facts, Truth, and Reality Are God-Terms: On Journalism's Uneasy Place in Cultural Studies." *Communication and Critical/Cultural Studies* 1 (1): 100–119.

INDEX

Abraham, Itty, 7, 71, 108, 234n7

accountability, 32, 58, 125–126, 130, 142, 180–181; crisis of, 36, 71

activism, 30, 35, 98, 162, 163–191; affinities and alliances, 18, 165–168, 171, 188; antinuclear as antinational, 84; in Canada, 49, 200; civil/political society categories and, 169–170; environmental, 28, 112, 167, 170, 179–180, 237n8; Japanese, 167, 200–201, 238n5, 238n6; media practices and, 82–91; styling, 37, 171, 189–190; witnessing, 86. *See also* anti–cell antenna movement; antinuclear movement

advertising, 2–3, 11, 36, 39–40, *40*, 68; call drop issue, *130*, 130–131, *131*, *132*; caricatures of, 77–78; foreign suppliers and, 140; Greenpeace, 20–21, *21*; middle class, appeals to, 71–72, 91, 140; National Geographic–NPCIL ads, 91–94, *92*, *93*, 103, 111, *139*; post-Fukushima, 111; "public sector," 94. *See also* publicity

affect, 13, 155, 160, 222n26, 227–228n2, 229n11, 235n11; flows between audience and cell towers, 145–146; mediation and, 143, 158–159; television shows and, 61–62

agency, 62, 187–188

Agni-5 ICBM, 115

Ahmedabad antinuclear conference, 34, 141, 163, 174, *175*, 186–188

air pollution, 1, 17, 136, 219n1

Airtel (cellular operator), 40, 109, 134; Open Network initiative, 129–133, *130*, *132*

Akhbarbaazi ("newspaper business"), 57–58

Akhtar, Farhan, 165

Akhtar, Javed, 165

Ali, Salim, 213

Alley, Jason, 153

alliances, 18, 164–168, 170–171; fishermen-student, 188; translocal, 200–201

alpha particles, 10–11, 148, 233n4

aluminum foil shielding, 41, 49–50, 67, 68, 192

Amudhan, R. P. (filmmaker), 102, 217, 230n21; *Radiation Stories*, 4, 13, 97–99; *Radiation Stories 1: Manavalakurichi*, 98, 150–153, *152*, *153*; *Radiation Stories 3: Koodankulam*, *140*, 140–141, 175–179, *176*, *177*

Anand, Nikhil, 35, 237n2

anecdotal evidence, 143–148, 146–148

Anthropocene, 9

anti–cell antenna movement, 37, 67–69, 162–171, 227n14; apartment rooftop meetings, 18, 22–23, *23*, 48–50, 67; celebrities and, 165–167, 186, 189–190; civil society privileges, 169; as "elitist," 183; visuals/banners, *172*, *173*, 173–174. *See also* cell antennas/towers; cell antenna/tower controversies; Kasliwal, Sudhir; television shows

anti-dam movements, 84–85, 167, 170

antinuclear movement, 19–20, 229n15; Ahmedabad conference, 34, 141, 163, 174, *175*, 186–188; as antinational, 84; celebrities and, 163–164, 166–167;

antinuclear movement (cont.)
    as environmentalism of the poor, 28–29,
    170, 223n28; historical trajectories of,
    170–171; as political society, 169. *See also*
    expertise
Anumukti (antinuclear journal), 200–201,
    222n27
apartment rooftop meetings, 18, 22–23, *23*,
    48–50, 67
Appadurai, Arjun, 54–55
Arabian Sea, 208
Areva (French corporation), 3, 103–104,
    172, 195, 230n18, 231n27; Sakhri-Nate
    nuclear plant location, 3, *5*, 103, 208–209
Are-Vah! (documentary, Patault and Irion),
    195–197, *196, 197*, 208, *209*
Arnall, Timo, 49
Arya, Yashvir, 89–91, 141
assemblages: material, 50, 192, 209–210; of
    media, 22–24, 33, 42, 134
Atom Bomb (film), 212
Atomic Bomb Survivor Study, 150
Atomic Energy Act of 1962, 180
Atomic Energy Regulatory Board, 47, 108,
    135, 146, 204
audience(s), 27; affective flows between
    cell towers and, 145–146; agency of, 62;
    emplacement/situation of, 12–13; for
    English media, 30–31; as media publics,
    60–61; middle-class and upper-middle-
    class, 143–144; as subject of infrastruc-
    ture, 119–120; for talk shows, 59–60; for
    vernacular media, 30–31. *See also* media

Bagla, Pallava, 20, 107, 112–115, *113*, 118
Barad, Karen, 142
Barthe, Yannick, 24, 59, 168
Bauman, Zygmunt, 203–204
Baviskar, Amita, 170, 185
beautification concerns, 182–185
Bee, Rashida, 166
Bell, Genevieve, 15
Bennett, Jane, 48
Bennett, Jill, 20, 222n21

beta particles, 10–11, 233n4
Bhardwaj, S. A., 114, 135
Bhatia, Gaurav, 198–199
bhatti mein shahar (city inside the furnace)
    campaign, *31*, 31–32
Bhopal gas disaster, 94–97, 165–167, 170, 180
Big Data, 137
bioelectromagnetic terrain, 16
BioInitiative Report 2007, 47
biomedical imaging, 7, 33, 75, 138,
    156–158, 162, 217, 218, 222n20; magnetic
    resonance imaging (MRI), 156–157, *157*;
    X-rays, 9, 11–12, 143, 145, 158, 220n9,
    220n10, 234n10
Birulee, Ghanshyam (Jadugoda inhabit-
    ant), 201–205, *203*
bodies, 35–37, 137, 230n23; affect, two
    aspects of, 143; of animals, 25–26,
    37, 138–139, *139, 140*; brain and heart
    activities, 162; dosage and, 148–153;
    "downwind," 142, 234n8; electromag-
    netic waves inside, 153–158; embodied
    publics, 158–162; gendered, 161, 238n6;
    internal radiation, 148, 162, 233n3;
    intimacy and, 138; at molecular level,
    14, 36–37; "nuclear body," 150–151, 153,
    234n8; outward appearance, 142–143; as
    part of environmental publics, 137–138;
    proximity and, 138; "standard body," 150,
    160–161; testimonies of, 6, 12–14, 36–37,
    97–99, 138, 143–153, 235n11; (un)con-
    trolled emissions and, 12–14; "unwanted
    intimacy," 14, 35–36, 142–143, 189–190,
    233n2; visualization of radiation in, 145,
    149–158. *See also* exposure
Bollywood, 163, 165, 170, 212–213, 231n29,
    236n5, 239n15
Bose, Jagdish Chandra, 14, 216
boundaries, 204, 221n13; epistemological,
    146; experts and nonexperts, 32–33, 58;
    national, 28; public-private, 5, 234n10;
    radiant energies and, 158
bourgeois environmentalism, 28–29, 170,
    185–186, 190, 223n28, 223n29

Bowker, Geoffrey, 110
Bradbury, David, 102
Braidotti, Rosi, 214
Breckenridge, Carol A., 25, 54–55
Brihanmumbai Municipal Corporation of
    Mumbai, 198–199
Bruns, Axel, 19
Buddha Weeps in Jadugoda (documentary,
    Shriprakash), 99–102, 104, 148–153, 151,
    201–205, *203*, 231n26
Burgess, Adam, 159
Burgess, Jean, 19

call drops, 35, 39–42, 64–67, 225n1; Open
    Network initiative, 129–133, *130, 132*
Callon, Michel, 24, 59, 168
Canada, antiradiation activism, 49, 200
cancer, 22, 25–26, 138, 200–205; bodies as
    testimony, 13–14; correlated with radia-
    tion detection, 46; disruption, concerns
    as, 10, 41; Hodgkin's lymphoma, 17; in
    Jadugoda (Jharkhand province), 99–101;
    Kasliwal family, 50–51; media reporting
    on, 42; as metaphor for encroachments,
    185–186; *Patrika* coverage of, 30, 35;
    slum residents and, 186; stigma of, 148;
    testimonies of patients, 6, 12–14, 36–37,
    97–99, 138, 143–153, 235n11. *See also* bod-
    ies; carcinogens; exposure
Canetti, Elias, 112
carcinogens, 1, 10–12, 182; cell antenna
    signals, fear of, 10, 15, 24, 26, 39, 103,
    144–145, 163, 182–183; chemical modifi-
    cation of DNA, 12; gamma rays, 10, 148,
    200, 233n4; radiant infrastructures as
    emitters of, 6–7; slums equated with,
    185–186; types of radiation, 10. *See also*
    cancer
cartoons, 95–97, 103–104
Castaing-Taylor, Lucien, 209
casteism, 90, 103, 136
celebrities, 37, 163–164, 166–167, 170
cell antenna signals, 35, 39; aluminum foil
    shielding, 41, 49–50, 67, 68, 192; disclo-

sure about, 107; "fear psychosis" about,
    144–145; microwave ovens compared
    with, 23, 42, 44, 47–49, *48*, 200. *See also*
    call drops
cell antennas/towers, 1, 39–69; affective
    flows between audiences and towers,
    145–146; as base stations, 45; clustering
    of, 42–43, *43*; dish antennas, 45; electro-
    sensitivity to, 12, 45, 155–158, 214, 234n9;
    increase in, 39–41; monitoring of signals,
    51–52, 127–129, 132, 134, 137; nonion-
    izing radiation, 10; park locations, 42,
    65–67, *66*; sector antennas, 45; urban
    location, 3–4. *See also* anti–cell antenna
    movement; call drops; cell phones; radi-
    ant infrastructures
cell antenna/tower controversies: begin-
    nings of, 42–43; call drops, 35, 39–42,
    64–67, 225n1; interrogating expertise in
    talk shows, 57–63, *60*; scare, 50. *See also*
    anti–cell antenna movement; expertise
cell phones, 2, 4–5; call drops, 35, 39–42,
    64–67, 225n1; as equalizers, 199–200; in
    fiction, 212–215; Indian mobile phone
    market, 8. *See also* cell antennas/towers;
    nonionizing radiation
"Cell Phone Towers: India's Safety Check"
    (*We The People* talk show episode),
    57–63
cells (geographic areas), 45
cellular operators, 18, 35–36, 39–40, 68,
    227n1; Airtel, 40, 109, 129–133, *130, 132*,
    134; Open Network initiative, 129–133,
    130, 132; perceived as rich and uncaring,
    27; Reliance Jio, 2, 39, *40*, 199; secrecy
    and, 12, 108–110. *See also* advertising;
    emissions
Cellular Operators Association of India,
    18, 43
Cellular Telecommunications and Internet
    Association, 26
Center for Environmental Oncology,
    161
Center for Internet and Society, 132

Center for Nuclear Disarmament and Peace (CNDP), 171–172, 182

cesium, 162

Chai Kadai blog, 82–83, 228n5

Chakrabarty, Dipesh, 81, 179, 236n7

Chandrashekhar, T., 58, 59, 60

Chatterjee, Partha, 28, 29, 169, 172, 188–189, 223n30, 223n31

Chaudhary, Anil, 181–182

Chawla, Juhi, 37, 58, 108–109, 173

Chemmencheri, Sudheesh Ramapurath, 189

Chennai Solidarity Group for Koodankulam Struggle, 83, 228n5

Chernobyl (television miniseries), 217–218, 240n21

Chernobyl nuclear disaster (Soviet Union), 70, 141–142, 215, 232n5, 238n5, 238n8

Chingari: Award, 166; Rehabilitation Center (Bhopal), 166

Chipko ("tree hugging") movement, 170

Chitti (andro-humanoid robot character), 213–214

chronic exposure, 18, 45

Citizen (Tamil film), 205

citizen participation, 23–24, 32–33, 129, 224n34

citizen-sensing/crowd-sensing projects, 24, 129, 132, 134, 136–137

citizenship, 29, 33, 35, 162, 171, 235n14; narrow view of, 237n8; scientific, 201, 238n6; "subaltern citizens," 187–188. *See also* civil society; political society

civil society, 28–29, 82; intersections with political society, 186–188; NGOs and, 180; political society binaries, 30, 32, 169–170; public interest litigation (PIL), 180, 182–183; rupture with political society, 183–186

climate change, 1, 9, 232n10

CNDP. *See* Center for Nuclear Disarmament and Peace

CNN-IBN (CNN News 18), 4, 143, 190. See also *Living It Up* (television show)

Coimbatore Institute of Technology (CIT), 79, 211

Cold War era, 215

collateral damage, 99, 225n39, 228n2

collectives of people, 32, 55, 91, 167, 221n17, 226n8

colonial legacies, 172

Commerzbank, 94

compensation, 12, 20, 28, 85, 95, 222n25

compliance, not linked to environmental responsibility, 125

Constitution, Indian, 180

containment, 12, 43, 106, 118, 135

contamination, 201, 206–208

controversies. *See* anti–cell antenna movement; antinuclear movement; cell antenna/tower controversies; environmental controversies; nuclear controversies; protests

Convention on Supplementary Compensation for Nuclear Damage, 95–96

coproduction model, 73

corruption, 80, 135, 180, 193, 197, 213, 225n38

Cram, Shannon, 142, 150

crowdsourcing/crowdmapping initiatives, 129–133, 134, 232n11; Japan, 201

cultural imaginaries, 7, 35–37

Cumbria, 141–142

Curie, Marie, 9–10

Cvetkovich, Ann, 143

Daily News and Analysis, 120–121

Davis, Devra, 161, 200

decibel-milliwatts (dBm), 45–47

Deepak, J. S., 199–200

Defense Research and Development Organization, 115

de la Cadena, Marisol, 203

Delhi, India. *See* New Delhi, India

Delhi nuclear reactor, 34. *See also* New Delhi, India

Delicath, John W., 85

DeLoughrey, Elizabeth, 10, 220–221n13

DeLuca, Kevin Michael, 85

democratization: of access, 54; of monitoring, 90; of risk, caste and, 129; of science, 59, 136–137

Deora, Milind, 44

Department of Atomic Energy, 108

Department of Telecommunications (DoT), 44–45, 59, 109, 127, 198–200; "awareness sessions," 199, 200

development, 2–3, 7–9, 29, 34, 65, 72–73, 164, 168, 222n24; displacement of vulnerable people, 167; engineering student views, 72, 79–81; "green," 71; mediated radiance of, 7; nuclear nationalism, 79–81, 134, 232n3; slums as polluters, 182–183, 185–186; symbolic radiance of, 9; techno-fetishism, 79–80; urban, as damaging, 183. *See also* middle class

Devi, Mahashewta, 228n5

Dewan, Leslie, 215–216

Dewey, John, 15–16, 221n17

diegetic sounds/voices, 46, 177, 238n9

digital divide, 199–200

"Digital India" program, 2

Dinamalar (Tamil media), 82, 84

direct-reading dosimeter (DRD), 149–150, *150*

disclosure, staged presentations of, 106–107

discourse, circulation and, 6; experience privileged over, 138

displaceable populations, 16, 28, 167

dispositions, 192, 210–211

disruption, 14–15, 40–41, 229n11; call drops as, 131; cancer concerns as, 10, 41; infrastructural breakdown as, 224n37; protests and, 84; uncertainty, public cultures of, 24–27

disruptive infrastructures, 14–19, 164; cell towers as, 18, 41, 131; nuclear power plants as, 136

documentaries, 72, 97, 222n22; "committed," 98; ethical considerations, 100–101; "right to complex personhood," 152–153; spaces of reticence, 153; style of, 77–78; visible surfaces, 148–149. *See also specific documentaries*

Doron, Assa, 8

dosage, 148–153, 159

dosimeters, 27, 121, 149–150, *150*, 158, 200

Dourish, Paul, 15

Dow Chemical, 94, 166

Dowie, Mark, 26–27

Down to Earth (science and environment magazine), 34

"downwind" bodies, 142, 234n8

D'Souza, Faye, 17, *18*

Durkheim, Émile, 134

Dutt, Barkha, 57–63, 236n6

Dutta, Arnab Pratim, 106

Earth-Vision International Film Festival, 204

Easterling, Keller, 192

eco-cosmopolitanism, 205

ecological metaphors, 67–69, 89

e-governance projects, 109

Ek Tha Budhiya animated cartoon series, 74–78, 103, 104

electricity, 195–197; distribution infrastructure, 196–197; shutoffs, 83, 194; workarounds by low-income households, 197–198

electrocardiogram (EKG), 154

electromagnetic fields (EMF), 9–11, 44–45; danger sign, 66; hypersensitivity/electro-sensitivity to, 12, 45, 155–158; mediation of EMF and LED lights, 45–48

electromagnetic spectrum, 9, 220n8

electromagnetic waves, 153–158

electro-sensitivity, 12, 45, 155–158, 214, 220n10, 234n9

embodied publics, 158–162. *See also* bodies

emissions, 39, 106–137; bodily exposure to, 6; e-portals, 124–129; fear of, 107, 145–146; government "leaks" to media, 179–181; information leaks, 36, 106, 135; intermediality and infrastructural governance, 133–137; leakiness of knowledge, 12; measured revelations, 108, 110, 111–118; secrecy, 106–110; steam, 106–107;

emissions (cont.)

tactical trespass, 111, 116, 135; tritium leak, Rawatbhata reactor, 120–121; (un)controlled, 12–14; (un)regulated, 36, 42–43, *43*, 107, 133, 135; visibility and, 110–111, 122, 125–126, 131; willful withholding of information about, 27

emplacement: of audience, 12–13; of bodies, 85–86, 139

energetic environments, 158

English-language media, 29–31, 53, 82

Enthiran (film), 213–214

environmental controversies, 3–7, 14–17, 37, 217; critical infrastructure studies, 34–35; intermediality in, 20–24. *See also* antinuclear movement; cell antenna/tower controversies

environmental disasters: Bhopal, 94–97, 165–167, 170, 180; Chernobyl nuclear plant (Soviet Union), 238n5, 238n8; Fukushima, Japan, 1, 36, 111–113, 117, 135, 167, 188, 232n5, 232n11

Environmental Impact Assessment (EIA), 174

environmentalisms, 35; bourgeois, 28–29, 170, 185–186, 190, 223n28, 223n29; differentiated, 28–33, 168–171; of the poor, 28–29, 170, 223n28; support for nuclear power, 215–216

environmental publics, 14–19, 164, 221n18; always-in-formation, 41; bodies as part of, 137–138; circulation of discourses, 41–42; democratization of, 129; ecological metaphors and, 67–69; expansion of, 57; expert-layperson divides, 206–208; hierarchies, 57; "Indian/ South Asian" character of, 164–165; as issue-based publics, 15–16, 19, 164; reconfiguring, 14–15, 17, 19, 35, 40–41, 48, 50, 54, 67, 72, 133; secrecy and, 106, 137; stakeholders, 14–15, 18–19

epidemiological studies, 146, 148

epidemiological surveys, 104

epistemological boundary making, 146

e-portals, 21, 36, 111, 124–129, 133–134

Escobar, Arturo, 11, 139

ether, 14

European pressurized reactors (EPRs), 103, 197, 231n27

everydayness, 25, 73, 89–90, 160, 235n12

evidence, 146–148

e-waste, 1, 227n15

experiences, privileged over discourse, 138; sensory, 26; of uncertainty 25–26; public sphere and, 160

expertise: boundary crossings with nonexperts, 32–33, 58; dependence on, 47; expert-layperson divides, 206–208; expert-layperson relationships, 58, 62, 71, 208–210, 226n3; interrogating in talk shows, 57–63, *60*; media dependent on, 111–115; performance of, 29–30

exposure, 6, 10, 12, 33, 36, 138–162, 234–235n10; accountability and, 142, 189–190; acute vs. chronic, 18, 45; affect and, 143; chronic, 18, 45; dosage level, 148–153; embodied publics, 158–162; interference, 153–158; measurement of, 142; "nuclear body," 150–151, 153, 234n8; situated testimonies and anecdotal evidence, 143–148. *See also* bodies

extremely low frequency (ELF) electromagnetic fields, 44

Facebook, 82, 84, 228n9

fears about radiation, 6, 220n10, 226n3; bodily sensations in response to media infrastructures, 158–159; cell antenna signals, 10, 15, 24, 26, 39, 103, 144–145, 163, 182–183, 234n9; emissions as fear, 107; "fear psychosis," 144–145; nuclear fallout, 19, 24, 70; pathologization of, 143; socialization of, 141; transparency and, 104, 107

Federal Communications Commission, 26

fiction, speculative, 211–215, *212*, *213*

films: fiction, 239–240n17; vigilante, 80. *See also* documentaries; television shows

fishworkers, 1, 30, 70, 77, 188–189, 208; civic organizations of, 237n9
fish yields, 1, 223n31
5G (fifth generation) wireless networks, 14, 216–218
Foreign Contribution Regulation Act (FCRA), 181–182
"foreign hand," 20–21
foreign suppliers and investors, 20–21, 71, 93, 222n25, 227n1; advertising directed toward, 140; liability, 94–97
Fortun, Kim, 127
4G LTE technology, 2, 199, 216
France, 94, 197, 219n3
Frankfurt School, 138
Fujiwara, Toshi, 239n12
Fukushima, Japan, nuclear disaster (2011), 1, 36, 70, 89, 135, 188, 232n5, 232n11, 233n2; forbidden "red" zone, 206, 239n12; ghost towns, 205–208; India, responses to, 111–113; Japanese government response to, 117; "lessons learned," 167. See also Japan
Fuller, Matthew, 22
furnaces (bhattis), metaphor of, 42
Furusato (documentary, Trimpop), 206–208, 238n10
future, 74; securitizing, 93, 113–114

Gabrys, Jennifer, 24, 158
Gadekar, Sangahmitra, 104–105
Gadekar, Surendra, 104, 174, 200, 202, 202, 222n27
gamma rays, 10, 11, 148, 200, 233n4
Gandhi, Mahatma, 85
Gandhi, Sonia, 228n5
Garg, Rabani, 12–13, 58–59
Gaurav tower, Malviya Nagar region of Jaipur, 122
Geiger counters, 110, 142, 201, 202, 206–207, 238n6
gender politics, 161, 238n6
geographies of unknowing, 27
Ghertner, D. Asher, 182

ghost towns, 205–208
Global South: environmentalism of the poor, 28, 170; informality of politics, 35
Goldman Environmental Prize, 166
Gorakhpur (Haryana), 90, 141
Gordon, Avery, 153
governance, 80, 105, 107–111, 122, 232n14; intermediality and, 133–137; media's role in, 193–194; of risk, 74. See also Tarang Sanchar e-portal; transparency
governed populations, 28, 169, 223n30, 235–236n3
government: abdication of responsibilities, 193–194; e-governance projects, 109; as infrastructure, 167; postcolonial governing institutions, 7–8, 27, 134, 232n3; state and public, 171–179; state-science-society contract, 168, 170
Graham, Stephen, 40
Green Bank, West Virginia, 156
Greenpeace, 20–21, 179, 181–182
Guha, Ramachandra, 170

Habermas, Jürgen, 138, 160
Haji Ali Juice Center, 43
Hale, Mike, 240n21
Half-Life in Fukushima (documentary, Olexa and Scalisi), 206
Hanford nuclear site (Washington, United States), 142, 150
Harvey, Penny, 34, 224–225n37
Hastie, Amelie, 157
Havas, Magda, 49, 200
Hecht, Gabrille, 233, 219n3
Heise, Ursula, 205
Helmreich, Stefan, 154–155
Herkman, Juha, 20, 222n22
Hermann, Rainer, 181
Hernan, Luis, 49
Hertsgaard, Mark, 26–27
Hess, David, 44, 156, 193
Hindu, The (English-language newspaper), 29–30, 95–97

historical context: antinuclear movement, 170–171; government anxieties, 180–181; media and publics, 29–33
Holby City (medical drama), 156–158
"home," 206–208
Hotel Supreme (Cuffe Parade area, Mumbai), 198–199
humanimal machine, 213–214, 239n16
hybrid forums, 32–33, 59

Idinthakarai village, 70, 102, 166, 187
image events, 85
imaginaries, 72; alternative, 202–203; cultural, 7, 35–37; infrastructural, 200; sociotechnical, 73. *See also* nuclear imaginaries
imperceptibility. *See* invisibility/ imperceptibility
India, 33; "idea of," 81; legitimization and mega-development projects, 7–8; media, 28–33; nuclear nationalism, 79–81, 134, 232n3; nuclear tests, 8, 104, 232n3; post-colonial governing institutions, 7–8, 27, 134, 168, 232n3; telecom revolution, 109
Indian Institute of Science (Bangalore), 146
Indian Penal Code, Section 144, 172
Indian Rare Earth Limited (IREL), 97–98, 102, 150
indigenous cosmopolitics, 203
Indo-US nuclear deal, 94–97, 166, 227n1
Indus Towers (mobile tower company), 8, 42
infra-ness, 33–34, 67, 107, 224–225n37
infrastructural publics, 16, 221n19
infrastructures, 5; approaching, 33–37; change and, 215–218; complexities of, 210–211; ecological and relational characteristics, 16; government as, 167; "in-between," 50; intimacy of mobilizations, 189–191; national, regulatory conundrums and, 195–200; national-cultural, 73; physical structures, differences between, 108; of power, 21–22; ruined, 195; as socializing force, 50; symbolic

radiance of development, 9. *See also* material properties of infrastructures; radiant infrastructures
"Inside Kudankulam N-Plant: How Safe Are Our N-Reactors?," 112–114
"Inside Protest Hit Kudankulam Nuclear Plant," 114
Inside series: "Tarapur Nuclear Power Plant: Unlock Power," 118–120, *120, 121,* 149–150, *150*
institutional relations, 15
intelligibility, infrastructural, 210–211
intercontinental ballistic missiles (ICBMs), 108, 115
interference, 153–159
intermediality, 19–24, 33, 41, 68, 71, 73, 222n21, 222n22; assemblages of media, 22–24, 33, 42, 50, 134; "in-between-ness" 158–159; infrastructural governance and, 133–137; of media objects, 9, 22, 47–50, 48, 67, 225n38; of radiation-sensing technologies, 22. *See also* media; mediation
internal radiation, 148, 233n3
International Coalition for Justice in Bhopal, 167
International Commission on Non-Ionizing Radiation Protection (ICNIRP), 44–45, 47, 61
International Journal of Epidemiology, 26
Internet of Things, 218
intertextuality, 20, 48, 71
intimacy, 138; of mobilizations, 189–191; "unwanted," 14, 35–36, 142–143, 189–190, 233n2
Investigative Bureau (IB) report, 179–181
invisibility/imperceptibility, 1–3, 6–7, 14, 16, 33, 35, 67–69, 73, 142–143, 182–183, 187, 210–211, 217–218, 220n9, 224–225n37, 238n9; emissions and, 110–111, 122, 125–126, 131; of radiation, 1, 43–44, 67–68, 110–111, 218; secrecy and, 110–111, 118–119; uncertainty and cell antenna radiation, 43–44
ionizing radiation, 10, 68; X-rays as, 145

Irion, Sarah, 103, 195, 208–210, *209*
issue-based publics, 15–16, 19, 164

Jadugoda, India: uranium mining effects
   on people, 97, 99–101, 118, *149*, 149–151,
   200–205, *203*, *204*. See also *Buddha
   Weeps in Jadugoda* (documentary,
   Shriprakash)
Jaipur, India, 30–32, *31*, 42, 172, 195; *Rajasthan Patrika* campaign, 50–56; slums,
   186. See also *Rajasthan Patrika* (Hindi
   newspaper)
Jaitapur, India, 3, 93, 103; Sakhri-Nate
   (village), 3, *5*, 103, 208–209
Jal Satyagrah, 84–86, 189
Japan: Hiroshima and Nagasaki bomb-
   ings, 175; media, 117; Minamisoma,
   206, 206–208, *207*; post-Fukushima
   documentaries, 205; translocal alliances,
   200–201. *See also* Fukushima, Japan,
   nuclear disaster (2011)
Japanese activists, 167, 200–201, 238n5,
   238n6
Jasanoff, Sheila, 73
Jatayu/Garuda (mythological figure), 214
Javeri, Pravet, 22
Jayalalithaa, M. S., 194
Jayaraman, Nityanand, 83, 89–91, 167,
   228n6
Jeffrey, Robin, 8
Jensen, Casper Bruun, 34, 110, 224–225n37
Ji, Govind (interviewee), 53–54
Jishnu, Latha, 106, 115–117, 135
Johnson, Jeromy, 156
journalists, 21; access to nuclear reactors,
   33, 36, 107, 111–115; Japanese, 117; in local
   newspapers, 31, 51–52; legitimacy of, 155;
   middle-of-the-road, 112; "trespassing" by,
   116–117. *See also* documentaries; media
Jung Aur Aman (*War and Peace*) (docu-
   mentary, Patwardhan), 104, 202

Kakodkar, Anil, 208–210
Kakrapar nuclear reactor (Gujarat), 135

Kalam, A. P. J. Abdul, 29–30
Kalapakkam nuclear reactor, 230n21
Kamanaka, Hitomi, 238n5, 238n6
Kapoor, Priti, 46, *46*
Kasliwal, Sudhir, 25, 50–52, 56–58, 122–123,
   214, 236n6
katiyabaaz(s) (experts in informal electric-
   ity workarounds), 198
Kaur, Raminder, 101, 108, 229n13, 236n7,
   239n15, 239n17, 240n21
Kenji (*Furusato* documentary participant),
   206–207
Keshav (cartoonist), *95*, 95–97, *96*, 104
khamosh khatra (silent danger), 1
Khan, Aamir (Bollywood actor), 163–164
Khanduri, Gairola, 95
Kholi, Anoop, 58
Kim Sang-Hyun, 73
Kimura, Aya Hirata, 238n6
Kirsch, Scott, 27
Kluge, Alexander, 138, 160, 235n12
knowledge, 47, 153, 235n11
knowledge systems, 28, 41, 77–78, *78*,
   208–209
Koide Hiroaki, 200, 201, 204, *204*,
   237–238n4
Koodankulam nuclear reactor (Tamil
   Nadu, India), 24, 29, 34, 70; defective
   parts, Russian, 180; Facebook groups,
   82; fish yields and, 1, 223n31; foreign
   suppliers and, 166; halt of construction,
   112–113; nuclear "hot run" test, 106;
   protests, 3, 20–21, *21*, 36, 70, 82–85, 165
Krishna, Sankaran, 79–80
Krtilova, Katerina, 23
Kuchinskaya, Olga, 35
Kudankulam, India. *See* Koodankulam
   nuclear reactor (Tamil Nadu, India)
Kumar, Girish, 18, 22, 45–47, 58, 61,
   108–109
Kumar, Neha, 47

Lakkad, Abhishek, 214
land grabs, 171–172

landline telephone systems, 61–62
language barriers, 82, 174, 190
Larkin, Brian, 7, 120, 224n37
Lascoumes, Pierre, 24, 59, 168
Latigowarkar, Majeed (Sakhri-Nate resident), 208–209
Latour, Bruno, 16
leakages. *See* emissions
legitimacy, crises of, 108, 112, 179
Leviathan (Castaing-Taylor and Paravel), 209
Lippit, Akira, 149
Little Voices of Fukushima (documentary, Kamanaka), 238n5, 238n6
Living It Up (television show), 4, 143–146, *144*, 161, 235n1; "Are Mobile Towers a Health Hazard?," 154; radiation detector demonstrations, 46; testimonies, 12–13
Livingstone, Sonia, 32, 59
local-local relations, 200, 205, 238n7
Lunt, Peter, 32, 59
Lynch, Lisa, 215

magnetic resonance imaging (MRI), 156–157
mahashakti (ultimate energy), 14
Manavalakurichi, people of, 97–98, 102
Mandal, Tridip, 154, *154*
Manhattan Project, 11, 220n11
Manju Das (documentary participant in *Buddha Weeps in Jadugoda*), 99–101
Mankekar, Purnima, 145
maps, 232n11; of cell towers, 109; Open Network, 129–133; of radiation, 21, 46, 122–123. *See also* Tarang Sanchar e-portal
Marres, Noortje, 16
Martinez-Alier, Juan, 170
Marupakkam (media activism organization), 98
Masco, Joseph, 73, 134, 139
material properties of infrastructures, 6–8, 12, 33–36, 67, 141, 162; assemblages, 50, 192, 209–210; emissions and, 12, 107,

110–111, 211; governance and, 126–127, 133; heuristics, 6–7, 36, 133, 214; sociomaterially situated practices, 21–22, 24, 50, 89–90, 227–228n2
Mathew, Dr. (president of New Link Road Forum), 183–184
Mathur, Shipra, 52–54, 122–123, 186, 193
Matru Ki Bijlee Ka Mandola (film, dir. Vishal Bhardwaj), 236n5
Matsumura, Naoto ("red zone" resident), 206
Mattern, Shannon, 218
Matthews, Rajan, 18, 43, 58, 61
Mazzarella, William, 25, 101, 109
Mbembe, Achille, 141
McKinzie, Matthew, 216
McLean, Lyn, 200
measured revelations, 108, 110–118
media: access to, 33, 54, 56–57, 172–173, 175, 190, 236n6; assemblages of, 22–24, 33, 42, 134; called on to intervene, 63; civil/political society distinctions and, 169–170; coverage, 222n20, 226n3; critiques of scientific establishment, 30; democratization of access, 54; effects, 159; emotional reporting, 52–53; English-language, 29–31, 53, 82; events, 41–42; governance, role in, 193–194; historical context, 29–33; Indian, 28–33; modes of address, 31–32; open-door policies, 1–52, 54; operation across scale, 6; performativity of, 55–56; political economy of, 68, 101; practices, 19, 24, 73–74, 82–91, 101–102; press-club systems, 117; representations, 71, 74, 81, 110, 119, 134, 189, 210–211; rival outlets, 56–57; scientific reporting, 52, 53; spectacles, staging of, 32, 62, 84–86, 94, 101; testimony of bodies, role in, 13–14; types of journalism, 113; vernacular, 30–31. *See also* audience(s); cartoons; documentaries; intermediality
media ecologies, 22, 47–50
media infrastructures, 68, 158–159

medial relations/systems, 22

media objects, 9, 22, 47–50, 67, 158–159, 225n38

media studies, 32, 217

mediated arenas, 6, 17–19, 30, 62–63, 108–110, 117, 168–170. See also *We the People* (talk show)

mediation, 7, 14–15, 74, 101, 103–106; affect and, 143, 158–159; electromagnetic, body and, 154–155; of EMF and LED lights, 45–48; "flows" and "cuts," 48; hyper-mediation, 107; interspecies turn, 26; of nuclear imaginaries, 103–105; publicity campaigns and, 36; of publicness, 57–63; of security regimes, 118–119; specific processes, 142; techno-politics of, 118–122. *See also* intermediality

medical radiology, 10–11

medical visualization techniques, 36–37

Meherabad apartment (Warden Road, Mumbai), 48, 49

Mehta, Nalin, 62

Men against Rape and Discrimination campaign, 165

microwave ovens, 23, 42, 44, 47–49, 200

Mid-Day (newspaper), 39, 42

middle class, 68, 165–166, 168, 225n39; alienation from state, 79–80; bourgeois environmentalism, 28–29, 170, 185–186, 223n28, 223n29; empathy for local communities and, 141; engineering students' film, 72, 79–81, 211; genocidal impulse, 81; as heterogeneous, 72, 169; high-level contacts, 56–57, 236n6; media avenues, 169–170; nuclear publicity campaigns directed at, 71–72; technocratic elite, 79–81. *See also* development; urban inhabitants

millimeter waves, 14, 216–217

Minamisoma, Japan, 206–208

Mirror Now (television show), 17

Mithi Virdi (village, Gujarat) public hearing, 174–179, *176, 177*

Mobilize (documentary), 161

modernity, 183, 200, 219n5

Modi, Narendra, 2, 126, 179, 232n10, 237n8

molecular bonds, 11, 145

monazite mining, 13, 97–99, 150–153, 233–234n6

monitoring, 24–52, 61; of cell antenna signals, 51–52, 127–129, 132, 134, 137; by citizens, 24, 110–111; of officials, 51–52

Moore, Alfred, 146

Morita, Asturu, 34, 224–225n37

Moskowitz, Joel, 161, 240n19

Movement of India (NAPM news magazine), 167–168

Mukherjee, Pranab, 141

multinational/transnational corporations, 94–97, 165–166, 170

multiple chemical sensitivity, 156

Mumbai, India, 1, 17, 22, 39, 41–42, *196*; apartment rooftop meetings, 18, 22–23, *23*, 48–50, 67; regulations flouted, 198–199; slums, 182–183, 185–186. *See also* anti–cell antenna movement; cell antenna/tower controversies; middle class

Munshi, Prakash, 18, 22–24, 48–49, 58, 60, 173, 186, 200; Bollywood celebrities and, 165–166

Murphy, Michelle, 27, 156

mutations, as result of radiation exposure, 10–12, 45, 68, 148, 151, 217, 238n8

Nabikei (Shriprakash), 204, *204*

Nadar villages, 24, 90

Nagercoil, India, 34, 188, 228n4

Nair, Karmel (participant in *Living It Up* show), 144–146, *145*, 161

Nandy, Ashis, 81

Narmada Bachao Andolan (Save the Narmada Movement), 86, 164, 167, 170, 180, 229n12

Narora atomic power plant (Uttar Pradesh), 91

Natarajan, Vasant, 146

National Alliance of People's Movements (NAPM), 167–168
National Geographic channel, 136; *Inside* series, 118–122, *120*, *121*, 149–150, *150*
National Geographic–NPCIL ads, 91–94, *92*, *93*, 103, 104, 111; bodies of animals in, 138–139, *139*
nationalism, nuclear, 79–81, 134, 232n3
national security, 20, 115; "energy security" discourse, 81, 222n24; media access and, 33; secrecy of, 107–108. *See also* security regimes
nature, discourse of, technology merged with, 11, 139
Navajo Nation, Churchrock tailings spill, 204–205
Nayar, Pramod, 239n16
necropolitics, 141
Negt, Oskar, 138, 160, 235n12
Nehru, Jawarhalal, 76, 134
neoliberalism, 109, 134, 136, 167, 224n36, 232n10
NESA Solutions, 22
New Delhi, India, 1, 34, 41, 52, 61, 65, *196*; South Delhi, 181–182. *See also* anti–cell antenna movement; cell antenna/tower controversies
New Delhi Television (NDTV), 119, 236n6; Bagla's nuclear reactor reporting, 112–115, *113*; *We the People* talk show, 32, 35, 57–63, *64*, 236n6
New Link Road Residents Forum, 183–184
Nizaruddin, Fathima, 77–78, 102, 205–206
No Man's Zone (documentary, Fujiwara), 239n12
nongovernmental organizations (NGOs), 20, 178–179; Investigative Bureau report and, 179–182
nonhuman actors, technologies as, 41–42, 48, 50, 239n13
nonhuman animals, 209; bird life, disruption of, 212–215, *213*, 240n18; bodies of, 25–26, 37, 138–*140*

nonionizing radiation, 10, 68–69, 154; directed beams, 142; electromagnetic fields (EMF), 9–11, 12, 44–48, 66, 155–158; specific absorption rate (SAR), 160–161, *161*, 235n13
Non-Proliferation Treaty, 219n6
normalcy, search for, 206–208
"nuclear body," 150–151, 153, 234n8
nuclear controversies, 19, 70–105; Environmental Impact Assessments (EIA), 174; protests, Koodankulam, India, 3, 20–21, *21*, 36, 70, 82–85, 165; Sakhri-Nate protests, 3, *5*; secrecy and, 107–110
nuclear enclave, 108
nuclear establishment, 70–72, 222–223n27, 231n28; accountability, crisis of, 36, 71; Atomic Energy Act of 1962, 180; damages inflicted by, 72; insularity of, 104; refusal to engage, 29–30; rule-flouting by, 174. *See also* advertising; emissions
Nuclear Hallucinations (documentary, Nizaruddin), 77–78, 104, 205–206, 212
nuclear imaginaries, 72–74; "background," 90–91; mediation of, 103–105; presenting, 89
Nuclear Liability Act/Bill, 21, 94–97
"nuclear nationalism," 8
Nuclear Power Corporation of India Limited (NPCIL), 71, 108, 194, 228n4; *Ek Tha Budhiya* series, 74–78, 103–104; failure to give warnings, 106; governance structures and, 110; National Geographic–NPCIL ads, 91–94, *92*, *93*, 103, 104, 111, *139*; restrictions on filming by outsiders, 102–103; secrecy, 231n1, 231n2; wind and hydropower investments, 116
nuclear reactors, 1, 69; displacement of fishing and farming communities, 3; foreign suppliers and investors, 71; hypervisibility of, 34; indiscriminate spread of radiation, 142; Kalapakkam, 230n21; Koodankulam, India, 1, 3, 11; leak, Kakrapar, 135; monumentality

of, 7, 34, 114, 119–120, 122; protests, Koodankulam, India, 3, 20–21, *21*; in public sector, 110; radioactive isotopes, 5–6; rural location of, 3; sanctioned without fair public hearings, 28; steam emissions, 106–107; techno-politics of mediation and, 118–122. *See also* Koodankulam nuclear reactor (Tamil Nadu, India); radiant infrastructures

Nuclear Suppliers Group (NSG), 8

nuclear testing, 8, 11, 73, 99, 212, 220–221n13, 230n22, 234n8; official secrets and, 134

nuclear waste, 73–74, 233n3

nuclear weapons, 8, 108, 230n22

nuclides, radioactive, 6, 12, 106, 138, 148–149, 200, 223n27, 234n8

Nussbaum, Emily, 218

Obama, Barack, 232n10

"objectivity," 53, 159, 223n32

Olexa, Mark, 206

Omkareshwar Dam, 84–85

Open Network initiative, 129–133, *130, 132*

Pakistan, nuclear tests, 8

Pakshi Rajan (character, *2.0*), 212–213

Pandey, Gyanendra, 187

Pandey, Harish, 183–184

Papacharissi, Zizi, 160

Parameswaran, Radhika, 58

Paravel, Véréna, 209

Parks, Lisa, 34–35, 210–211, 222n20

Parmanu (atom) (character), 80, 81

Parmanu (comic series), 80

Parmanu: The Story of Pokhran (film), 212

Parthasarathy, K. S., 47, 146

Patault, Micha, 103, 195, 208–210, *209*

Patwardhan, Anand, 98, 104, 202, 230n22

peacocks, return of, 25–26, 37

people's charter against nuclear energy, 141, 186–187

People's Movement against Nuclear Energy (PMANE), 33, 82, 84–89, 179, 187, 228n4, 229n15; RTI claims, 180

performativity: of expertise, 29–30; of media, 55–56; of revelation, 111

Piram, Prem, 171–172

plant sensitivity, 14

plutonium, 10–11, 220n11

PMANE. *See* People's Movement against Nuclear Energy

Pokhran nuclear tests, 212

police brutality, 84–86, 187

political society, 29–30, 169–170, 223n30, 223n31; intersections with civil society, 186–188; rupture with civil society, 183–186

politics: gender politics, 161; Global South, informality of, 35; indigenous cosmo-politics, 203; necropolitics, 141; techno-politics, 118–122, 135, 185, 235n3

Politics of Invisibility, The (Kuchinskaya), 35

popular culture, 25, 54–55

Popular Education and Action Center (PEACE), 181

"populars," 167

Powerplant by Powerplayers (film), 79–81

practices: media, 19, 24, 73–74, 82–91, 101–102; of secrecy, 106; subaltern, 169, 237n9

Prakash, Gyan, 7

Prasad, Ravi Shankar, 63

prehension: bodily, 7, 159, 189; in relation to comprehension, 159

Pripyat (Ukraine), 238n8

protests: anti-dam, 84–85, 167, 170, 229n12; antinuclear films as, 97–103; caricatures of, 79–81; collective efforts, 229n10; fasting, 82, 86, 189, 229n10; Jaitapur, 93; Jal Satyagrah, 84–86, 189; Koodankulam, 3, 20–21, *21*, 36, 70, 82–85, 165; Penal Code prohibitions, 172; post-Fukushima, 138; rights violations alleged, 70–71; social media use, 82–83, 229n9; Theripu tax system, 89, 189, 229n10. *See also* anti-cell antenna movement; antinuclear movement

proximity, 138, 145, 185

Public and Its Problems, The (Dewey), 15
public cultures of uncertainty, 24–28, 37, 73, 78, 193–195
public hearings, 28, 173–179
public interest litigation (PIL), 180, 182–183
publicity, 16, 36, 71–74, 101, 105, 134–135, 222n20; revelation as performative, 111; secrecy and, 105–106, 111; subaltern practices, 169, 237n9. *See also* advertising
publics, 14–16, 221n17, 224n36; ad hoc and post hoc, 19; affective, 160; differentiated, 28–33, 168–171; disappearing, 97–103; embodied, 158–162; historical overview, 29–33; infrastructural, 221n19; issue-based, 15–16, 19, 164; linguistic and cultural diversity of, 29; mediated national, 56–57; mediated publicness, 57–63, 178; mobile users in dead zones, 67; object-oriented notions of, 16; as poetic world-making, 56; quasi-publics, 29–30, 235–236n3; scientific-citizen, 29, 235–236n3; split, 31–32, 53; state and, 171–179. *See also* environmental publics
public sphere, 19, 143, 160, 220n10, 221n18, 223n29, 224n36, 235n12
Pujari, P. K., 126

quasi-publics, 29–30, 235–236n3

radiance, 220n9; as double-edged sword, 6–7; glow of development, 9; of infrastructures, 7–10; mediated, 7; metaphors and manifestations of, 7; symbolism of, 2
radiant energies, 5, 9–10; energetic environments, 158
radiant infrastructures: definitions, 5; governance of, 107–110; as heuristic, 6–7, 36, 133, 159, 214; infra-ness of, 33–34, 67, 224–225n37; intermediality and governance, 133–137; interrelationship of, 158; lack of comparison between, 3; leaks/leakiness of, 10; media discussion of, 1–4, *4*; persistence of debates, 225n38;

political subjectivities 37, 165–171. *See also* infrastructures; material properties of infrastructures
radiation: fish yield decreases and, 1; imperceptibility/invisibility of, 1, 43–44, 67–68, 110–111, 218; inability to measure properly, 35, 43; as natural, 11; nuclides, radioactive, 6, 12, 106, 138, 148–149, 200, 223n27, 234n8; Sanskrit word for, 10; "standard body" used to measure, 160–161; types of, 3, 10–12; uncanny quality, 69, 73, 211, 214. *See also* fears about radiation; nonionizing radiation
"Radiation: A Constant Companion in Our Life" ad, 11
radiation detection, 7; secrecy about, 108–109
radiation detectors, 1, 22–23, 25, 44–46; LED lights transform EMF, 45–48; maps, generation of, 21, 46
radiation discourse: analogies with sun, 11; naturalness of radiation, 11; (un)differentiation, 11
radiation maps, 21, 46, 110, 134
Radiation Stories (documentaries, Amudhan), 4, 13, 97–99
Radiation Stories 1: Manavalakurichi (documentary, Amudhan), 98, 150–153
Radiation Stories 3: Koodankulam (documentary, Amudhan), *140*, 140–141, 175–179
radio, 9; radio waves, 10
radioactive isotopes, 5–6; half-life of, *142*
radioactive particles, 9
radiogenic injury, *142*; seasonal workers blamed for, 150
radium, 9–10
Rajagopal, Arvind, 30–31, 53, 224n33
Rajasthan Patrika (Hindi newspaper), 35, *52*, *55*, 67, 122, 143; aggressive approach, 55–56; anecdotal evidence in, 146–148; *bhatti mein shahar* (city inside the furnace) campaign, 31–32, 42; campaign, 50–56; cell tower controversy, 42; idealistic and communitarian ethos, 53–54;

"Inki Jaanch Par Kaise Ho Vishwas" (How Can We Rely on Their Investigation?), 122–124, *124*; letters to the editor, 32, 63; open-door policy, 51–52, 54; trust of readers, 193

Raj comic series, 80

Rajnikant (cinema superstar), 79

Ramana, M. V., 108, 231n1

Ramjanmabhoomi (Birthplace of Lord Ram) movement, 30–31, 53

Rao, Ursula, 54

Raphael, Debbie, 161

Rawatbhata power plant (Rajasthan), 118; tritium leak, 120–121

reasoning, mode of, 172

Reference Man/Standard Man model, 150, 160–161

regulations, 225n1; antenna emission levels, 39; compliance not linked to environmental responsibility, 125; municipality, 17; national infrastructures and, 195–200

regulatory frameworks, 24

Reliance Jio (cellular operator), 2, *2*, 39, *40*, 199

Research Reactor Institute (Kyoto University), 200

resource extractivism, 170

Reynolds, Ann, 143

Right to Information (RTI) Act of 2005, 180–184

risk, 24; future, questions of, 74; hierarchized by caste, 90, 103; social amplification framework, 159; temporary/casual workers and, 120–121, 136; Western perceptions of, 28

rumor, as popular discourse, 19, 27, 107, 194–195

rural inhabitants, 1, 3–4, 225n39, 235n1; as "governed populations," 28, 223n30; livelihoods threatened, 4, 28, 36, 70, 103, 140, 167, 169–171, 190, 195, 209, 222n24, 231n28, 235n1; nuclear reactors sanctioned without fair public hearings, 28

Russian Atomic Energy Commission, 135

safety culture, lack of, 89–90

Sahni, Urmi, 154

Sahyadri Guest House, *172, 173*, 173–174

Sakhri-Nate (village, Jaitapur region), 3, *5*, 103, 208–209

Satyamev Jayate (*Truth Alone Triumphs*) (television show), 164

scale: interaction across, 19; local-global, 210; macro-level discourses, 6; macro perspective, 30; micro-level bodily encounters, 6; multiscalar infrastructural relations, 110; nation-states and mega-development projects, 7–8; spacetimemattering-scape, 142

Scalisi, Francesca, 206

Science magazine, 20

science reporting, 1, 192–193

science studies, 32, 168, 217

scientific-citizen publics, 29, 235–236n3

"scientific temper," 76–77, 134; "Scientific Nuclear Temper Act" (caricature), 78

scientists, dissident, 18, 35, 45, 129, 192, 200–202

seasonal/temporary workers, 120–122, 136, 150, 223n27, 232n5

secrecy, 12, 21–22, 106, 107–110, 231n1, 231n2; government "leaks" to media, 179–181; Japan and Belarus, 238n5; measured revelations, 108, 110, 111–118

securitization of future, 93, 113–114

security regimes, 118–119, 134. *See also* national security

Shankar (filmmaker), 79

Sharma, R. S., 126

Shriprakash (filmmaker), 97, 98–102, 104, 148, 151, 218, 231n26; bodies, exposure of, 148–153

Shukla, Champa Devi, 166

Sibal, Kapil, 61

sick building syndrome, 27

signaletic level, 158

Signal Traffic (Parks and Starosielski), 34–35

Simmel, Georg, 134

Simone, AbdouMaliq, 50

Singh, Manmohan, 20, 95, 141, 181, 222n24, 230n19

Sinha, Manoj, 126

Sivakasi fireworks factory accident, 89, 229n17

Sivakumar, Souwmya, 120–121

slums, 182–183, 185–186

smartphones, 2, 161

social media platforms, 160, 222n22; blogs by resident associations, 182–185; *Chai Kadai* blog, 82–83, 228n5; Facebook, 82, 84; time-stamped updates, 82–83; websites and blogs, 82–83, 228n5. *See also* Twitter

social movements, 164–167; intersections between civil and political society, 186–188. *See also* antinuclear movement

social relations, technical uncertainties shaped by, 24

sociology-of-risk literature, 159

sociopolitical life: corporeal/affective aspects, 25; discursive/ideological aspects, 25

sociotechnical entanglements, 42, 44–47, 54; uncertainty and, 24, 37

sociotechnical imaginaries, 73, 89

Soneryd, Linda, 159

South Mumbai: Usha Kiran building, 42

speaking truth to power (*Satyagrah*), 85

specific absorption rate (SAR), 160–161, 235n13

spectacles, media staging of, 32, 62, 84–86, 94, 101

Spivak, Gayatri, 187

split publics, 31–32, 53

Staiger, Janet, 143

stakeholders, 14–15, 19–20; cell tower and call drop controversies, 41; coproduction model and, 73; mediated national public and, 56–57

Star, Susan Leigh, 16, 110

Starosielski, Nicole, 34–35

state-science-society contract, 168, 170

Stengers, Isabelle, 203

Stephen, Amritharaj, 83, 86–89, *87*, 229n13

stigma, 156

Stilgoe, Jack, 146

St. Lourdes Mary Church of Idinthakarai, 83

"Stranger Electrifier" (character), 79–80, 211

strontium, 162, 221n13

students: engineering students' film, 72, 79–81, 211; fishermen-student alliances, 188

subaltern classes, 167; antinuclear movements of, 28; civil society practices, 169, 237n9; media avenues, 169–170

subalternity, media depiction of, 86; "subaltern citizens," 187–188

sublime, technological, 119–120

Sundar, Aparna, 189, 237n9

Sundaram, Kumar, 172

surveillance, 84, 182, 185, 237n7

Swacch Bharat (Clean India!), 237n8

Sweden, 159

symbolism of radiation and radiance, 2

talking groups strategy, 99, 230–231n24

Tamil diaspora, 83–84

Tamil film industry, 212–213

Tamil media, 82

Tamil Nadu, India, 34, 228n4; electricity shutoffs, 194; Kalapakkam reactor, 230n21; nuclear power plant construction halt, 36. *See also* Koodankulam nuclear reactor (Tamil Nadu, India)

Tarang Sanchar e-portal, 36, 111, 124–129

Tarapur nuclear power plant, 118–120, *120*, 163

"Tarapur Nuclear Power Plant: Unlock Power" (*Inside* series), 118–120, *120*, *121*, 149–150, *150*

Taylor, B., 153

Taylor, Charles, 72, 90

technical democracy, 168

techno-fetishism, 79–80

technologies, as nonhuman actors, 41–42, 48, 50
techno-natures, 11, 139
techno-politics, 118–122, 135, 185, 235n3
techno-struggle, 120, 185, 201–202
Tehelka magazine, 89
Telecom Enforcement Resource and Monitoring (TERM), 109, 122–123, 128–129
Telecom Regulatory Authority of India (TRAI), 11, 18, 65
television shows: affective elements, 61–62; bodies affected by, 145–146; participatory, 32–33; split-screen debate shows, 17–19, *18*; talk shows, 35, 59–63, 226n7, 226n8. See also *Living It Up* (television show)
TerraPower, 215
testimonies, 12, 104; of patient bodies, 6, 12–14, 36–37, 97–99, 138, 143–153, 235n11; situated, 12, *13*, 143–148
Theripu tax system, 89, 189, 229n10
thermoluminescent dosimeter (TLD), 121, 149–150, *150*
thorium, 150, 233–234n6
Three Mile Island nuclear reactor (United States), 215
3 Miles to Gorakhpur (documentary, Piram), 171–172
Times of India (TOI), 183
Tiwari, Harish Chand, 17
Tokyo Electric Power Company, 117
top-down model, 74
translocal connections, 105, 200–205, 218; local-local relations, 200, 205, 238n7
transmitter antennas, 45
transparency, 36, 107–111, 233n5; hiding of processes, 106, 118, 129, 134, 136, 232n10; Tarang Sanchar e-portal and, 36, 111, 124–129, *125*, *128*. See also governance
Travelling International Uranium Film Festival, 72, 163
trespass, tactical, 111, 116, 135
trials: in court, 180; by media, 179–182; public interest litigation (PIL), 180, 182–183

Trimpop, Thorsten, 206–208, 238n10, 239n12
trust, cultures of, 193–194
trust, secrecy and, 107–110
trust deficit, 90, 124
tsunami: December 2004, 24, 70, 90; threat of, 113
Tuticorin port, 85
TV9, 190
Twitter, 19, 27, 32, 84, 224n35, 226–227n9, 228n9; language barriers, 82; #MyClean-India, 237n8; *We the People* responses, 62–63
2.0 (film), 212–215, 239–240n17, 240n18

Udayakumar, S. P., 82, 84, 181, 187
uncanniness, 69, 73, 211, 214
uncertainty: "home" and, 206–208; imperceptibility/invisibility of cell antenna radiation, 43–44; latency period for radiogenic injury, 142; "overall," use of the term, 26; public cultures of, 24–28, 37, 73, 78, 193–195; rumor, as popular discourse, 19, 27, 107, 194–195; secrecy and, 106; sociotechnical, 24, 37; transparency produces, 136
(un)controlled emissions, 12–14
"undone science," 156, 192
Union Carbide, 94, 165–166
United Kingdom, 146, 159
United States, 26, 110; antiradiation activism, 200; atomic bomb tests, 134; Churchrock tailings spill, Navajo Nation, 204–205, *205*; Hanford nuclear site, 142, 150; nuclear reactors in India, 174
unknowability, 24
(un)regulated emission, 36, 107; clusters of cell towers, 42–43, *43*; entanglement of both kinds of emission, 135; as heuristic, 133
uranium, 10
Uranium Corporation of India Limited (UCIL), 99

uranium mining, 233n3; alpha particle and gamma ray exposure, 148; Jadugoda, 97, 99–101, 118, 149–151, 200–205, *203*, *204*; metaphors for, 202, *203*

Urban Debate, The (television show), 17–19, *18*

urban inhabitants, 1, 3–4; as concerned citizens, 37; slums, 182–183, 185–186. *See also* middle class

US Atomic Energy Commission, 220–221n13

US-India Nuclear Nonproliferation Treaty (2006), 8

Varughese, Shiju, 29

Victorian science, 9

Victor Shelter apartments, 183

vigilante characters, 79–80

Vigyan Prasar (government science publicity wing), 11, 74–78, 111

violence, radiological, 35, 218

visibility, 67; emissions and, 110–111, 122, 125–126, 131; hypervisibility, 122, 138, 233n5; limited, 132–133; techniques of, 44–47

visualization of radiation in body, 145, 149–158

visual pollution, 66

Visvanathan, Shiv, 89

Vodafone, 165

voluntary associations, 180

Von Schnitzler, Antina, 35

Wadia, Homi, 212

Wales, 141–142

Walter, Tom (Bollywood actor), 163

Warner, Michael, 56

watts per square meter (W/m^2), 44–45

Waugh, Thomas, 98

Web 2.0, 126, 232n10

Welsh, Ian, 103

Weston, Kath, 47, 143, 201, 233n2

We the People (talk show), 32, 35, 57–64, 67, 226–227n8, 236n6; "Cell Phone Towers: India's Safety Check," 57–63; Twitter responses, 62–63, *64*

Wi-Fi signals, 49

wind and hydropower, 117

wireless signals, 9, 14, 27, 48, 216

wireless smart meters, 44

working-class issues, 167–68

World Health Organization (WHO), 26

Wynne, Brian, 103

Xavieramma (community member), 141, 187–188

X-rays, 9, 11–12, 143, 145, 158, 220n9, 220n10, 234n10

youth, 72, 79–81, 188, 211, 224n35

YouTube, 49

Zio-Podolsk, 135